Arthur Henderson

LIVES of the LEFT is a new series of original biographies of leading figures in the European and North American socialist and labour movements. Short, lively and accessible, they will be welcomed by students of history and politics and by anyone interested in the development of the Left.

general editor David Howell

published:
J. Ramsay MacDonald Austen Morgan
James Maxton William Knox
Karl Kautsky Dick Geary
'Big Bill' Haywood Melvyn Dubofsky
A. J. Cook Paul Davies
R. H. Tawney Anthony Wright
Thomas Johnston Graham Walker
Arthur Henderson F. M. Leventhal
William Lovett Joel Wiener

forthcoming, to include:
John Strachey Michael Newman
Tom Mann Joseph White
John MacLean Brian Ripley and John McHugh
Eugene Debs Gail Malmgreen

Arthur Henderson

F. M. Leventhal

Manchester University Press
Manchester and New York
Distributed exclusively in the USA and Canada by St. Martin's Press

Copyright © F. M. Leventhal 1989

Published by Manchester University Press, Oxford Road,
Manchester, M13 9PL, UK
and Room 400, 175 Fifth Avenue, New York, NY 10010, USA

Distributed exclusively in the USA and Canada
by St. Martin's Press, Inc., 175 Fifth Avenue, New York, NY 10010, USA

British Library cataloguing in publication data
Leventhal, F. M. (Fred Marc), *1938–*
    Arthur Henderson. — (Lives of the left)
    1. Great Britain. Politics. Henderson, Arthur, 1863-1935
    I. Title   II. Series
    941.082'3'092'4

Library of Congress cataloguing in publication data
Leventhal, F. M., 1938–
    Arthur Henderson / F. M. Leventhal
    p.   cm.   — (Lives of the left)
    ISBN 0-7190-2150-2. ISBN 0-7190-2151-0 (pbk.)
    1. Henderson, Arthur, 1863-1935. 2 Statesman—Great
    Britain—Biography. 3. Labour Party (Great Britain)—History
    —20th centry. 4 Great Britain—Politics and government—
    1910-1936. I. Title II. Series
    DA566.9.H4L48 1989
    941.083'092'4—dc 19

ISBN 0 7190 2150 2 *hardback*
ISBN 0 7190 2151 0 *paperback*

Set in Perpetua
by Koinonia Ltd, Manchester

Printed in Great Britain
by Hartnoll Ltd, Bodmin, Cornwall

Contents

	Preface	vii
1	Political apprenticeship	1
2	Building the party	19
3	War leader	49
4	Uncle Arthur	79
5	Foreign secretary	137
6	Tribune of peace	182
7	Conclusion	217
	Notes	223
	Bibliography	232
	Index	236

For David

Preface

It is now fifty years since Mary Agnes Hamilton published her biography of Arthur Henderson. A Newnham graduate and sometime Labour M.P., Mrs Hamilton was a writer and journalist who knew and admired her subject. Although her tone was occasionally patronising, she offered an affectionate portrait of a faithful, if somewhat dull politician, committed above all else to promoting the interests of the workers through the emerging Labour Party. Far more emotionally detached than her earlier sketches of Ramsay MacDonald as the man of destiny, the biography was written under the shadow of the 1931 crisis and the abortive Disarmament Conference, from both of which Henderson emerged as something of a tragic hero. The author never idolized him as she had MacDonald, but by 1938 many of the references to the latter bore the mark of rueful disenchantment. In her discussion of the growing enmity between the two leaders it is Henderson who is cast invariably as the injured party, the selfless servant of the movement contemptuously treated by the ungrateful MacDonald. Mrs Hamilton wrote as a friend and an advocate, not as a dispassionate scholar. Her proximity to her subject gave her work an immediacy that compensated for the lack of primary sources. The book, begun shortly after Henderson's death, relied not only on her own recollections, but those of other public figures, like Gilbert Murray, to amplify her interpretation.

Unfortunately, Henderson left little in the way of private papers, that vital grist to the biographer's mill. He was neither a voluminous nor a lively correspondent and never kept a diary. Surviving letters generally concern routine matters, the significance of which has often been lost with the passage of time. Much of his business was conducted through personal contact, and little evidence survives to document the daily encounters of Labour Party activity. The glimpses of him that appear in other people's diaries, notably those of MacDonald, Beatrice Webb, and Hugh Dalton, are enlightening, but none of these could profess to objectivity: MacDonald's references are usually derogatory, Webb's critically favorable, and Dalton's laudatory, though often condescending. Even Henderson's public writings and speeches generally bear the mark of other hands at work, aides and colleagues more articulate or less preoccupied than he usually was. Unlike MacDonald, he rarely engaged in political polemics; he was a trade unionist, a party manager, and a politician, never a writer. Lacking literary facility, he was content to let others give expression to his public views, although he did not hesitate to vent them at annual conferences or meetings of the National Executive Committee. The lack of controversy surrounding his life may help to explain why he has sparked so little historical investigation.

Despite its defects, Mrs Hamilton's biography has held sway for half a century. Its only rival, E. A. Jenkins's *From Foundry to Foreign Office,* published while Henderson was still alive, was a popular work intended to glorify and, somewhat implausibly, to romanticize, its subject for a working-class audience. Margaret Cole included a sketch of Henderson in her *Makers of the Labour Movement* (1948), while later historians, such as Henry R. Winkler, Ross McKibbin, and Kenneth Morgan have analyzed particular episodes of his career. Although long overdue, there has been no biographical reappraisal, no attempt to modify the outdated and partisan views that underscore Hamilton's work.

Such neglect stems in part from the shortage of sources, in

part from Henderson's somewhat bland and unreflective personality which tended to discourage psycho-biography. However significant his career, his was not a sufficiently provocative personality to entice biographers into reconstructing his life. Yet he is perhaps the most significant neglected Labour leader. In recent years Keir Hardie, Ramsay MacDonald, Ernest Bevin, Clement Attlee, Aneurin Bevan, Hugh Dalton, and Hugh Gaitskell have all been the subjects of major, full-scale studies and others are under way. Labour biography has now become respectable; it is no longer left to popularizers and apologists impervious to academic criteria of evidence. It is time to make restitution to Uncle Arthur, the last Labour leader to have begun his working life as an industrial worker, the only politician to have both managed the party as Secretary and served as its national leader, aside from MacDonald, whose tenure at Head Office was comparatively brief. With some gaps, Henderson served in the Commons for approximately thirty years and as Secretary for more than twenty, a record unmatched in Labour history. He was also the first Labour M.P. to serve as a Cabinet minister, the only prominent British Labour politician to have won a Nobel Peace Prize or to have presided over the Workers' International.

This biography does not profess to be either exhaustive or notably revisionist. Within the limits imposed by the series in which it is published, it seeks to update Mrs Hamilton's version and to incorporate the important and mostly quite recent scholarship that sheds light on Henderson's career. I am more concerned with casting a contemporary eye over his life than with overturning established opinion. I have largely excluded mention of his private life, happy and unexceptionable as it was, because there is nothing to add to the earlier account. Although I have examined scattered correspondence – little, in fact, survives – and made extensive use of the diary sources mentioned above, I have relied chiefly on the research of others. I am deeply obliged to a number of historians who have illuminated aspects of twentieth-century labour history and rendered my task considerably easier. It would have been impossible to write this book without the invaluable scholarship of Reginald Bassett, David Carlton, Christopher Howard, David Marquand, Ross McKibbin, Ben Pimlott, Philip Poirier, A. W. Purdue, A. F. Thompson, Henry R. Winkler, and J. M. Winter. If I have tried to modify Mrs Hamilton's judgments, I have rarely found it wise to tamper with theirs, and these historians would all recognize many of their own ideas in my work. I have also shamelessly borrowed much of the evidence that underpins their analyses. I would particularly single out Ross McKibbin, who did much of the groundwork for a reassessment of Henderson, and David Marquand, with whose interpretation of events I sometimes differ, but whose biography of Ramsay MacDonald is an essential landmark in Labour history. The late Reginald Bassett enlivened my interest in Labour politics many years ago with idiosyncratic recollections of MacDonald and Henderson. I owe an enormous debt to all of them which I am pleased to acknowledge. I also appreciate the efforts of archivists and librarians at Labour Party headquarters, the London School of Economics, the Bodleian Library, and the Public Record Office in helping me to locate material essential for my research.

I would further like to thank David Howell and Alec McAulay for inviting me to undertake this study and historians at the Australian National University, the Institute of Historical Research, London, and the Pacific Coast Conference on British Studies for valuable criticism of some of the views expressed here. Boston University provided a faculty research grant at the start of my investigation and the opportunity to spend a year in London where much of the writing was completed. I am grateful to my wife Jean for her unfailing encouragement and for her meticulous reading of the text. This book is affectionately dedicated to my son David.

1 Political apprenticeship

Arthur Henderson was, like Keir Hardie and Ramsay MacDonald, the only leaders in the early history of the Labour Party of greater prominence, a Scotsman. Born into poverty in a slum area of Glasgow on 13 September 1863, he was one of four children of David Henderson, described alternatively as a cotton spinner or a manual laborer. As in so many similar Victorian families, economic survival was invariably precarious, and the early death of his father, when Arthur was nine, reduced the household to virtual penury. He soon ceased attending the local St Mary's School and went to work in a photographer's shop. When his stepfather, Robert Heath, found employment in Newcastle, the family left Scotland for the North-East of England, the region with which Arthur's career as an industrial worker and novice politician became identified.

In Newcastle he secured a job as a messenger boy until the local educational authorities, more concerned with implementing the objectives of the National Education Act than with the exigencies of family earnings, compelled him to attend school. His formal education was, however, short-lived, and at the age of twelve he was apprenticed as an iron-moulder, first at Clarke's, a local foundry which soon failed, and later at the larger, renowned locomotive and foundry works of Robert Stephenson and Son. The work, six days a week from 6 a.m. to 5 p.m., was arduous, but Henderson acquired the reputation as a steady worker and 'good, clean moulder'. During his early years at the Stephenson works, he continued his schooling in evening classes and played local football. He helped to establish the Newcastle East Club, which subsequently became Newcastle United, and was in later years president of the Northumberland Football Association. Unlike some early labour leaders, he does not appear to have demonstrated any hunger for education and was more concerned to obtain practical knowledge than to develop his intellect. His home life, despite the death of his father, was harmonious: the children were raised on the Bible by their mother and regularly attended services at a Congregational chapel.

Until the age of sixteen Henderson's life was unexceptional, providing scarcely any intimation of the purposefulness and capacity for leadership so marked in later years. It was at that impressionable age that he encountered Rodney 'Gypsy' Smith, a celebrated Salvation Army evangelist, who converted him from conventional religious views to reborn faith in Jesus Christ. Having once testified publicly to his renewed conviction, he began to attend services at the Elswick Road Wesleyan Methodist chapel, where he was soon acknowledged as a member and invited to teach Sunday School. Like so many other Labour pioneers, Henderson was to discover in Methodism a focus for his energies and a guide to conduct. Instead of squandering resources on minor vices, he resolved to abstain from gambling and drink and to devote himself to open-air preaching, debating, and ministering to the poor. 'In those days the money was shared out in a public house,' he later recalled.

> I had to join in, and in a small way I began to drink. I am thankful to say it never got very far. But I asked myself one day where was this going to lead to? I determined to give it up. I turned, as it were, right round about. I determined to follow Christ.[1]

In a world hitherto circumscribed by the drudgery of the foundry and the claustrophobic environment of a working-class dwelling, the chapel offered an alternative community – embracing, uplifting, and useful. Wesleyanism gave him a place in society, enriching his life with the companionship of similarly inclined young people (including Eleanor Watson, his future wife) among whom he seems to have been quickly recognized as a leader. His closest friendships were made within the chapel, with those who shared his unswerving faith, rather than in political circles. The personal attributes acquired as an adolescent, all associated with Methodism, were to become life-long traits: neatness, methodical work habits, and rigid teetotalism.

In the same way the formative intellectual influences on him were religious ones. His reading consisted primarily of the Bible and the sermons of Wesley and Nonconformist preachers, although the seriousness of his social preoccupations was reflected in his reading of the Radical *Newcastle Chronicle,* whose contents he imparted to fellow workers. Sermons and religious tracts were an inadequate substitute for more traditional learning, but unlike MacDonald, Henderson's intellectual horizons were limited. As he admitted in an autobiographical sketch written in 1906,

> Being brought at sixteen years into active church and social work and engaged in serving my apprenticeship in the foundry, my time for exceptional reading was limited. My Bible has ever been an immense help, not only for its great influence but for its literary helpfulness. My best book has been my close contact with, and deep interest in, the spiritual, moral, social and industrial affairs of life.[2]

Never questioning the tenets of his Methodist faith, he absorbed its values, which gave him a moral certainty and fixed purpose evident throughout his life. Untroubled by doubt, Henderson possessed a mental stability that enabled him to endure economic and political vicissitudes with remarkable equanimity. It was not so much that Methodism transformed him into a socialist, but rather that it evoked a political response from him and helped him to articulate an ideology. It was Methodism which shaped the content of his democratic, social reforming beliefs, ideas always closer to Liberal than to socialist precepts. While political reforms might ameliorate social conditions, spiritual renewal was the precondition for a genuine transformation of community life. In addition to this fusion of Christian piety with democratic doctrine, Henderson was to obtain the kind of speaking experience in the pulpit, during his stints as a lay preacher, which provided valuable preparation for addressing labour audiences. Methodism defined his rhetorical style, taught him organizational skills, furnished experience in running meetings. His missionary activities could be adapted without much modification to the needs of a party still in its evangelical phase, as others, like Keir Hardie and Philip Snowden, also discovered.

Henderson's term as an apprentice lasted until he was seventeen. Then, according to traditions operative in his trade, he was obliged to work elsewhere for a year to gain additional experience before eligibility for a standard journeyman position. Invited by a former manager at Clarke's foundry to join his works, he travelled to Southampton where he was to remain for a year. At its end he was re-engaged at Stephenson's, this time as a skilled moulder, with acknowledged competence in all aspects of the craft. As a butty-man he soon became virtually a sub-employer within the works, with responsibility for other workers. It is important to remember that although he soon abandoned his trade to work as a union organizer and later within local politics, he did earn his living for more than a decade as a skilled craftsman. His credibility as a union official and as a party functionary derived in part from having pursued a craft. He also had first-hand experience of unemployment when the slump of the 1880s hit the North-East, heavily dependent on shipbuilding. Henderson, out of work for six months in 1884 and another eight in 1885, was quick to learn that qualifications did not guarantee a job. 'I shall never forget,' he wrote years later, 'the humiliation with

Political apprenticeship

which I used to return home every evening, and say I had been unable to find a job.'³ His mother, again widowed, depended on her sons' earnings, the loss of which meant immediate privation. In this sense, with direct experience of industrial poverty, he was a genuinely representative figure within the British labour movement, capable of identifying, as MacDonald never could, with the experience of ordinary workers.

In 1883 Henderson, fully qualified as a journeyman, joined the Friendly Society of Ironfounders, the very year that its longtime leader, Daniel Guile, one of the original Junta leaders of the 1860s, died. Under his benevolent direction, the union had pursued a course of deliberate moderation. Imbued with a strong sense of craft dignity, it had devoted itself chiefly to providing friendly benefits and avoiding clashes with employers by recourse to conciliation in disputes. The policies Guile fostered were perpetuated after his death, not least by Henderson himself, a staunch advocate of conciliation machinery. During the mid-1890s a conciliation board – of which he became chairman in 1908 – was established for the entire north-east coast. Industrial relations in the region were notably harmonious even during the years of militant New Unionism. The singular exception was the 1897 engineers' strike. Northumberland and Durham miners, politically cautious at all times, continued to adhere to the ethos of the sliding scale of payment and disavowed legislation for an eight-hour day until 1908, when statutory enactment left no alternative to compliance.

Nor was it only in trade union policy that the North-East exemplified the moderation so characteristic of the late Victorian labour movement. Ever since Thomas Burt, secretary of the Northumberland Miners, became one of the first two working-class M.P.s in 1874, the region had been receptive to Lib–Lab collaboration. There were soon four mine union M.P.s for Northumberland and Durham returned with Liberal cooperation, in addition to the moderate secretary of the Seamen's Union, Havelock Wilson, returned for Middlesbrough in 1892. Yet despite the working-class vote, local Liberal associations only gradually overcame their resistance to working men as candidates, even though the concentration of miners in certain constituencies rendered the selection of union candidates inevitable. Despite the recalcitrance of entrenched Liberal elites, many of the newly politically-conscious workers identified with the fortunes of the Liberal Party and particularly with Gladstone.

In October 1891 Henderson attended the ceremonies conferring the freedom of Newcastle on the Liberal leader. When the National Liberal Federation promulgated its Newcastle program in the same year, he applauded its call for Irish Home Rule, temperance reform, manhood suffrage, the payment of M.P.s, a platform devised to attract working-class no less than middle-class voters. It was here that he came to the attention of Robert Spence Watson, the Federation's shrewd president, whose patronage he was to enjoy in years to come. Ross McKibbin has argued that Henderson never escaped Watson's influence, and that his later preoccupation with international relations can be attributed to the pacifist radicalism absorbed from Watson and his circle in the 1890s.[4] Certainly it was as early as 1892 that he was tapped by Watson as having a political future within the Liberal camp. In the general election of 1892 Henderson worked hard to secure John Morley's re-election as one of the Liberal members for Newcastle and was invited to address a public meeting in his behalf. Morley praised his speech as possessing 'the ring of the true democrat and a workman who respects himself and respects his order'. When Morley's elevation to the Cabinet occasioned a by-election, Henderson again figured prominently in his campaign, thereby increasing his own visibility in Liberal circles.

In the autumn of 1892 two Liberal councillors invited him to stand for the Newcastle City Council, the election which launched his political career. Despite some resistance from workers who did not want to be represented by a member of their own class, he was pleased that fellow foundry workers requested a holiday on polling day in order to cast their votes and help to ensure his election. It was through his experience on the Newcastle and later the Darlington Councils that he learned the fundamentals of political compromise that shaped his outlook. Right from the start he perceived that the essential work of the council was carried on in committees and that the most effective politicians operated behind the scenes rather than indulging in speech-making. Although council work was arduous for someone like Henderson, still employed at Stephenson's for eleven hours a day, it provided essential practical experience for an aspiring politician.

At the same time he was regarded by his own union as a man of considerable abilities, although this may simply have reflected his growing local reputation. He had won recognition as secretary of his local lodge, a position involving responsibility for correspondence and finance, for arranging meetings and adjudicating disputes. He often represented the lodge at district conferences and transformed it into a model of good management and prudent expenditure. In 1892 the Ironfounders had singled him out for appointment as district organiser for Northumberland, Durham, and Lancashire. Accountable to the General Secretary in Manchester, he was obliged to travel around the region and to report regularly to union headquarters. Since the position was salaried, it enabled him to forsake foundry work. While keeping him in contact with his trade, it meant that at twenty-nine Henderson's life as a manual worker had ended. For the next eleven years trade union activity was the focus of his energies. It kept him in touch not merely with his own union, but with the labour movement throughout the region, furnishing the contacts and experience of industrial negotiation. From 1902 to 1911 he held the position of National Organiser for the union, although by the latter date his party and Parliamentary functions rendered his union role rather more perfunctory. The combination of union functionary and local councillor, coupled with his continuing commitment to lay preaching and temperance reform, gave Henderson a political base in which he felt secure, developed his instinct for the handling of administrative business, and nurtured his self-confidence. It was incomparable training for a future labour politician.

Before leaving Stephenson's, Henderson helped to devise conciliation machinery and, although it was ineffective at the time, he was in a key position to continue efforts when he became district delegate. In October 1894 a Conciliation Board was established for the entire North-East, including not only Newcastle, but all the lodges in the region, to deal with industrial problems. Installed as its secretary, Henderson intervened to prevent a strike among foundry workers. Even though the machinery eventually broke down, it was reconstituted in 1907, with Henderson becoming its chairman. It remained in his own mind, long after he ceased to be involved with local industrial grievances, the model for dissolving industrial conflict, resuscitated in the schemes he sought to promote after the First World War. In 1894 he attended the T.U.C. for the first time as delegate of the Ironfounders. Despite his Liberal affinities he endorsed a resolution in favour of nationalization of the means of production, but nothing in his career at that time indicated any predisposition towards labour independence, which the I.L.P., launched the previous year, avowed. Unaffiliated with any socialist group, he was friendly with local socialists, whose deputation to the Newcastle Council he sometimes led.

What is most notable about Henderson's politics in the 1890s is his unflagging Liberalism. Liberal patrons, at Stephenson's, within the Newcastle party organization, in his own union, and later the Pease family, fostered his career, and neither through intellectual inclination, nor personal conviction was he disposed to betray his patrons. Lacking any formulated ideology, his tacit support of nationalization notwithstanding, Henderson was a pragmatic politician, invariably disinclined to theory. He regarded politics as an extension of trade union activity, at least at this stage of his career, and in both his objectives were identical – the improvement of working conditions. There is little evidence at the outset of a broader national, still less an international, perspective. In so far as he could articulate general issues, the Newcastle Programme measured the extent of his objectives.

The Liberals had lost one of their Newcastle parliamentary seats in 1892, possibly because of working-class abstentions over the party's continued social exclusiveness. It was for that reason that Watson, Morley and the Liberal Association executive began to promote Henderson's candidature for the second seat. Addressing an executive meeting on 15 February 1895, he made a favorable impression, speaking, as J. L. Garvin later noted, 'to the top-hatted, not in tones of petition, but on direct Labour representation as a right'.[5] It was, however, significant that he was insisting on direct representation rather than on the need for an independent labour candidacy. The executive, doubtlessly manipulated by Watson, recommended Henderson for adoption by a vote of 84 to 3, but a meeting of the whole Liberal Association a week later rejected the proposal and, by an overwhelming majority, selected former M.P. James Craig instead. A ship broker and successful fund raiser for party coffers, Craig had proven ineffective during his term in the Commons. His readoption in 1895 was less a mark of residual loyalty than a repudiation of the clique within the Newcastle executive eager to foist working-class candidates on a recalcitrant party machine.

In the event both Morley and Craig were defeated in the 1895 election, which returned the Conservatives to power nationally. However promising his career, it was hardly surprising that Henderson, still unknown to voters, lacking funds and influence, and then only thirty-two, should have been at a disadvantage compared to a familiar, well-heeled local notable. Despite the espousal of working-class candidates by progressive elements within the party leadership, Henderson's claim was hardly irrefutable. The Liberal Association which disavowed his nomination was more representative of local party opinion than figures, like Watson, who were trying to popularize its image. The leading Newcastle paper, moreover, waged an unscrupulous campaign against Henderson, which was hardly calculated to help his cause. Nor is there any reason to doubt that the local party functionaries genuinely believed that Craig was more likely to secure victory than the untried union official whom party bigwigs were trying to impose on them. Henderson accepted the negative decision without bitterness, placing himself at the disposal of both Liberal candidates during the campaign. Morley and Craig were unable to buck the national Tory tide, and it seems unlikely that Henderson would have been capable of reversing the trend locally.

Despite his failure to secure the nomination – or perhaps because of it – Henderson was drawn even more deeply into party politics when he was appointed as agent to Sir Joseph Pease, the Liberal member for Barnard Castle, at a salary of £250 per year, twice his trade union earnings. As a mining and agricultural constituency, strongly imbued with Methodism, it was well suited to Henderson's background. The Pease family were Quaker industrialists in the region with a financial interest in Stephenson's, his former employer. It was Jack Pease, Sir Joseph's son and a director at the foundry, who recommended him as a natural organizer who retained the confidence of fellow workers. Reluctant at first, Sir Joseph consulted local political activists, who confirmed his son's estimation. Henderson accepted the offer on the understanding he could remain active within his union. The appointment, which obliged the family to relocate to Darlington, extended Henderson's own political base. In 1897 he was elected a member of the Durham County Council, and the next year gained a seat on the Darlington Town Council. By 1903 he had become a J.P. and Mayor of Darlington, the first working man so honored.

Pease certainly had no cause to regret his choice. Not only was the constituency better organized than before, but Henderson was unfailingly loyal to the party. Despite Mrs Hamilton's assurances to the contrary, there is nothing to suggest that he was disenchanted with Liberalism. Indeed he encountered criticism from more militant elements in his own union who disliked his professed Liberalism and disapproved his working politically for a leading industrialist. But if his union occasionally challenged his cautious policies, his religious proclivities suited the temper of the region. He identified with the strong sense of fellowship, the habit of plain speaking, and the simple Methodist piety of the colliery villages. He was in constant demand as a preacher, often preaching several times on a Sunday with temperance meetings interspersed. He travelled around Northumberland, Lancashire, and Yorkshire, taking an active role in chapel affairs. His faith never lost its sustaining certitude, and his unanalytical cast of mind did not dispose him toward metaphysical speculation. His reading was largely restricted to theological tracts, to the works of Fox and Wesley, and, above all, to the Scriptures. The core of his Wesleyan faith was an abiding commitment to fellowship and cooperation. It was his profound sense of solidarity with working people that Henderson translated from religion to trade union activity and then to politics, and there was nothing in Liberal doctrine inimical to such religious views. In the 1890s Nonconformists still found a refuge in the Liberal Party, and if many chapel-going workers resented its social exclusiveness, they found little to repudiate doctrinally.

In spite of stalwart efforts to increase Pease's Liberal majority at the 1900 general election, Henderson was by no means impervious to labour initiatives. In his role as union delegate he attended the inaugural meeting of the Labour Representation Committee, to which the Ironfounders affiliated from its inception. In fact, L.R.C. provisions did not unequivocally preclude continued Liberal membership however much its intentions, as articulated by more militant socialists, diverged from such a policy. The Liberals did not challenge the return of David Shackleton of the Weavers as L.R.C. nominee for Clitheroe, recognizing perhaps that the candidate was a Liberal rather than a socialist. Nor was there anything incompatible in Henderson's continuing in Pease's employ and campaigning for L.R.C. candidate Will Crooks, who, in any event, contested Woolwich in March 1903 without Liberal opposition.

By the end of 1902 the Ironfounders had resolved to put forward their own candidates who would contest seats under the L.R.C. banner. To this end they agreed to impose a levy of threepence a quarter on their 18,000 members, with each branch having the right to nominate candidates who might then campaign within the union at large. Henderson garnered a majority of branch nominations and polled first in a field of six, despite criticism from dissidents who complained that he was no longer actively associated with the union. Although some branches demanded a second ballot, Henderson was officially declared the union nominee in November 1902 with instructions to find himself a constituency. This did not involve a conflict in loyalties, since union candidates were guaranteed a free hand as long as they voted with labour on issues pertinent to union welfare. Anyone still oblivious to Henderson's Liberal leanings was disabused of any misconceptions during the selection process, when he emerged as the favorite of the union's Liberal wing and of its president, Fred Maddison. Despite the understanding that the candidate would fight under the L.R.C. label, it was by no means certain that this implied opposition to the Liberals, and Henderson felt no compulsion to resign his Barnard Castle agency merely because he had been selected.

While the Woolwich by-election was still under way, the L.R.C. convened in Newcastle, with Henderson representing the Ironfounders. This conference moved more decisively towards independence, when it adopted Pete Curran's resolution that members of the executive and officials of affiliated organizations should neither identify themselves with, nor promote the interests of the Liberal Party, a gesture whose implications were sufficiently opposed to the underlying loyalties of trade unionists that it was repealed the next year. Furthermore, the 'party pledge' was introduced, binding successful candidates to abide by the majority decisions of the L.R.C. contingent in Parliament or resign their seats. The delegates also accepted the executive's proposal to establish a Parliamentary fund. Based on a voluntary levy of 1d per affiliated member, it was designed to cover part of electoral expenses as well as to support M.P.s with a £200 annual salary. Although he had failed to win an executive slot, despite his nomination by the Ironfounders, Henderson made an impression on the assembled delegates when he moved an amendment to the rules urging that affiliation fees be raised to fourpence and pleading for adequate election machinery. As an experienced agent, he was painfully aware of the deficiencies of Labour organization. 'If we are going to do something more than simply play a game,' he told the gathering, 'we cannot do it on a penny contribution' or on an electoral register devised by the other parties. The amendment was defeated by the unions in alliance with the I.L.P., whose secretary, John Penny, labelled Henderson's suggestion as extravagant. This rebuff did not prevent his election as L.R.C. Treasurer and an invitation to put his experience as an election agent to good use by collaborating with MacDonald on a pamphlet on *Organization and the Law of Registration and Elections*. Curran's resolution would have appeared to preclude membership of both the L.R.C. and the Liberal Party, but this did not prevent Henderson from continuing as Pease's agent even after he became Treasurer.

In December 1902 J. A. Pease had informed Herbert Gladstone that his ailing father was unable to stand again at Barnard Castle. While recognizing that Henderson might be obliged to resign his position should his union invite him to become a formal candidate, Pease predicted that a fund would be raised to ensure his retention as election agent. His employer had the impression that should Henderson follow a policy of independent labour representation, it would be against his personal inclinations. Events moved more rapidly than Jack Pease anticipated, and in February 1903 Sir Joseph announced his impending retirement. Although some local Liberals (including members of the Pease family) clearly regarded Henderson as a plausible Liberal nominee, the L.R.C. intervened to render such an outcome impossible. In March Henderson was certified as an eligible L.R.C. candidate by its executive, and on 1 April a hastily formed Labour and Progressive Association, representing local trade unionists as well as some Liberals and members of the I.L.P., adopted him as the official candidate at Barnard Castle itself, something Pease does not appear to have foreseen. Shortly thereafter the L.R.C. executive gave its official blessing to his nomination, although not without some misgivings. The S.D.F. journal *Justice* had derided him as 'a camp follower of the Liberal party',[6] but even the I.L.P.'s less inflammatory Bruce Glasier had recently dismissed him as 'backboneless'.[7] Henderson was still Sir Joseph's agent at the time he was selected as L.R.C. nominee and would probably have felt more comfortable were he to enjoy Liberal sponsorship. At that point he was approached by Jack Pease, who informed him that the local Liberal Association proposed to invite him to contest Barnard Castle as a Lib–Lab. Whatever his own inclinations, Henderson declared that as a consequence of union and L.R.C. decisions, such an option was no longer open to him.

Once he had been nominated as an independent Labour candidate, the Liberals retaliated by adopting Hubert Beaumont, a protegé of Samuel Story, the Chairman of the National Liberal Federation and an avowed opponent of the L.R.C. He was selected against the wishes of important elements within the local Liberal caucus who favored allowing Henderson a straight fight against the Conservative candidate, a policy that had succeeded in the Clitheroe by-election. Henderson, on the other hand, fearing possible Liberal reprisals if the L.R.C. contested too many Durham seats, warned H. D. Hughes, the L.R.C. agent at Darlington, that his union would not allow him to contest the seat if he were to face Liberal opposition.[8] Convinced that he had no chance of winning a three-cornered contest, he pleaded with MacDonald to allow him to withdraw, prompting L.R.C. leaders to doubt that he would stick it out. Keir Hardie, certain that Henderson would ultimately withdraw, thought that Labour should concentrate its efforts on Darlington and Stockton. Were Henderson to retire, it would leave the L.R.C. with the unenviable task of finding another candidate, presumably one without his local visibility. Encouraged by initial local enthusiasm for his candidacy, he quickly changed his tune, and by the end of May he could see 'no other course than that of going full steam ahead'. He now insisted that the L.R.C. and his union 'will have to drag me out by the neck' if they now decided to abandon the race.[9]

When the death of Sir Joseph in June precipitated a by-election, Jack Pease and Spence Watson tried to induce Beaumont to stand down on the grounds that his candidacy violated the Liberal policy of accommodation with Labour. Herbert Gladstone, Liberal Chief Whip, hesitated to intervene directly but suggested that the party would be indebted to Beaumont were he to withdraw in favor of Henderson, 'who is sound on Free Trade, Educn., and Temperance and the leading questions which interest progressive politicians'.[10] In the belief that Henderson should be allowed a straight fight with the Tories, party leaders warned that Beaumont's candidacy would have a disastrous impact on the working-class electorate, which the Liberals were assiduously courting. There is little doubt that Henderson would have preferred closer links with the Liberal Association than independence allowed. But while they were dismayed by his tendency to distance himself from avowed socialists, I.L.P. members had to concede that for such a recent convert from Liberalism, he seemed 'remarkably straight on independence'.[11]

Thus he enjoyed the advantage of Labour solidarity and Liberal encouragement at the same time. MacDonald, Crooks, and Shackleton addressed enthusiastic crowds, but Labour ebullience did nothing to dissuade Cadbury's *Daily News* and Rowntree's *Northern Echo* from endorsing him. No prominent Liberal speakers appeared to rally the faithful on Beaumont's behalf, and disaffected local Liberals formed a Barnard Castle Labour and Progressive Association to work for Henderson. On the other hand, the *Leeds and Yorkshire Mercury,* lamenting the apparent desertion of Beaumont by the party executive, warned that if the 'Socialist wreckers' won at Barnard Castle, 'there is not a liberal constituency in the country safe from their attack'.[12] Henderson qualified his independence by promising to support the Lib—Lab miners' candidate at the next election, a pledge calculated to appease Liberal voters. With his election address, which featured his picture in full regalia as Mayor of Darlington, endorsing trade union legislation, a universal system of old age pensions, poor law reform, and modification of the 1902 Education Act, Henderson scarcely diverged from the Liberal platform. Indeed his staunch advocacy of free trade made him appear more Liberal than Beaumont, who, by embracing Joseph Chamberlain's tariff reform proposals, forfeited not merely working-class votes but those of traditional Liberals. As A. W. Purdue has noted, 'What Liberal voters in Barnard Castle had, in fact, to choose between was a candidate orthodox in name but heretical in policy and one who, though wearing the L.R.C. label, was very close to Liberalism.'[13]

While sections of the Liberal press urged voters in Barnard Castle to resolve their differences and unite behind Henderson, Beaumont's increasingly blatant support of protection earned the hostility of Liberal leaders. Henderson could look forward not merely to votes from avowed radicals but even to those of disaffected moderates, who followed the promptings of the party managers and the Liberal press. Although his campaign speeches did little to set him apart from orthodox Liberalism, Beaumont and Story attempted to malign him as an opportunist and traitor to the Liberal cause with which he had hitherto been identified. Shifting their attack from the Tory to Henderson, the Liberals also sought to embarrass him by distributing a fly-sheet enumerating his earlier attacks on the I.L.P. In fact Henderson had as little as possible to do with the I.L.P., and local activists thought it expedient to warn prominent members to stay away to avoid alienating voters. At the urging of MacDonald, Henderson grudgingly agreed to invite Snowden and other I.L.P. speakers, but he relied mainly on trade unionists like Shackleton and Crooks for platform help. As the first by-election since Joseph Chamberlain pronounced in favor of tariff reform, the campaign was dominated by the fiscal question, a considerable advantage for Henderson in a traditionally Liberal constituency. His victory by the narrow majority of forty-seven over the Tory, with Beaumont coming at the bottom of the poll, vindicated the policy of Labour independence. It was the first time that an independent candidate, standing in a single member constituency, had defeated both major parties. It was equally a striking defeat for the autonomy of local Liberal leaders, still reluctant to sanction the shift towards Lib–Lab electoral accomodation. Never concealing their preference for Henderson, national party leaders virtually withheld support from their official candidate at Barnard Castle, encouraging those Liberals who favored a Labour representative with orthodox Liberal principles. What the results indicated was that an informal alliance had already evolved, and that constituency organizations which refused to recognize the new political alignment faced a loss of safe seats for the sake of exclusiveness. Finally, by pursuing the policy of independence, the L.R.C. ensured that Henderson entered Parliament not as the Lib–Lab M.P. he might have become, but as a pivotal member of the small band of five – soon to be reduced to four – Labour members, marked for leadership in the years to come.

2 Building the party

Henderson was a man who knew his place, not in terms of deference to his social betters, but rather in the congruence of public and private roles. His sense of his own class identity gave him confidence, a sureness of touch in politics that differentiated him from other labour leaders, like Ramsay MacDonald, who felt no such kinship with working men. As a trade union official, a Methodist teetotaller and lay preacher, and a pragmatic political moderate, he typified the prevailing currents in the labour movement. He derived strength from his own experience, applying the lessons he had learned in his craft, his union, and in local politics to the national stage. To be sure, his election to Parliament in 1903 under the auspices of the Labour Representation Committee was fortuitous. His conversion to independent labour representation was the result not of an ideological progression, but of his union's decision to sponsor candidates who would fight under the L.R.C. banner. While Henderson might have found association with the Liberals equally, if not more, congenial, he willingly deferred to the dictates of his union. Nor was this merely opportunism. Throughout his career he deliberately subordinated his own personal inclinations to the interests of the labour institutions to which he belonged. As Ross McKibbin has observed, 'The unequalled authority he came to possess in the Labour movement was perhaps less a result of his ability to lead it in the direction he wanted than of his sensitivity to its wishes.'[1]

As an official of the Friendly Society of Ironfounders, he entered politics with a solid trade union base and understood the value of maintaining close ties not only with brother unionists, but with organized labour. In return for his loyalty, the Ironfounders gave Henderson their full confidence. More than any of the other party founders, he became the spokesman and the embodiment of the trade union element, a source of power in his early years in Parliament and even more when he became a spokesman of the movement during the First World War. After David Shackleton of the Weavers, who preceded him to the House of Commons and whose pre-eminence he acknowledged, became a government official, Henderson emerged as the most influential trade unionist politician of his generation, striving to promote the unity between the industrial and political wings on which the ultimate success of the Labour Party depended.

If trade union ties defined his political identity, it was his religious convictions which shaped his political outlook. His affinity for Liberal values stemmed in part from their harmonious resonance with the moral precepts of his Methodist faith. Although he never hesitated to deplore the 'slavery of an uncontrolled competitive system', he diverged from those socialists who looked to 'a social and economic salvation' as the goal of human endeavor. Even a more equitable distribution of wealth and a higher standard of education would accomplish little without the spiritual deliverance that adherence to the doctrines of Christ made possible. The social efficiency of the state, he asserted, depended on the moral fitness of its citizens, a view more closely aproximating traditional Liberal precepts than socialist ideology.[2] While recognizing that the masses were all too often alienated by the indifference of institutional religion, he believed that Christianity, sustained by its innate sympathy for the wretched and its belief in universal brotherhood, might yet rekindle the ebbing faith of the working class. 'When Christianity is shown in its real nature,' he wrote,

Building the party

...gressive force, destroying the evil of the individual life, ...orming the character of the workers' environment, taking ...ance of social defects, seeking to right industrial wrongs, and ...ng the injustices under which the workers suffer, then it ...ail to command the sympathies of the common people.³

...strove to bridge the gulf between Christianity and working class politics by preaching in Methodist chapels, addressing temperance gatherings, and participating in the Brotherhood movement. When the Wesleyan conference launched the Union for Social Service in 1903 to undertake social work under Methodist sponsorship, Henderson became one of its most ardent proponents, speaking on its behalf at demonstrations up and down the country. These religious pursuits not only suited his evangelical temper; they were inseparable from his political activity, and, like his trade union affiliation, helped to extend his personal following throughout the movement.

Despite the applause his electoral victory evoked among those seeking to promote independent labour representation, Henderson remained suspect in the eyes of socialists. He was unenthusiastic, to say the least, about the resolution passed at the 1903 Newcastle L.R.C. conference stipulating that M.P.s and party officials should refrain from identifying with or promoting the interests of the Liberal Party. His own union had imposed fewer restraints, offering him a free hand in politics as long as he voted with Labour on issues involving trade union welfare. Although he had affirmed his independence during the by-election, he certainly courted Liberal support and, even after his election, continued to speak on temperance platforms and under the auspices of the Free Trade Union, conduct hardly likely to endear him to I.L.P. militants. When Henderson and Shackleton seemed tacitly to endorse Liberals in by-election contests, Bruce Glasier suggested that they be offered I.L.P. platforms or else cease campaign speeches altogether. MacDonald, prone to extol the

Arthur Henderson

virtue of independence until his own election to P[...] disparaged their 'tendency to merge in the Liberals'.[4] By no[...] intimidated by such criticism, Henderson insisted that it was [...] to give a lead to Labour voters in contests without independe[nt] Labour candidates, a policy implicitly condoned in the covert agreement concluded by MacDonald and the Liberal Whip, Herbert Gladstone, in September 1903. This arrangement, which gave the L.R.C. a free run in certain identified constituencies, presupposed electoral cooperation, but also some element of mutual support of Labour and Liberals within Parliament.

The fact that Henderson appeared ideologically undistinguishable from the Lib–Labs in the Commons in no way vitiated his allegiance to the fledgling Labour group. Even before his election he had begun to collaborate with MacDonald on the handbook for L. R. C. election agents which was published in August under the title *Organisation and the Law of Registration and Elections*. Applying his own experience as a Liberal agent, Henderson wrote the sections on registration and advised MacDonald on matters of organization. In June he had criticized the Secretary's draft for implying that voluntary workers would be sufficiently devoted and efficient to perform the necessary functions. As he noted in an illuminating passage:

> ... if we have come to stay (and that I cannot doubt) then the movement as a whole is large enough, and ought to be generous enough to do its work in such a way as to bring conviction to the outsider that we know the task we had undertaken, and we were going about it in a business way. Then I would like you to consider for a moment the immense advantage it would be in the event of a sudden By-Election, to be in a position to bring a dozen of these paid Agents into the Contest, giving one to each polling District, it would mean the difference between winning and losing. I think you would improve your otherwise excellent paper by pointing out the need of the paid Registration Agent.[5]

In his own constituency he began to consolidate a local party organization after his election, based on individual members paying direct contributions, permanent ward committees, and a women's section. Although his popularity derived from trade union links, his ties to the district and prominence as a lay preacher helped enhance the personal loyalty he commanded as an M.P. Whereas most constituencies which Labour contested before 1914 depended at election time on loosely-knit trades councils or on I.L.P. branches to mobilize working-class voters, Barnard Castle, with its well-managed electoral machine and evangelical style, established a pattern for local organization that other districts came to emulate. In 1904, anxious to safeguard his own constituency party, he proposed to the L.R.C. executive that local Labour associations be permitted to affiliate with the central body in those districts not covered by trades councils. The plan, adopted by the executive, was passed at the 1905 national conference despite some union opposition. Thus right from the start Henderson put into practice the plan he would try to implement nationally in 1918: a permanent constituency party with a professional agent, relying on the active support of local trade unionists and individual members. Never a dynamic speaker, he understood that elections were won through effective organization and local activism rather than in response to the inspirational qualities of the candidate.

With his knack for organizational detail, it was inevitable that Henderson would immediately be drawn into that facet of L.R.C. activity. In 1904 he was chosen as party Treasurer, and in late 1903 and early 1904 he found himself supervising much of the work of the L.R.C. while MacDonald was incapacitated by appendicitis. Succeeding Shackleton as Chairman of the L.R.C. in 1905, he assumed a central role in developing the electoral machinery of the party during the critical months before the general election.

Without becoming reconciled to socialist doctrine *per se,* he certainly took the idea of independence seriously. Like others who joined the party in its early days, he had an acutely developed working-class consciousness. For him labour representation meant more than simply the political expression of trade union interests; it meant a sense of identity with working class traditions and the democratic impulses of ordinary people. If this did not necessarily imply a rejection of the constitution or of capitalism, it did connote a championing of the interests of his fellow workers. 'What we want,' he told the 1904 L.R.C. Bradford conference, 'is to get away as far as possible from mere trade representation. We want Labour representation, in the proper sense of the term.'

In the House of Commons his success was, at first, less palpable. When Henderson was elected in 1903, he joined a small band of four L.R.C. members: Keir Hardie, elected for Merthyr Tydfil, Richard Bell of the Railway Servants, who sat for Derby, and two earlier by-election victors, David Shackleton in Clitheroe and Will Crooks in Woolwich. Their number was depleted when Bell joined the Lib–Labs, although he remained in the Commons until the end of 1909. Too small a group to make a serious impact, they also disagreed as to which legislative measures should be accorded priority. Nor were Henderson and Crooks predisposed to flamboyant political conduct, as Keir Hardie often was. They were bound to work closely with Liberals in order to secure a place on the ballot for Labour-sponsored bills, but their influence with the opposition party was inevitably less than it would become when the Liberals came to power at the end of 1905. Furthermore, even Henderson found it difficult to devote his complete attention to Parliamentary business, assiduous though his attendance was. Until 1906 his family remained in Darlington, while he shared digs in Lambeth during the short Parliamentary sessions with Shackleton. Increasingly organizational responsibilities took him away from London, while temperance activity and preaching continued to be a drain on his time.

During his first year in the Commons trade union-sponsored M.P.s were for the most part unorganized. Hardie was frequently absent because of illness, and his behavior was erratic. It was Shackleton and Henderson who gave the group what cohesion it had, although Hardie continually sniped at his colleagues for their lack of aggressiveness. 'The group,' he wrote Glasier in July 1904, 'doesn't appear to be making much of a show.'[6] Henderson's contributions to debates were cogent, frequently grounded in personal experience, but tended to be dull, unlikely to dazzle his audience. Even Mrs Hamilton was obliged to concede that 'his speeches did not set the Thames on fire'.[7] His maiden speech in February 1904, a resounding defense of free trade, warned that declining output was the result of inefficient management rather than international competition. Protection, opposed by the workers he represented, would be injurious to national well-being. Several months later he spoke against a Tory-sponsored licensing bill, which, he claimed, constituted unwarranted protection to the liquor industry and a hazard to working people, who were its greatest victims. Both of these interventions were in accord with Liberal objections and, although couched in terms of concern for workers, did not specifically pertain to labour legislation.

II

It was in the office of the Labour Representation Committee, not in the halls of Westminster, that Henderson and MacDonald began their fruitful, if always problematic partnership. At this stage the talents of the two men complemented each other admirably. Although both were Scottish in origin and close in age, the contrasts between them were profound. MacDonald, handsome and mercurial, restless and moody, fought to overcome the handicaps of his upbringing. A magnetic speaker with serious intellectual pretensions, he gained ascendancy over the more parochial labour figures who populated the movement. They were attracted to his visionary socialism, however vague its objectives, and recognized his mastery of political strategy and knowledge of international affairs. Despite his charm, MacDonald could be petulant and suspicious, easily wounded by imagined slights to his self-esteem. Contemptuous of Henderson's pedestrian intellect, he relied on his judgment and grasp of political detail. If Henderson appreciated MacDonald's charismatic qualities and deferred to his authority, MacDonald in turn came to recognize that Henderson was 'a rock of steady strength' who was not a competitor for the leadership of the party. Mrs Hamilton described the two, perhaps over-vividly, as 'a race-horse and a cart-horse, a tiger and an elephant in yoke'.[8] Until 1914 they were, more often than not, in agreement about political strategy, committed to the uneasy balance between Labour independence and cooperation with the Liberals both in and out of Parliament. More than that, despite recurrent clashes, they offered each other support against the recriminations of socialist militants who balked at the policy of caution both leaders espoused.

The 1904 L.R.C. conference decided to make contributions to the Parliamentary fund, used to finance electoral contests and to pay salaries to M.P.s, compulsory, but the beneficiaries of this decision bridled at attempts by the I.L.P. to monitor their conduct. To be sure, the same conference repealed a 1903 resolution binding M.P.s to obey the decisions of the majority of the Parliamentary group, thus allowing some room for individual conscience. What troubled Henderson was not the insistence on conformity – he was always a team player – but the snide remarks about dereliction of duty. He had not only been censured for appearing on free trade platforms but was now criticized for insufficient diligence. 'I see in the *Labour Leader*,' he grumbled in a letter to MacDonald, an article headed 'Gentle Art of Avoiding Labour Meetings'. I don't know if it is intended for me but it is so put that it [is] calculated to give many the impression that I am the delinquent... If the *Leader* is going to advocate that because we receive from the Parliamentary fund we should give up going to Church and Chapel meetings to speak and should this be the decision of the movement I for one shall find another means of support than the Parliamentary fund. It is not Independence they want it is automatic machines into which the £200 can be put and Labour service of one particular brand will be supplied.[9]

After the 1906 general election the position of the Labour Representation Committee, renamed the Labour Party, substantially changed. In place of the paltry four members, twenty-nine were returned, their number subsequently reinforced after the miners, hitherto identified as Lib–Labs, resolved in 1908 to affiliate with Labour. An independent group, representing organized labour, had arrived and could no longer be discounted. On the other hand, the fact that the great majority of Labour M.P.s held their seats only on Liberal sufferance suggested at least an implicit alliance. Labour was also dependent on the new Liberal government to introduce a trade disputes bill to reverse the detrimental Taff Vale decision. In effect, therefore, Labour's freedom of action – both in terms of electoral strategy and parliamentary action – were circumscribed by the ascendancy of the Liberals.

It was not merely the secret pact with the Liberals which accounted for the increase in Labour victories. Thanks mainly to Henderson's skilful manipulation of local organization, Labour was poised to take advantage of the free run the Liberals had conceded in thirty seats, many of them in Lancashire. The fifty official candidates represented a significant increase over the dozen who had gone to the poll in 1900 and stretched the campaign resources of the party to its limits. MacDonald secured one of the two Leicester seats, while Henderson, unopposed by the Liberals this time, increased his poll to 5,540 and his majority to 1,605, making Barnard Castle virtually a safe Labour seat. He was now a national figure, able to fight on his record, and the mainly working-class electorate, with no Liberal deflecting progressive sentiment, responded decisively. In his election speeches he attacked the Taff Vale judgment, defended the maintenance of free trade in the face of Tory protectionism, pleaded for better education and the emancipation of women.

As Chairman of the L.R.C. executive, Henderson, who presided over the annual conference held in London on 15 February, set the celebratory tone. Success at the polls provided clear evidence that 'a real, live Labour Party' was now 'an accomplished fact in British politics'. He proclaimed a willingness to support the Liberal Government, but equally a sense of responsibility to keep the ministry 'up to the scratch of its own professions'. Admitting that the assembled trade unionists and socialists did not agree on all points, he spoke of the overriding need for unity 'to break down the forces of privilege and monopoly that have for so long dominated the political life of our country'. Despite his Liberal roots, he insisted that the party should 'guard as a sacred right the principle of independence which has assured the success of our movement'.

Lest his audience question his own allegiance, he told a Queen's Hall gathering ten days later that 'the return of Labour members to Parliament marks an important epoch in the progress of Socialism'. Thus by 1906 Henderson had shed the Liberal trappings of his youth and embraced the doctrines – and even colleagues – from which he had recoiled in 1903. In principle his views altered very little, if at all, but he now saw Labour as the inevitable instrument of working-class advancement and recognized a kind of pragmatic, non-revolutionary, classcollaborationist socialism as its ideological basis. Even now he did not, in contrast to most of the early party leaders, join a socialist society. MacDonald's prominence stemmed in part from his links with both the I.L.P. and the Fabian Society; Henderson belonged at this time only to his trade union, which had sponsored his Parliamentary candidacy. It was not until 1912 that he joined the Fabian Society and then perhaps only because his eligibility to serve as Secretary of the British section of the International might have been questioned had he remained unaffiliated to any socialist organization.

When the new Parliament convened, Keir Hardie insisted on standing for Chairman, a position to which he was incontestably entitled, but for which he was constitutionally unsuited. He was elected by a majority of one vote over David Shackleton, a more capable leader, if less revered figure. Much of the more mundane work fell to Henderson, who had been chosen as Chief Whip. Prone to bully Labour M.P.s, whose attendance, once the initial excitement wore off, was intermittent, Henderson earned their respect for his diligence and patient service to the party. He began to demonstrate his capacity for the management of men, the mixture of benevolence and disciplinary rigor that earned him the sobriquet of Uncle Arthur, which was to serve him in good stead during his long stint as party Secretary. Once he had become convinced that his own future and that of the Labour Party were inextricably linked, he devoted himself to it unstintingly. As Mrs Hamilton noted,

> He cared for the Party as most people can care only for persons. He saw it as a potential instrument of purposes that had a Divine sanction, worthy of all a man could give to its service. He, on his own part, gave all he had... He was there for the Party, not the Party there for him. This was the root of the unequalled authority he built up.[10]

Aside from the demand for protection of the legal status and financial assets of trade unions, which the Liberal Government promptly conceded in the Trade Disputes Act, nullifying the effects of the Taff Vale judgment, Labour's main concern was unemployment. In April 1905 the Balfour Government had introduced an Unemployed Workmen's bill containing a provision for employing men in farm colonies and supporting them with payments from rates. Although Crooks and Henderson supported the measure, some of the trade unionists remained critical of projected labour exchanges. When the measure was passed, the provision of work at public expense was eliminated, and the Local Government Board decided that destitution, rather than joblessness, was to be the test of eligibility. Thus instead of grappling with the growing problem of unemployment, the Government offered only a minor supplement to traditional poor relief. When John Burns, the ineffectual President of the Local Government Board under Campbell-Bannerman, rejected Labour's demand for a bill embodying the right to work or maintenance by the state, Henderson, Shackleton, and MacDonald organized a petition signed by 115 M.P.s demanding that the Government disclose its intentions. Burns remained obdurate, and the Government limited itself to providing a £200,000 grant under the terms of the 1905 Unemployed Workmen's Act. In 1907 MacDonald introduced a Right to Work bill on behalf of the Labour Party, and during the next two years Henderson and others hammered away at the failure of the Liberals to enact remedial legislation. It was an example of Labour's inability to influence the content of Liberal legislation in those areas which would have a serious social and fiscal impact. The Trade Disputes Act had been a concession of enormous significance, but without direct economic ramifications; a commitment by the state to furnish work or maintenance would have constituted a major encroachment on the autonomy of capitalism. Instead the Liberal Government chipped away at the problem: through old age pensions, labour exchanges, and insurance schemes they offered palliatives which, while not liquidating unemployment, mitigated its effect. Nor was it much consolation that Labour initiatives sparked eventual remedial action, since the legislation all too often diluted the intentions of its proponents. In April 1907 Henderson introduced a bill to secure joint boards with statutory wage-fixing powers in the area of sweated labour. A select committee was appointed to investigate home work, and its deliberations foreshadowed the passage of the Trade Boards Act in 1909.

As part of Labour's effort to seek information about solutions to the unemployment problem, Henderson and G. N. Barnes, an official of the Amalgamated Engineers and a Glasgow M.P., were sent to Germany in 1907 to investigate insurance schemes and labour exchanges. Their report suggested that labour exchanges had worked effectively in the cities they visited, gaining the confidence of both employer and workmen, but that unemployment insurance was still in too experimental a stage to provide any useful lessons. In stressing the effectiveness of labour exchanges, the two trade unionist politicians were seeking to allay the suspicions of fellow unionists at home, who feared that they would weaken the bargaining power of organized labour. They also noted, in a pointed reference to the free trade controversy, that, despite protective tariffs, there was widespread unemployment in Germany, but that the use of labour exchanges had diminished its incidence.[11] Previously Henderson, who had never really travelled abroad, had drawn upon his own industrial experience when speaking in Parliament; his exposure to Germany initiated him into a wider industrial community, making him less parochial in his outlook. The Liberals did introduce labour exchanges in 1909, but more in response to the persuasive testimony of William Beveridge than at Labour's behest. While conceding that the proposal had merit, Labour continued to reproach the Liberals for failing to concede work or maintenance.

When the labour exchange bill was brought in, Henderson, for example, dismissed it as 'the Right to Work Bill in penny numbers'.[12]

While Labour M.P.s blasted the Government for inaction, they often discovered that more could be obtained through patient negotiation than expressions of outrage. In 1908 Henderson tried to persuade Liberal ministers to increase the Exchequer grant and permit local authorities to use revenue from rates to pay wages to those employed in relief schemes. Winston Churchill and Charles Masterman welcomed his suggestion, but Burns vetoed any concession beyond an increase of the grant to £300,000. The lack of tangible accomplishments frustrated those Labour M.P.s unaccustomed to the dilatory practices of Parliamentary rule. By 1908 morale and cohesion within the Parliamentary Labour Party were disintegrating, with much of the blame levied at Hardie for the divided counsels and ineffective strategy that hampered its efforts. But Hardie, frequently neglecting his duties and taking independent initiatives, had irritated his Parliamentary colleagues almost from the outset. In 1907 Henderson informed him that he could not support his re-election as Chairman,[13] and although Hardie survived a second year, he wisely decided to resign the post in 1908. When Shackleton refused to accept nomination, Henderson was elected as the best available substitute, but he too was soon at loggerheads with some of his colleagues. Whereas Hardie had offended by failing to consult, Henderson was unable to satisfy the militants who believed that Labour should do more than encourage the radical policies of the Liberal Government. The I.L.P.'s Bruce Glasier confided to MacDonald in October 1908 that Henderson 'is not popular – he is reckoned perhaps quite unjustly to be playing the Liberal game... [Henderson] should appear to lead the party as a fighting force, and he cannot do that if he is always side by side with Liberals on virtually Liberal [Temperance & Methodist] platforms'.[14] At the end of the year Hardie, who invariably doubted his successor's socialist commitment, bemoaned the fact that 'we are in for another year of Henderson's leadership, which means that reaction and timidity will be in the ascendancy with disastrous effects on our side of the movement in the country'.[15]

MacDonald, who had earlier shared Henderson's misgivings about Hardie's leadership, now grumbled about Henderson's failure to inspire Labour M.P.s as he believed he himself could do if given the opportunity. The two quarrelled, and MacDonald charged Henderson with being 'a bloody liar' in the presence of several witnesses. When Henderson was named acting Secretary in 1909, during MacDonald's Indian trip, the latter was said to have described the appointment as 'an insult' to him, presumably because of his low estimation of his deputy's abilities. The incident was smoothed over by intermediaries, but not before Henderson resigned from the party executive, demanding that it investigate the allegations in the interests of the 'harmonious working' of the party.[16]

Yet internecine squabbling, endemic among the leaders, could usually be overcome in the face of common enemies. When Ben Tillett, the Dockers' leader, who was 'more concerned to maintain his reputation as an ageing *enfant terrible* than to show solid qualities of leadership',[17] excoriated the Labour M.P.s as flunkeys and hypocrites, the I.L.P. joined Henderson and Shackleton to parry the attack and defend the Parliamentary Labour Party against any attempt by the annual conference to dictate policy.

Personal disagreements notwithstanding, MacDonald and Henderson shared a common outlook on electoral strategy. Both recognized that, however grandiose the ambitions of socialist militants, Labour could not expand the number of candidacies without provoking Liberal retaliation. Committed though they were to Labour independence, they also shared a belief that support for Liberal policies might not only achieve desired legislative goals, but reap electoral dividends as well. As in 1906, independence did not preclude some arrangement regarding the disposition of seats. MacDonald's concerns were personal as well as practical: he might jeopardize his Leicester seat were he to condone a serious increase in the number of Labour candidacies. Some of Labour's gains had been in two-seat towns, like Leicester, where Labour and the Liberals might share the representation and keep out the Tories. Henderson's perspective derived from his keen sensitivity to electoral details. As early as 1906 he was urging 'the unwisdom of contesting Bye-Elections, [sic] unless the soil has been well prepared and every part of the constituency is sufficiently organised to ensure the gathering in of the fruit'.[18] He spelled out the components of effective organization in a speech to a Labour Party special conference, held in Hull in January 1908. While he agreed that the enthusiasm and devotion characteristic of the movement's pioneers was a force in promoting independent labour representation, future success would hinge on such factors as capable permanent constituency agents, ward committees, canvassing of voters 'to counteract the shameful misrepresentation to which our candidates are subjected', and finding conveyances to bring electors to the polls.[19] Furthermore, in the years before the Lib–Labs affiliated to the Labour Party, the segment of the movement most ardent for increasing the number of candidacies was the I.L.P., whose prestige Henderson was reluctant to enhance.

When Liberal intentions to call an election at the beginning of 1910 became clear, MacDonald hastened back from India to support Henderson's efforts to limit Labour's electoral expansion as much as possible. The party executive did endorse several candidates against the wishes of the Secretary and Treasurer, but Henderson and MacDonald succeeded in restricting the party to seventy-eight candidates in January and reducing that number to fifty-six in the second 1910 general election. In defense of his actions, MacDonald argued that constituencies had no right to ask for candidates until they were prepared to support them with organization and votes. The leaders had no desire to squander limited resources in fruitless contests merely for propaganda value or to appease socialist activists. Henderson's own Barnard Castle political machine functioned smoothly in both elections, with an enthusiastic working men's club and adequate committee rooms reinforcing the efforts of the local party, but in most places organization was haphazard at best. In most constituencies Labour relied on the public meeting, bringing in a party leader who would marshal support with rousing speeches.

Henderson's growing involvement in organizational matters made MacDonald suspect that his colleague had his eye on the secretaryship, especially after Henderson, emulating Hardie's practice, resigned the Parliamentary chairmanship after two years. Convinced that his skills could be exercised more effectively as Secretary than as Chairman, he had opted for the lesser Parliamentary role of Chief Whip. Although MacDonald was at first unwilling to relinquish the secretaryship, with its permanent control over the party machine, he aspired to the leadership, which he rightly concluded he could wield more forcefully than any of his predecessors. In 1910 a hesitant MacDonald found his path blocked by Barnes, who was unanimously chosen to lead the Parliamentary party. But when Barnes tactlessly attacked his colleagues for slackness and timidity, he forfeited whatever support he had garnered. By January 1911 Henderson, who had opposed Barnes in 1910 because he 'lacked those qualities necessary to the position', refused to support him any longer. Barnes, he told MacDonald, had 'proved a conspicuous failure and now seeks to blame the Party for all the failures and blunders of leadership'. Whatever his personal qualms, he concluded by the beginning of 1911 that MacDonald was the obvious choice, the only candidate likely to reconcile the I.L.P. and the trade unionists, and he urged him 'in spite of all the drawbacks to throw yourself into the breach and accept nomination'.[20] That MacDonald would be obliged to yield the secretaryship to him was no doubt a factor in his calculation as well. In addition MacDonald had now decided that the chairmanship might be transformed into the dominant position in the party and need no longer be tenable on a temporary basis. He was willing to trade the mundane work of constituency management, the tiresome negotiations with agents and committees, for the more visible role of party leader, especially if sufficiently long tenure would enhance his national prominence. Henderson, on the other hand, distrusted by the I.L.P., had failed to keep the Parliamentary forces united, and his two years of leadership in the Commons had not been a notable success. One of his greatest gifts as a politician was to be able to take the measure of his colleagues and, indeed, of himself as well. It was not that Henderson himself lacked ambition for it, or that he was not on several occasions – especially after 1914 – tempted to seek it, but rather that he had a greater affinity for the behind-the-scenes management of the party machine than for the rough and tumble of Parliamentary battles. He realized that his own talents could best be fulfilled in the Head Office and in the committee rooms, rather than on the platform or the floor of the Commons.

Henderson's support may well have been decisive in securing the chairmanship for MacDonald in 1911, and it is clear that until 1931 he continued to believe that, on balance, MacDonald was the politician best suited to fill that role. Without envy, he realized that MacDonald's natural endowments far exceeded his own and that, however unpredictable his behavior could be, he had the power to inspire an audience that Henderson did not possess. If Labour was to become a genuine political force, rather than simply a sectional interest group, it needed a leader with MacDonald's compelling personality. David Marquand contends that the real partnership between the two began with Henderson's overture to MacDonald in 1911. He also persuaded trade unionist M.P.s, who looked to him for a lead, that their suspicions of MacDonald were unwarranted. At the next annual conference he proposed that henceforth the party Treasurer should be elected by the mass vote of the delegates, rather than be selected by the executive from among their number. In 1912 MacDonald, nominated by the executive, was elected Treasurer in succession to Henderson at the party conference and thus acquired a secure position within the executive, one he was able to retain even when he resigned the leadership in 1914.

MacDonald did not hold Henderson in equal regard. He undervalued his more pedestrian gifts and took him for granted, but he realized that they could accomplish a good deal for the party if harmony was maintained between them. Even Keir Hardie was sanguine about the future, when he told Bruce Glasier that there was 'quite a new spirit in the party' now that MacDonald and Henderson were working together.[21] MacDonald was relieved to be able to relinquish some of the detail that distracted him from the pursuit of high politics, and Henderson was now free to carry on the management of the party with the minimum of interference. No one had his knowledge of constituencies or of local agents, his immense capacity for work, his sureness of touch in dealing with all facets of party activity. He was, as McKibbin has observed, 'indispensable in the creation of the system: he recognized faces, organized votes, found money, and put the right men in the right jobs'.[22]

Henderson was not only an energetic, but an extremely mobile Secretary. During the years before the war he made extensive tours of constituencies, often accompanied by Arthur Peters, the National Agent. He met with local union and trades council officials, persuading them to permit the establishment of constituency Labour parties, teaching them organizational techniques, and bringing news of Westminster politics. Uncle Arthur was their link with the national party, able to explain national issues to provincial working men whose allegiance to the emerging Labour Party might yet waver. Many of the organizational plans bruited by MacDonald before 1910 were implemented by Henderson as Secretary, but some of them had also been prefigured in Barnard Castle and in Henderson's speeches and reports. A scheme to have local agents appointed and controlled by Head Office was carried through in 1912, supplemented by a program of financial assistance to local parties. At the urging of Head Office local trades councils and Labour parties were amalgamated to achieve greater efficiency and avoid duplication of effort. The 1912 party conference rejected the idea of individual membership, which both Henderson and MacDonald favored, but they were prepared to await a more propitious moment to introduce so radical a change on a national scale. The general pattern that Henderson promoted was clear: between 1910 and 1914 the number of affiliated trades councils declined, while the number of local Labour parties increased. A major accomplishment was the launching of central party structures in London in 1913 and in other cities.

After 1910 Henderson and MacDonald maintained that as long as Labour remained electorally weak and the political mood was unfavorable, there was nothing to be gained from fruitless by-election demonstrations. Their focus on reforms in party structure and improvement in local organization looked toward the long term enhancement of Labour's prospects, but they saw little likelihood that these could be translated into immediate gains. In several contests they strenuously opposed official Labour candidacies, most notably in the 1913 by-election to fill the second Leicester seat formerly held by a Liberal. The Head Office was encouraging Labour candidates in vacant mining constituencies to replace former Lib–Labs in what seemed to be 'natural'

Labour seats, but in Leicester a Labour candidacy might jeopardize the agreement to share the representation that had secured MacDonald's election. When Henderson went to Leicester, he chastized those who would risk a fight irrespective of the views of the executive or its impact on MacDonald's position. He further warned that if Labour insisted on intervening, it would ensure a Tory victory. Such a result would bring a general election appreciably nearer at a time when the party was in no condition to fight. Although Henderson's estimation that the Leicester party was in no shape to contest the seat was probably correct, his action aroused a storm of indignation. Eager to avoid another Leicester situation, the executive overruled the Secretary when he tried to prevent a three-cornered contest later that year in Keighley. Once again Henderson had questioned whether a local organization was suffficiently sound to undertake an electoral battle. He suspected that the I.L.P. was trying to force a candidacy in the hope of embarrassing the leaders:

> I have seen for some time [he told his assistant] a deliberate attempt to exploit the larger movement in the interests of the I.L.P. The policy is all the more freely pushed if it can in any way harrass MacDonald or conflict with his position. This vacancy was too good an opportunity for them to miss.[23]

It was not that Henderson was opposed to maximizing Labour's opportunities or that he was hesitant in his pursuit of a policy of independence. His assessment of electoral prospects depended on his perceptions of the state of party organization. Before 1914 it was simply not ready to undertake a campaign on anything more than a limited scale. Aside from the embryonic state of local organization, Labour's financial position was rendered precarious by the 1909 Osborne judgment which restricted the abilities of unions to spend their funds for political purposes. The effect was not merely to deprive the party of secure revenue for its Parliamentary fund, but to call into question the political affiliation of the unions so vital to its survival. Although legislation in 1911, providing annual salaries of £400 to M.P.s, alleviated the pressure on party finances, the overriding concern of the leaders was to nullify the Osborne decision. By freeing the party from the need to pay Parliamentary salaries, the new law did reduce its financial obligations and made it possible for Henderson to introduce grants of 25 per cent towards the support of local party agents, as well as to appoint two national organizers. But although the Liberals were committed to remedial legislation, a Trade Union Act restoring the financial link between the unions and the party was not enacted until 1913. Hence these financial constraints coupled with the desire to avoid antagonizing the Liberals while the Osborne judgment was still in effect militated against three-cornered contests.

If Henderson and MacDonald both saw the value of accommodation with the Liberals, the leader may have had something more than the allocation of seats in mind. Like Lloyd George, he was intrigued by the prospect of a political reorientation, with a new radical party superseding both parties of the left. Whether this was ideological pipe dreaming or the elusive goal of hard bargaining is unclear, but rumors of a coalition government were in the air in 1911, perhaps as a way of resolving Irish and other problems. Years later Henderson recalled that MacDonald was proposing to enter, possibly as Chief Secretary for Ireland, a coalition headed by Lloyd George and Arthur Balfour. One version has MacDonald offering Henderson an under-secretaryship, with a variation suggesting that he could have 'any job he liked outside the Cabinet if he would put the Party machine at the disposal of the new government'. According to both versions Henderson declined the offer, warning MacDonald that any such departure would shatter the Labour Party.[24]

III

As a typical trade unionist politician, Henderson's interests before 1914 rarely extended to international problems. A few examples of involvement with defense or foreign issues suggest a fairly conventional radical perspective, generally hostile to needless expenditure and favoring a non-belligerent policy. In 1909 he sent a message to the National Peace Congress deploring the popular clamor for increased armaments as based on an unjustified suspicion of German intentions. His own encounters with German trade unionists had persuaded him that the militarist tide had been exaggerated. He intervened in a debate in the Commons that year on the issue of naval estimates in which he sought to mediate between the alarmist response of the pacifists and the Government's readiness to expand the number of battleships. While condemning any militarist policies, he would not go as far as Hardie, who was willing at least to investigate the possible use of a general strike as a device to stop war, a watered down version of a recommendation by the International. At a special conference on armaments Henderson argued that a general strike was unacceptable as a weapon because it violated Labour's commitment to Parliamentary action. On this issue he remained consistent throughout his career: direct action whether in industrial affairs or as a preventative against war was totally unacceptable. The core of his belief was in democratic procedures, either through the accepted channels of collective bargaining and arbitration in industry or Parliamentary debate in national concerns. For the labour movement to defy accepted methods for registering opposition was not merely un-British: it was a betrayal of the struggle for equality within the national community.

Between 1909 and 1914 the Parliamentary Labour Party operated under difficult conditions. In most of the serious constitutional questions of the day they could only play a secondary role, limited by their number and identity of view from exerting much influence over the Liberal majority. Even after the changing complexion of the House of Commons in 1910 made their votes more crucial, there was little incentive for them to oppose the Government on the central issues of the budget, House of Lords reform, or Irish Home Rule. If the Liberals could no longer neglect Labour proposals with impunity after 1910, they determined the legislative timetable. As long as the spectre of the Osborne judgment dominated Labour strategy, they hesitated to defy the Government. Thus while the Asquith ministry rejected work or maintenance as a solution to the unemployment problem, Labour could either accept the modest legislative package or risk jeopardizing any reform at all.

While Labour endorsed the principle of unemployment insurance, the I.L.P. and the Webbs united in opposing its contributory aspect. Henderson and most of the trade unionists believed that the benefits of the scheme outweighed the disadvantages, whereas both Hardie and Snowden denounced it. Although Labour had agreed to support the bill, Hardie and others denounced it in committee, much to the dismay of MacDonald, who feared that such insubordination signalled the fragmentation of party unity. Hardie, by now a habitual rebel, had also indicted the Asquith Government for its bloody handling of the railway strike in a pamphlet called *Killing No Murder*. Henderson, who was involved in helping to mediate that dispute and who served on a royal commission on the railway crisis, complained that 'the Hardie episode will exercise a damaging influence upon our deliberations'.[25] As a trade union leader as well as a politician, he had to step warily to avoid alienating his diverse constituencies. Ever since his early days with the Ironfounders he had contended that the strike should not be abandoned as a weapon, but that it should only be used in the last resort. He believed in negotiation, and had, as President of the Ironfounders, secured a wage improvement when he put the workers' case before the Conciliation Board in 1910. Moreover, he remained convinced that, despite renewed outbreaks of industrial unrest, the moderation of organized labour would ultimately prevail. Having long shared MacDonald's distaste for Hardie's inflammatory rhetoric and recently clashed with him over the use of a general strike as an anti-war weapon, he warned that 'it is going to be impossible for any of us to conduct negotiations for the party if this sort of line is going to be followed'. Even though the requirement that M.P.s abide by the decisions of the Parliamentary Labour Party had been eliminated, he further contended that the conduct of Hardie and Snowden during the insurance debates was provoking so much discord that a party meeting should 'take the matter in hand'.[26] The conflict was brought out in the open at meetings of the Parliamentary Labour Party, where both MacDonald and Henderson repudiated the conduct of the increasingly isolated Hardie.

Tensions mounted within the Labour Party during 1911-12, intensified by Hardie's quasi-syndicalist pronouncements and George Lansbury's futile sacrifice of his Bow and Bromley seat to the cause of the militant suffragettes. After the Parliamentary Labour Party refused to subordinate its legislative agenda to the women's movement, Lansbury had resigned his seat and, disowned by the party, lost the by-election to a Unionist. With the I.L.P. dissociating themselves from the official strategy of accomodation to the Liberals to avoid a premature general election, disaffection within the ranks seemed to cloud future prospects. The internal rancor may have been one of the factors that prompted MacDonald to hint that he might abandon the leadership in 1912. Amid rumors that Snowden would stand against him, Henderson urged MacDonald to buck yourself up and go through with it however 'unpleasant' it may be. If you do not those members of the Party who have interested themselves in getting to know the mind of the majority of our members will be greatly disappointed. However if the Snowden-Lansbury policy has to obtain in the House some of us must consider our positions with regard to our responsibilities outside. It is now sufficiently difficult and certainly not promising. What it would be if we had some more of their insanity with official sanction I don't know. It does not represent my views and never could.[27]

Despite the Bow and Bromley by-election, women's suffrage had become an issue which united Labour more than it divided it and which increasingly separated it from the Liberals. Initially its reactions had been something less than enthusiastic. Many trade unionists, as hostile to political equality for women as they were to equal wages, regarded the suffrage issue as an irrelevant distraction from industrial issues. Although Henderson and Snowden favored the enfranchisement of women, they looked with suspicion on any scheme designed to give the vote to a limited body of property-owning women. When the National Union of Women Suffrage Societies urged the leaders to press the Government for full facilities for a women's suffrage bill in 1908, Henderson reaffirmed Labour's disapproval of any measure that merely abolished the sex disqualification and extended the vote on the basis of the existing property qualification. While such a measure might bring sex equality, it would not only keep millions of adult workers disfranchised, but was prejudicial to the growth of the Labour Party. Henderson himself, a committed democrat, eager to see the elimination of all restrictions, whether based on property or sex, detested militancy as a threat to Parliamentary democracy no less grave than syndicalism. His stubborn opposition to militant tactics earned him the enmity of the W.S.P.U., who heckled him at suffrage rallies.

While adultists, determined to wait for a measure that included all men as well as women, and militants, demanding some remedial action immediately, quarrelled at party conferences, Henderson sought a mediating role. Once persuaded that a limited bill was practicable, he lent his name to the efforts of the non-partisan Conciliation Committee and spoke in support of its 1910 bill, introduced in the Commons by David Shackleton. Framed so as to preclude wrecking amendments, the Conciliation Bill, devised by H. N. Brailsford in consultation with Millicent Garrett Fawcett of the N.U.W.S.S., proposed to extend the existing Parliamentary franchise to women occupiers. It sought to meet Liberal and Labour fears of giving undue advantage to the propertied by excluding ownership or lodger qualifications. Since all householders would be admitted, even if they occupied only part of a house, the provisions would apply to working as well as to upper-class women. Although carried on its Second Reading by a majority of 109, the bill was referred to a committee of the whole House, effectively extinguishing hope of further progress.

Henderson participated in a deputation to Asquith in 1911, where he was informed that the Government now envisaged the introduction of manhood suffrage, despite earlier pledges to the women. At the Birmingham party conference in January 1912 he appealed to the delegates to proclaim that a reform bill that excluded women would be unacceptable to the labour movement, a resolution enthusiastically endorsed. Although this was not a promise to vote against a Liberal manhood suffrage bill, it warned the Government that Labour would no longer acquiesce in the Prime Minister's dilatory tactics. The strong conference declaration, supported by Snowden and other avowed adultists, paved the way for an accommodation with the N.U.W.S.S., hammered out by Brailsford in discussions with MacDonald and Mrs Fawcett. In recognition of Labour's past efforts to promote votes for women, an Election Fighting Fund would be launched to assist Labour candidates, although not in constituencies already represented by a known suffragist. MacDonald was apprehensive about how much say Labour would have as to which seats were contested, the party fearing the loss of autonomy, but he also had trepidations about risking an open breach with the Liberals. Although not averse to accepting subsidies, MacDonald and Henderson at first sought to avoid too close an affiliation, hoping to delete from the N.U.W.S.S. resolution any indication that it was trying to promote party interests. Brailsford warned Henderson that N.U.W.S.S. members would be indignant if they knew that Labour welcomed the women's money, but not their public endorsement.[28] A compromise was reached when the architects of the Fund specified that it would be used to support individual Labour candidates rather than the party. Just how decisive that intervention was cannot easily be determined: in the eight by-elections in which the Election Fighting Fund was employed the Liberals lost four seats to the Tories. Labour, despite an increased vote, captured no additional seats. On the other hand, the Fund may well have strengthened the party's resolve. By August 1912 Henderson could assure Catherine Marshall that there was a growing sentiment among Labour M.P.s to vote against the Third Reading of the Government's reform bill if it excluded women.[29] Less flamboyant than Hardie or Lansbury, Henderson was well placed to cement an effective alliance between moderate suffragists and the Labour Party and continued to play a crucial role in mobilizing Parliamentary support for an extension of the vote to women. Looking toward the next general election, the Fund's organizers had identified a number of critical constituencies, including Barnard Castle, where Liberal intervention might endanger the survival of noted suffragists. Henderson, who believed that the Liberals would be compelled to go to the country in 1914 or 1915 'by sheer force of political circumstances',[30] no longer expected an electoral compact with the Liberals and believed that the women's support might prove significant. Both he and MacDonald were committed to fighting the election as a genuinely independent party and expected to contest at least 120 seats. They had rebuffed overtures from Lloyd George because of the hostility of Labour's rank and file, but also because they doubted that Lloyd George could deliver on his political promises. Both leaders, anticipating the imminent demise of the Liberal Government, felt that Labour would benefit from electoral autonomy, not only in the number of seats won, but also in terms of renewed party unity.

By 1914 then, although Labour had not improved its Parliamentary position, it could look to the future with a new confidence. Henderson's organizational efforts had done much to transform Labour from a sectional pressure group to a national party. Many of the reforms implemented in the 1918 constitution were begun before the war, with local constituency parties proliferating and replacing trades councils. Mining districts were shifting their loyalty to Labour, and major cities were subjected to serious organizational initiatives. Although the quarrels over national insurance and women's suffrage, the tensions among leaders, and the lack of electoral gains seemed evidence of diminishing effectiveness, the truth was that the leaders used these years to build a solid foundation for the future. Even its legislative achievements were substantial. The Taff Vale and Osborne decisions had been overturned, the party emerging from those judicial reversals with renewed solvency. Labour pressure had prodded the Liberal Government to pass social legislation that might otherwise have been further delayed. It is true that the more propagandistic of Labour's legislative proposals, such as the Right to Work bill, never had a chance, but its preoccupation with the employment question influenced the Government's decision to introduce labour exchanges, a minimum wage for miners, trade boards in sweated industries, and unemployment insurance.

For Henderson these were years of political apprenticeship. He had entered the Commons in 1903 as a virtual unknown, although admittedly one with close ties to several of the components of the labour movement. As a trade unionist with a strong industrial and regional base, as a Wesleyan Methodist with ties to temperance agitation, he was well positioned to assume a key role in the fledgling party. Despite his lack of I.L.P. or socialist roots, he was able to refashion his ideological image so that he emerged during his first decade in Parliament as an identifiably middle-of-the-road Labour M.P., sufficiently anti-capitalist to satisfy working-class audiences, but avoiding any extremist rhetoric. He was, above all, a conciliator, whether representing his union or negotiating with the Liberal Government or building party unity. If conciliation meant avoiding divisive clashes, it did not mean avoiding confrontation. Henderson was outspoken, even blunt at times, in defending his viewpoint, challenging Hardie, Snowden, MacDonald, and the Government where appropriate. That his position within the party was immeasurably strengthened during these years was the result of his consummate political skills. He knew how to wield authority, usually behind the scenes and often by what Mrs Hamilton referred to as 'sledgehammer' methods.[31] But he understood the men with whom he had to contend, had an instinctive appreciation of Labour sentiment, and exploited opportunities to make himself not only the architect, but the master of its internal organization.

3 War leader

In contrast to MacDonald, Henderson had few contacts in Europe before 1914, was appallingly ignorant of geography, and spoke no foreign languages. Like many British working-class politicians, he was notably insular, and whatever internationalism surfaced before 1914 stemmed from moral conviction rather than from direct experience of foreign countries. He had travelled to Germany with Barnes in 1907 to investigate labour exchanges and returned there in 1912 on an expedition of Labour M.P.s and trade union officials organized by the Warden of the Browning Hall Settlement. They were received hospitably by their German Social Democratic counterparts, and the contacts established made Henderson less wary of enemy socialists than many of the right-wing union leaders were during the war. Once the Labour Party affiliated itself with the Second International, Henderson, who became Secretary to the British section, began to broaden his horizons, to feel more of a sense of class solidarity across international lines than he had as a provincial Northern union leader. As his biographer observed, 'Islander as he was, at this stage, he yet had the *feel* of internationalism in his bones.'[1]

Until its outbreak there was no way of determining what his attitude towards a war might be. Although certainly not a pacifist, he might well have chosen the path of Morley or Ponsonby or MacDonald. In the final days of peace he sought to mobilize organized labour in favor of neutrality, voting with his Parliamentary colleagues on 30 July 1914 to demand that Britain remain neutral even if a European war was inevitable. Two days later the British section of the International issued a manifesto, over the signatures of Hardie and Henderson, calling on workers to 'compel the governing class and their Press who are eager to commit you to cooperate with Russian despotism to keep silence and respect the decision of the overwhelming majority of the people'.[2] Henderson, addressing the anti-war Trafalgar Square rally on Sunday 2 August, moved the resolution which sought 'to unite the workers of the nations concerned in the efforts to prevent their Governments from entering upon war'. Moreover, he convened a meeting of Labour leaders on 5 August to make a concerted protest against war and consider the formation of a National Peace Emergency Committee.

By 5 August England was at war, Labour had agreed to support the Government's request for war credits, MacDonald had resigned the party chairmanship, and the emergency committee had been transformed into the War Emergency Workers' National Committee, constituted to safeguard labour interests during the war. Henderson, elected leader in place of MacDonald, was named Chairman of the Emergency Committee.

Why did Henderson support the war? The simplest answer is patriotism. Stirred by the violation of Belgian neutrality, he accepted Grey's rationalizations for British intervention. Despite his own pronouncements about Britain not being implicated in European quarrels, he could feel that the honor of the nation was involved in defending innocent Belgium. Whatever he had said in the past, there was now a higher duty as a British citizen which he could not evade. Nor was he surprised when his three sons joined the Honourable Artillery Company in September 1914. MacDonald, rejecting the Foreign Secretary's view that Britain was obliged to support the French, had by contrast resigned his position rather than sanction a war for which he felt that allied statesmen were almost equally culpable. But that analysis, attributing the conflict to secret diplomacy and the alliance structure, was too subtle for the majority of the labour movement, which rallied to the Government's appeal.

In some ways, as David Marquand has argued, 'politically, his position was only a hair's breadth away from Henderson's'.[3] Both deplored the policy of armaments and mutual suspicions that had divided Europe into armed camps; both blamed the entente with Russia for precipitating the war. Henderson found no inconsistency between supporting British involvement in the war and endorsing the platform of the Union of Democratic Control, on whose General Council he sat. Neither politician subscribed to the tenets of Grey's foreign policy, and MacDonald was certainly no more willing than Henderson to contemplate a German victory. But there were sharp differences between the two as well. Whereas MacDonald did not believe that war against Germany would foster peace and democracy, Henderson convinced himself that the defeat of Prussian militarism was a pre-condition for European peace.[4] Furthermore, he believed, as MacDonald never did, that 'Great Britain entered upon this war with clean hands in support of high ideals and great principles',[5] and although he came to criticize the Government's reluctance to articulate credible war aims, he never disavowed the war effort.

It was not so much their responses to the war as its implications for the Labour Party that divided the two leaders. MacDonald wanted Labour to become the fulcrum of opposition to the discredited Liberal Government and imagined himself as the leader of a reinvigorated radical party. Labour's vote in favor of credits seemed to contradict MacDonald's expectation that the majority would follow him, but he did not lose hope that anti-war idealism would revive. If MacDonald's conscience prompted him to defy the mainstream of Labour opinion, Henderson was equally determined to follow the party come what may. McKibbin has argued that Henderson's union connection was strong enough to push him into support for the war,[6] and it was certainly true that he shared the viewpoint of the majority of British workers. At the same time he attempted to resist the unabashed bellicosity of those trade unionists who regarded criticism of the war as treachery and overtures to European socialists as fraternization with the enemy. Equally he feared that if the party failed to respond to the national summons, a vindictive electorate might someday exact retribution and undo his constructive efforts of the previous decade. While MacDonald viewed himself as a symbol for those who continued to oppose the war, Henderson aimed to perserve unity and, at the same time, to enhance the party's national image. Only by participating fully in the struggle could Labour protect the gains of recent years and stake its claim to future benefits. Thus he saw his role as mediating between the pro- and anti-war elements within the movement and between Labour and the government. But while MacDonald perceived Henderson's conduct as unprincipled and spineless, Henderson, who regarded MacDonald as perverse and self-serving, angrily denounced him on one occasion as 'the most treacherous man in English political life'.[7]

Henderson had two aims: to preserve party unity and to ensure that Labour performed a useful role in the national effort; once Britain was at war, it was the obligation of the movement to help achieve victory. More than anyone else, he was responsible for ensuring that the Labour Party, in contrast to European socialist parties, did not split. As he remarked in a conciliatory letter to MacDonald,

> I am apprehensive that we are dividing ourselves off into small groups which, unless care is exercised, can only have a destructive effect upon the influence of the Labour Party. I have done what I could to follow the line which would leave the Party at the end of the War as strong, if not stronger than we were before hostilities broke out.[8]

Besides defending his unpopular stance and helping him retain the post of party Treasurer, he urged MacDonald in the early weeks of the war to resume the chairmanship. Despite recurrent clashes, he refused to sever their association or to sanction any policy that would have made MacDonald's continued involvement in party affairs invidious. MacDonald did modify his initial criticism of recruitment, but reconciliation became more difficult after the party issued a manifesto recognizing England's moral obligation to resist German aggression militarily. While hoping to avoid an irreparable breach, he not only declined to return to office, but refused to promise that he would resume it after the war. Clearly he was persuaded that if he resumed the leadership in 1914, it must be on Henderson's compromising terms and would violate those convictions that had prompted his resignation in August.

A less scrupulous or more personally ambitious politician might have isolated MacDonald or driven him into the political wilderness, but Henderson continued to acknowledge him as the one figure capable of keeping socialists and trade unionists together and had initially agreed to resume the chairmanship on the understanding that it was to be temporary. He also sensed that together they had a better chance of preventing jingoist trade unionists from stampeding the party into an avowedly pro-war position than if he were on his own. While it may be true, as historians have noted, that Henderson regarded himself simply as a caretaker for MacDonald, he became less willing to defer to his former leader. It soon became apparent that MacDonald's stance was too inflexible for him to play that mediating role Henderson deemed essential in a party leader. Furthermore, a taste of power inevitably spurred his own ambition, although he still preferred to control the party from behind the scenes as Secretary, a post he insisted on retaining, than as Parliamentary spokesman. MacDonald was not, of course, the only obstacle to party unity. Under Henderson's leadership during the early months of the war, the W.E.N.W.C. worked hard to prevent a breakdown of communication between pro- and anti-war elements in the movement in part by concentrating on those issues where there was general agreement and avoiding discussion of British participation in the war.

The second feature of Henderson's policy was his determination to cooperate with the Government even if it meant temporarily sacrificing political or economic objectives. If Labour could survive intact, it would ultimately benefit from the war. In the meantime it should concentrate its energies on safeguarding union funds and relieving distress of working-class families. The accepted political truce protected Parliamentary seats, but at the price of cooperation in the Government's enlistment campaign. Henderson's agreement to serve with Asquith and Bonar Law as a joint President of the Parliamentary Recruiting Committee underscored the commitment to share in the burdens of war. He regarded the campaign as a lesser evil than a possible election fought over the issue of conscription or solidarity in wartime. Almost from the start of hostilities he argued that because of its determined opposition to compulsory military service, Labour had incurred a special obligation to make the voluntary system work. As President of the Ironfounders, he was one of the most prominent union negotiators in the early months of the war and was chosen to serve as chairman of the union side at the Treasury Conference in March 1915. It was here that more formal cooperation with the war effort was contrived on lines drawn up by Henderson and his trade unionist colleagues. According to its provisions, voluntary at first, organized labour consented to forgo strikes and waive restrictive practices for the duration of the war. At the same time he assumed the chairmanship of the National Labour Advisory Committee, devised to implement the industrial truce. From then on he had the unenviable task of combining the positions of Labour Party leader with *de facto*

Industrial Advisor to a government in which the party was not officially represented. Yet even before he was invited to join the Asquith coalition in May 1915 he had obtained an unprecedented concentration of power: he was still the titular head of a major union, Parliamentary leader, Secretary of the Labour Party and of the British section of the International, Chairman of the Workers' Emergency Committee, and Chairman of the National Labour Advisory Committee, which helped Lloyd George draft the Munitions of War Bill in order to put teeth into the Treasury Agreement. Later he was appointed to chair the Central Munitions Labour Supply Committee, with a mission to formulate proposals for more equitable wage rates for women and unskilled workers brought into the munitions industry under dilution. One of its first circulars specified that women employed in skilled or munitions work should be paid at the same rates as the men they were replacing, a path-breaking step in the economic progress of women that was carried through despite trade union apprehension.

II

In May 1915 Henderson was invited to join the Asquith coalition as Labour's representative in the Cabinet. Although anti-war leaders like MacDonald were hostile and others warned that Labour representatives would have responsibility without actual power, the Executive favored participation, and the Parliamentary party endorsed it as well after initially expressing misgivings. Henderson joined the Cabinet nominally as President of the Board of Education, a position for which he had little obvious qualification and which he was reluctant to accept. The office was intended as a sinecure, since he was to serve as advisor on labour matters and largely to ignore educational matters. Nonetheless he was subject to unwarranted criticism as both an absentee minister and the defender of inherited and often reactionary policies.[9]

Not until August 1916 was he able to prevail upon Asquith, by threatening resignation, to relieve him of his department portfolio and to appoint him as Paymaster-General. This permitted him to function exclusively as labour advisor without being encumbered by responsibilities he was not actually expected to fulfil.

Such a fusion of authority enhanced Henderson's prestige in the labour movement, where he had begun to outdistance MacDonald in reputation, but it also reinforced his indispensability as Lloyd George's industrial conciliator. Yet he was soon to discover the peril of serving two masters. Representatives of the building trades unions were dismayed to receive a memorandum from him in November 1915 recommending the introduction of blackleg labour in order to meet the shortage of manpower on construction projects, a proposal abandoned after joint protests from the party, the T.U.C., and individual unions. When the Clyde Workers' Committee agitated against dilution, Lloyd George, as Minister of Munitions, and Henderson organized a counter-propaganda tour of munitions factories in December 1915. Although he had not been consulted when the Government decided to deport some of the Clydeside ringleaders, Henderson was subjected to considerable opprobrium for apparent complicity in the repression of radical shop stewards.

It was, however, the crisis over conscription that magnified and underscored his political dilemma. In common with most leaders he had publicly opposed compulsory military service, but once in the Government he was subjected to increased pressure from those elements favoring at least a modified form of conscription. After being sounded out about Labour's attitude to the manpower crisis, Henderson assumed the role of honest broker, seeking to reconcile the Government's sense of urgency about recruitment with Labour's antipathy toward compulsion. Following Lloyd George's meeting with Labour leaders on 8 June 1915 to urge greater cooperation, Henderson asserted that the Govern-

War leader

ment must protect the established position of workers and that excessive profits and exorbitant prices must be curtailed. When the Asquith ministry introduced the National Registration Bill later that month, it was generally perceived as an initial step on the road to compulsion. Snowden and other dissident Labour leaders denounced the measure, but Henderson defended it on the grounds that national registration would enable the authorities to obtain the information necessary to continue the war on voluntary principles. In August Asquith appointed him as Labour's representative on the War Policy Committee chaired by Lord Crewe and containing a majority favoring compulsion. The Committee's findings laid out three alternative schemes: a voluntary army frozen at current size, compulsory service, or a compromise proposed by Henderson, which the Prime Minister accepted as a way of buying time. What Henderson suggested was that the unions would undertake to recruit an additional half million men, and that only if the effort failed would conscription be introduced. By now he had become aware that, despite strong resistance from the I.L.P., many union leaders were prepared to endorse conscription should it be shown to be essential. In his memorandum – in effect a minority report – he counselled:

> Our aim must be to handle the situation so that compulsion, if it comes, comes by the action of the people themselves. On the alternative of conscription or defeat they will be united again. But they cannot be brought to that alternative suddenly, or apart from the conviction that it is a military necessity. They must have time. And if time is spent... I believe that one of two results will follow. Either conscription will be accepted without serious injury to the nation, or it will be proved to be unnecessary.

He further arranged a secret meeting at which Kitchener and Asquith addressed representatives of the Parliamentary party and the unions regarding the emergency in the hope of overcoming

Labour's opposition. Privately convinced that some measure of compulsion was inevitable, he tried to prevent its imposition against the wishes of organized labour and was instrumental in assuring the movement's compliance with the Derby scheme, essentially a means of implementing the Henderson compromise. He told C. P. Scott that labour was not 'irreconcilably opposed to compulsion' and would acquiesce if 'the Cabinet were unanimous in supporting it and Kitchener recommended it'.[10]

By January 1916 military and political pressures had converged to make conscription inescapable. The Prime Minister, yielding to political exigencies, introduced a bill imposing conscription on single males between eighteen and forty-one. Affirming his belief in the voluntary principle, Henderson nonetheless endorsed the bill, arguing that such modified compulsion did not violate any principle to which he was committed. He added that workers had not hesitated in supporting compulsion in the past to enforce temperance reform or secure trade union rights. Morever, he dismissed as groundless any fears that compulsion would remain after the war. While publicly espousing conscription, Henderson attempted to intercede with his Cabinet colleagues: before the debate he circulated a memorandum urging postponement of the Second Reading pending a final effort to satisfy manpower quotas through voluntary recruitment, a plea rejected by a Cabinet more apprehensive about Tory compulsionists than Labour voluntarists. He also extracted a promise that skilled workers would be exempted wherever possible from conscription.

Despite his unequivocal endorsement, a special conference on 6 January instructed Labour M.P.s to oppose the bill, and the N.E.C. and the Parliamentary Party subsequently decided that Labour ministers should withdraw from the Government in protest against the measure. In an impassioned speech Henderson declared that he would vote for conscription whatever the conference decision and offered to resign his seat in order to seek the approval of his constituents. Goaded by interruptions from unruly anti-war militants, he lost his temper and angrily hurled a challenge to I.L.P. socialists to resign their seats to test the popularity of their views with the voters. The conference rejection of the bill made Henderson's position all the more invidious: he had joined the Government to symbolize the unity of the war effort, had come to believe in the need for compulsory service, and never doubted that the inarticulate mass of workers shared his views.

In his letter of resignation Henderson made it clear that his decision was prompted not by personal inclination, but by the decision of organized labour. Noting that he had supported the Military Service Bill in the Cabinet, he promised to continue to do so in the Commons 'on grounds of military necessity'.[11] During the next few days the Government struggled to retain its Labour adherents, despite the apparently clear negative mandate. Henderson was urged not to press his resignation until he saw the final shape of the bill, and Labour members were invited to propose any amendment deemed necessary to protect the interest of workers. On 11 January Cabinet members lauded Henderson's loyalty and courage, and on the next day the Prime Minister, pledging not to impose compulsion on married men, implored Labour leaders to reverse their decision and allow their representatives to remain in the Government. At Henderson's insistence Asquith agreed to insert a clause into the bill disavowing any intention of introducing industrial conscription. Somewhat mollified, a joint meeting of the N.E.C. and the Parliamentary Party reversed its earlier resolution, resolving instead that Labour ministers withdraw their resignations. This decision was confirmed by the party conference in Bristol at the end of the month, which reaffirmed its opposition to conscription without committing the party to resist its implementation. It was now apparent that Henderson's continued participation had become for the Liberals security against the threat of Lloyd George and for the labour movement insurance against industrial conscription. Far less opposition was aroused by the extension several months later, despite all pledges to the contrary, of compulsion to married men. Henderson again supported the measure, representing the dilemma this time as a choice between conscription and a German victory.

If the introduction of conscription discredited the Prime Minister for his willingness to sacrifice Liberal principles to political expediency, it scarcely revealed Henderson in much better light. Whether for patriotic reasons or not, he had abandoned his commitment to voluntary recruitment with unseemly haste after a few half-hearted attempts to delay conscription. In the conflict between his loyalty to the Government and his loyalty to the movement, the war seemed to justify a stance that smacked of political opportunism. While Henderson genuinely sought to safeguard the interests of the movement he represented – especially over industrial conscription – he found it impossible to persist in his opposition to compulsion against Kitchener's immense authority. Having joined the Government, he had little choice but to support its policies, realizing that resignation would foment disunity that might jeopardize the British war effort. Above all, he believed that the need to defeat Germany took precedence over compunctions about voluntary recruitment. By 1916 all three of his sons were in military service, and the urgency of the struggle had acquired a personal dimension for him. Nonetheless anti-war critics could only bemoan the fact that 'Labour's walls of Jericho had crumbled at the first blast of a ministerial trumpet'.[12]

Henderson's loyalty to the Government stemmed in part from personal admiration for Asquith, who had throughout the coalition treated him with respect and consideration. He avoided any intrigue and was only brought into discussion concerning the looming political crisis on 6 December 1916, when leaders met at Buckingham Palace. Having told a Labour Party gathering only a week before that Asquith was 'indispensable', he was reluctant to abandon him to the last. Yet now Henderson consented to do Lloyd George's bidding: in return for Labour support, he was promised more ministerial offices than in the previous Government and reforms the movement had long been demanding, including state control of mines and regulation of food distribution. Despite his distrust of the distinctly Tory cast of the new ministry, Henderson believed that the change of administration had created the possibility of 'Labour securing a greater opportunity to mould policy and exercise executive authority'.[13] When a Labour contingent met Lloyd George, however, they found him evasive, and it took Henderson's persuasive gifts to convince them that adequate concessions had been offered. If Labour were to remain aloof from the new Government, it would convey the impression to the Allies that the nation was divided and that the coalition lacked popular support. His colleagues should, he contended, concern themselves more with what they were to give to the national effort than with what they were likely to receive in concrete benefits. Yielding to political pressure, the N.E.C. sanctioned participation by a narrow majority, and Henderson joined the five-man War Cabinet. MacDonald, lamenting the 'feebleness' of the trade union leaders, found even more galling the alacrity with which Henderson accepted Lloyd George's invitation after having publicly professed loyalty to Asquith.[14] By entering a coalition which did not include the Asquithian Liberals, he and his colleagues were betraying the principle of national unity and calling into question the very basis of the Labour Party.[15] These rumblings of discord notwithstanding, the transition went smoothly. Henderson himself objected when it appeared that the projected War Council was merely being restructured as a conventional, if more compact, cabinet. Such a change, which seemed to undermine the pretext for the new ministry, would, he demurred, 'lay us open to a charge of bad faith, and it would be mercilessly used by the minority of our Party against us at future conferences'.[16]

Although the party Executive had confirmed his appointment, Henderson had at first more difficulty with the movement he represented than with Lloyd George. The hostile mood of the Manchester annual conference in January 1917 was underscored in David Kirkwood's claim that by associating with Lloyd George, Henderson had forfeited the confidence of the party. Conceding the difficulty of reconciling his duties as Secretary with those of a cabinet minister, he rebuffed his critics:

> If he had to resign he would be resigning every day to please some of them. He was not sure he would not resign if he were to please himself, but he was not there either to please himself or them, he was there to see the War through.[17]

Alienated from the movement he served, under attack from anti-war socialists, from trade unionists, and from those who simply distrusted Lloyd George, his bitterness was compounded by grief for his eldest son David, who had been killed on the Somme. Haunted by doubts about his effectiveness, he clung to office in the hope that he could uphold the interests of the labour movement whether or not he retained its confidence.

Within the War Cabinet he successfully countered Curzon's attempt to restrict franchise extension to men and deciphered the state of labour opinion for his not always sympathetic colleagues. He continued, moreover, to support the Government's war policy, turning a deaf ear to those who urged peace by negotiation. When the radical politician Noel Buxton urged him to embrace Woodrow Wilson's appeal for an exchange of view between belligerents, on the grounds that their stated war aims were similar, Henderson anticipated the official reply when he told Buxton somewhat brusquely,

> I quite agree that there is much misunderstanding as to the attitude of President Wilson, though I cannot disguise from my mind the fact that he is largely responsible for such misunderstanding. No one doubts his good intentions but the phrasing of his Note, especially the reference to the objects of the two sets of belligerents, was, I think, unfortunate. Surely all the world knows that the motives which actuated Germany in August 1914 were as wide as the poles from those which actuated either Belgium, France or Britain.[18]

Nor was he any more receptive to radical initiatives within the Labour Party. When a special convention in Leeds in June 1917 called for the creation of extra-parliamentary Soviets, Henderson insisted that if councils were established on the Russian model, no one would oppose them more forcefully than he. He was determined to fight against 'any course of action which would paralyse our military force as it had paralysed the military force of Russia'.[19]

His loyalty to the Government was no security against pressure from Lloyd George, with whom his relations were never as amicable as they had been with Asquith. When the Home Secretary was tempted to suppress the *Labour Leader* and the *Tribunal* for publishing seditious articles, Henderson warned that such proceedings would render intolerable the position of Labour members of the Government. 'No one has come in for more criticism,' he wrote the Prime Minister, 'than myself personally, but I am prepared to face the Conference [and] to defend the Government.' If the Home Secretary crushed the radical press, however, it would have a highly inflammatory effect and totally undermine his own position.[20]

III

In April 1917 Henderson, still Secretary of the British section of the International, received a telegram from Camille Huysmans informing him that the neutral Scandinavian and Dutch socialist parties proposed to convene an international conference in Stockholm. The French, unwilling to sit down with German and Austrian socialists, were not disposed to attend, and Henderson persuaded the executive to pass a resolution 'that the British Labour Party should not be represented at the Stockholm Conference'. In the meantime the Petrograd Soviet decided to announce its support for a world-wide socialist conference at Stockholm to define war aims. As an alternative Henderson favored an inter-allied gathering to be held in London and agreed to lead a deputation to Russia to convince the Kerensky government to support the counter-proposal. Kerensky's accession to power and the prospect of Russian withdrawal from the war prompted Lloyd George to dispatch Henderson, not merely to assess the Russian situation, but with the further stipulation that he might remain there as replacement for British ambassador Sir George Buchanan should such a step seem appropriate. While the Prime Minister's motives remain obscure – Mrs Hamilton suggests that Lloyd George was eager to get Henderson out of his hair – it may well have been that he believed a prominent British trade unionist would make a more suitable envoy to the socialist government than a more traditional diplomat like Buchanan, who had been long associated with the Tsarist regime.

With his mission ambiguously defined and his inclination strongly against the Stockholm meeting, Henderson arrived in Petrograd on 1 June 1917. It was his first exposure to foreign negotiations, and he had little conception of the gravity of the problems confronting the Kerensky government. Rather than give Buchanan his marching orders, he tended to rely on his expertise, especially after determining that the new Russian authorities had a high regard for the ambassador. To recall him at this stage would have been deemed a concession to Bolshevik extremists who had clamored for his removal and would, Henderson concluded, actually diminish British influence with the fragile and suspicious government.[21] Despite his lack of Russian, he did manage to interview Prince Lvov, the head of the provisional regime, Kerensky, Miliukov, its first Foreign Minister, his successor Tereschenko, as well as manufacturers, professors, and workers' representatives; he addressed the Petrograd Soviet, the Moscow Soldiers' Council, and several gatherings of workers. He tried to bolster popular support for the moderate socialist leaders, warning that if the provisional government collapsed, it would lead to a victory for the extremists. He soon came to appreciate how precarious the political situation actually was and how imperative external support was. Employers were 'resolutely opposed to anything in the nature of that State control which at home we have found so essential for the successful prosecution of the war'.[22] There were 'no steadying influences akin to our Trade Unions' and the demands put forward to the employers by undisciplined workers were 'outrageous'.[23] Everything was muddled and inefficient; defeatism was rampant; and Bolshevism was gaining ground in an atmosphere of exhaustion and despair. The provisional government struggled to maintain themselves in power and outflank the Leninists by pressing simultaneously for a peace without annexation and defense of Russia against foreign invaders, the only apparent justification for remaining in the war. G. M. Young, the civil servant who assisted him, believed that his superior's views about Russia's prospects were altered by 'hearing 180 million Russians chant in chorus "Peace without annexation or indemnities"'.[24]

If Henderson tried to convey British enthusiasm for the war and solidarity with their Russian allies, they in turn tried to enlist his support for the Stockholm conference, which many of the moderates believed essential not merely to keep Russia in the war, but for the survival of democracy. In the face of Bolshevik attacks on the whole Stockholm concept, Henderson concluded that the Russians would only continue to fight if their faith in the war aims could be rekindled. Even if Russia ceased to to be 'an effective ally',[25] he believed that 'a crippled partner ruled by men sympathetic to the Allied cause and western democracy was far preferable to a Bolshevik Russia'.[26]

Satisfied that the British could neither prevent, nor delay the Stockholm meeting, he returned to England committed to Labour participation provided it could be made consultative rather than mandatory. At his instigation, the N.E.C., overriding minority objections, agreed to summon a special delegate conference on 10 August in order to persuade the party to reverse its earlier decision. On 25 July, after notifying the Prime Minister, then in Paris, of his plans, he reported to a hostile War Cabinet his intention of acccompanying MacDonald and G. H. Wardle, acting chairman of the Parliamentary party, to Paris, along with several delegates from the Petrograd Soviet, to confer with French socialists about the projected Stockholm meeting. Had it been possible, his War Cabinet colleagues would have prevented his departure, but Lloyd George's response to Stockholm had been ambiguous, and in his absence they were unable to curb Henderson's initiative and had no authority to accept his proferred resignation. He reminded them that he was visiting Paris not as a member of the government, but as Secretary of the Labour Party, underscoring his dual – and increasingly incompatible – loyalties.

Although a compromise was reached about the procedure for the Stockholm conference, by the time he returned to London the Cabinet were outraged at the spectacle of their colleague consorting abroad with foreign socialists and defeatists. Summoned to a Cabinet meeting on 1 August, he was then kept waiting for an hour – the infamous doormat incident – while his colleagues discussed the impropriety of his conduct. Only after voicing his indignation was he admitted and allowed to defend himself. Under pressure from hard line Cabinet members, the Prime Minister declined to say whether he would even permit the issue of passports for British delegates to attend a meeting in Stockholm at which enemy socialists would be present. Henderson later told Tom Jones that this was his first inkling that Lloyd George had hardened his views against Stockholm, having earlier encouraged exploratory approaches.[27] In reply to critics Henderson also justified his conduct during a Commons debate that evening, reiterating that his mission to Paris had been entirely consistent with his duties as party Secretary. He warned that the allied cause would be jeopardized at Stockholm unless it were represented by those capable of correcting the misapprehensions that existed among Russians and Germans regarding British war aims.

Considerable confusion still surrounds the events of the next fortnight. By now unyielding as to the wisdom of participation in the Stockholm conference, Henderson refrained from raising the issue again, although he did plead with the Prime Minister to grant passports to delegates if the Labour Party agreed to send them. Despite clear evidence to the contrary, Lloyd George later professed to believe that Cabinet opposition had dissuaded Henderson from persisting with his support for Stockholm, a change that he was expected to convey to the party at the special conference. If the Prime Minister was in this case propagating a deliberate misconception, he may have been on stronger ground in regard to two other accusations. Henderson was charged with concealing from the conference the depth of Cabinet hostility to Stockholm, thus betraying his duty as a member of the Government. More misleading was Henderson's failure to apprise the delegates of the apparent Russian change of heart.[28] Lloyd George subsequently claimed to have received a telegram from Kerensky distancing himself from the projected meeting, but this purported telegram never materialized and was, in any event, disclaimed by the Russian leader. All that can be conclusively proven was the receipt of a message from the Russian *chargé d'affaires* confirming that the Russians envisioned Stockholm as a party concern, not a gathering that would bind the Government, a position close to that posited by Henderson and ostensibly less objectionable to British leaders. In any event that was the only communication which Henderson actually saw, despite the Prime Minister's allusions to the contrary. Whereas Lloyd George later construed the telegram as a clear disavowal of the conference, Henderson merely reported it as a slight modification in the Russian position, insufficient to warrant jettisoning Stockholm.

On 10 August the special Labour Party conference was convened at Central Hall, where Henderson reminded the assembled throng that before going to Russia, he had opposed the conference, but owing to the determination of the Russians, he had come around to their point of view. As long as certain safeguards were retained, it was far better for the Allied case to be represented directly than to abandon the Russians to the blandishments of delegates from enemy and neutral countries. He pleaded with the party not to respond to the Russian initiative with a 'blank refusal' and to supplement their military effort with the 'political weapon' in order to secure a victory that would 'ensure for the world a lasting, honourable and democratic peace'.[29] Although Henderson expected his effort to be defeated by a belligerent trade union bloc, the conference, swayed by his impassioned advocacy, voted by a three to one majority to accept the Russian invitation, adding the proviso that no representatives of other British bodies affiliated to the Socialist International, including the I.L.P., would be allowed to attend.

War leader

Lloyd George, who had implausibly gambled either on Henderson urging rejection of the invitation or the delegates dissociating themselves from it, was furious at the outcome. That evening Henderson went to see the Prime Minister, who angrily reproved him for 'selling out' the Government and demanded his resignation from the War Cabinet. Charging him with having deceived his chief, his colleagues, and the conference after he, Lloyd George, had defended his unauthorized Paris trip, he described Henderson's conduct as 'something very like treachery'.[30] The latter's resignation letter conceded 'the embarrassing complications arising from this duality of office' but trusted that he might continue to render assistance in a non-governmental capacity.[31] In the days that followed a carefully orchestrated campaign of vituperation was levied against him in the press, where he was denounced as a traitor, a liar, and a pacifist. Two days later he rose to defend his action in the House, but Cabinet secrecy prevented revelations about its deliberations, and he decided that it would be improper to disclose contradictory evidence concerning the disputed Russian telegrams, even though this left him vulnerable to the charge of deception. Moreover Henderson, wounded by popular calumny, was no match as a debater for the adroit and devious Prime Minister. He intimated to Jim Middleton, the acting Secretary, that had he divulged Lloyd George's pro-Stockholm May telegram to him, it would so embarrass the Government as to cause its downfall.

Having endured recriminations from the left for his loyalty to the Government for three years, Henderson now found himself the target of attack by the very elements he had striven to defend, and his temporary disgrace rankled. As he told Walter Runciman,

> ... you know from experience the kind of politician into whose hands I unfortunately permitted myself to fall. However much appearances may be against me I have the inward consciousness

that I did not intentionally withold [sic] any information from the conference which I was entitled to give. . . . I have paid the penalty of trying to serve two Masters, the Government and the Labour Movement. I got wrong with one in seeking to be loyal to the other. Yet if I had to go through it again the only thing I would do would be to tender my resignation a little earlier. I wanted to leave before going to Paris and ought to have done so. Everything I did from that moment left me subject to misunderstanding and suspicion.[32]

IV

If his resignation released Henderson from the collective responsibility of a cabinet minister, it also unmuzzled him. He was now free to criticize Lloyd George's handling of the war and to conciliate some of his more radical antagonists. As Arthur Ponsonby told C. P. Trevelyan, 'I believe labour will rally to Henderson & new recruits will come in & H himself will be forced more & more in our direction'.[33] His writings in the coming months reveal an attitude much closer to that of the Union of Democratic Control than his statements as a minister. In September he wrote that 'if we intend to come out of the war with clean hands there can be no good reason against the Government stating clearly and publicly the fundamental issues for which we fight'.[34] This echoed the spirit of Stockholm, but it reflected equally his *rapprochement* with the idealists of the U.D.C. In November, insisting that everything must be done to prevent the division of Europe into hostile economic camps after the war, he condemned the Allied proposals which envisaged an 'organized systematic commercial and economic boycotting' to destroy German commerce.[35] The special 10 August conference had drawn up a draft memorandum on war aims which served as the basis for a fuller statement formulated by Henderson, MacDonald, and Sidney Webb and later approved by another conference on 28 December. It proposed a League of Free Nations, a policy of no annexations, the re-drawing of frontiers on the basis of self-determination, a repudiation of indemnities and secret diplomacy, the adoption of the open door principle in international trade, and socialist representation in delegations to the peace conference.

Nonetheless some differences with MacDonald and the I.L.P. could not be circumvented. Henderson believed that Labour should attempt to influence the peace settlement by applying pressure to the allied governments, whereas the more radical elements urged socialist movements to disavow their governments and to negotiate directly among themselves. When MacDonald and Henderson went to Paris in February 1918 as part of a deputation to consult with French socialists, they quarrelled about the need for a common stance in support of the British war aims memorandum. MacDonald affirmed the right of the dissident minority to express its views even where they contradicted avowed Labour policy. Typically, Henderson was more concerned to maintain a facade of unity than to provide a forum for ideological wrangling. He could barely repress his sense of irritation when he wrote MacDonald,

> The deputation goes to Paris to induce all sections to agreement upon our basis, but it must be obvious to you that it would be inconsistent for the promoters of the Conference to reveal and discuss their own differences on details at such a stage... I should view with great regret any action which might lead our Allied friends to imagine that there was no real unity in the Labour, Socialist and Trade Movement in this country, as would undoubtedly be the case if the deputation did not speak with a unanimous voice...[36]

The very notion of publicizing internal dissension at an international gathering, however typical of socialist parties, was entirely repugnant to him. Having imposed a statement of principles on the party, Henderson had no wish to see old quarrels rekindled and resented MacDonald's assumption of the mantle of socialist purity.

The articulation of enlightened war aims marked the first stage in Labour's assertion of independence; at Henderson's instigation it was adopting a foreign policy clearly at variance with the Government of which he had so recently been a member. But however incisive its critique or clamorous its resistance to an uncompromising war policy, it was essential to restructure Labour into a national party competing for power if its goals were to be implemented. While he had perceived Labour's function before the war as prodding the Liberal Party to respond to working-class needs, Henderson recognized by 1917 that Labour itself must be the instrument of social amelioration. He had become convinced that the war had engendered a new democratic consciousness which Labour could exploit, especially once the impact of the extended suffrage was felt in electoral terms. Echoing his own disenchantment with the established order, he asserted that the party was now capable of representing the mass of ordinary people who no longer regarded the traditional parties as suitable vehicles for democratic policies. His first concern was to transform Labour into an effective electoral machine, able to mobilize the new voters among the working class and women. For this reason he stressed the creation of local Labour parties in every Parliamentary constituency as the 'cardinal feature' of the scheme. Although the financial strength of the party would still rest on the unions which would remain 'the final repositories of authority in determining the direction of party policy', the main burden of electoral organization and political propaganda would fall on the constituency bodies.[37] Whereas party organization had been of secondary interest to him once he had entered the government in 1915, he now plunged into that familiar territory with renewed vigor. Labour had fought only three by-elections from the start of the war until August 1917, but it was the next general election to which he now turned his attention.

From the outset Henderson envisaged the expanded Labour Party as a coalition. Local parties would attract activists not necessarily affiliated with either trade union or socialist society, especially the female voters in whose interests he had struggled since pre-war suffrage battles. In addition he saw the need to attract middle-class support, both in order to enlarge the candidate pool and to generate new ideas. From his own collaboration with Sidney Webb during the early days of the W.E.W.N.C. to his association with men like G. M. Young and Tom Jones within the Government, Henderson came to appreciate the need for receptivity to fresh thinking. As Jones recorded their conversation, he intended after the war 'to re-cast Labour representation in such a way as to bring in a larger infusion of the non-trade-unionists. He mentioned no names, but was clearly referring to the younger intellectuals who are keenly sympathetic to Labour.'[38] C. P. Scott also had the impression that Henderson's policy was 'to enlarge the bounds of the Labour Party and bring in the intellectuals as candidates'. With additional talent and resources, it might be possible to contest as many as 500 seats in the next election.[39]

V

It seemed as though Henderson's resentment at his mistreatment by Lloyd George not only altered his perspective on Labour's future, but energized him as well. Shortly after leaving the Cabinet, he abandoned the chairmanship of the Parliamentary Labour Party to Willie Adamson in order to devote himself to the task of reorganization. He was soon meeting regularly with a number of Labour supporters, including Webb, G. D. H. Cole, R. H. Tawney, and J. J. Mallon, to revise Labour's constitution. On 26 September, barely a month after his resignation from the War Cabinet, he was ready to present a memorandum to the

N.E.C. calling for

> the re-organisation of the Party with a view to a wider extension of membership, the strengthening and development of local parties in the constituencies, together with the promotion of a larger number of candidates, and the suggestion that a Party programme be adopted.

The sub-committee appointed to consider details was dominated by trade unionists, but it also included MacDonald, whom he consulted at each stage of program development. But, as Marquand observed, 'their cooperation was uneasy, spasmodic, and punctuated by bursts of sharp mutual hostility'.[40]

No longer the lonely dissenter, MacDonald was increasingly eclipsed by the newly militant Henderson and was clearly jealous of his rival's new-found popularity in the movement. That same month Henderson received an ovation at the T.U.C. conference in Blackpool, where he repaired his relations with the trade unions, so often strained during his tenure as a minister. He told an attentive audience that some kind of international organization was imperative after the war and insisted that he would rather consult with the German socialist minority before peace was achieved than to meet the representatives of a discredited regime after military victory had been secured. Scott subsequently reassured him that 'as leader of the Labour party he was far away more powerful than as a member of the Government'.[41] Little wonder then that he had begun to harbor wider ambitions, no longer content to view himself as a surrogate for MacDonald. After the Nottingham conference Beatrice Webb observed that Henderson, for whom she and Sidney had developed considerable affection, was 'ambitious: he sees a chance of a Labour Party government, or a predominantly Labour government, with himself as Premier'.[42]

Much as he aspired to broaden the national constituency for

the Labour Party, Henderson recognized that trade union support was the precondition of political viability. Tempting in principle, the idea of replacing the existing machinery with a constitution based entirely on individual membership was clearly unfeasible. The unions, wedded to the existing structure, were suspicious of attempts to enhance the power of local activists and feared that the growth of constituency parties would weaken their traditional authority. In order to win union consent to the higher affiliation fees needed to finance the party's electoral operations, he retained the provision, which he had previously fought as too drastic a change, that all members of the Executive be elected by the conference at large, thus ensuring that the unions would determine its composition. Although MacDonald would have preferred to strengthen the constituency parties at the expense of the unions and derided the proposals as 'an election agent's document', even his biographer concedes that 'Henderson's constitution was probably the best obtainable'.[43] Five seats were allocated to divisional parties, four would be reserved for women, and eleven were to represent affiliated organizations, including both unions and socialist societies. Without the protection of reserved seats, socialist bodies might find themselves excluded by the trade union majority. If the trade unions were victorious in the struggles over the constitution, the I.L.P. and the socialist societies were the losers, a shift in power that reflected Henderson's own biases. Working with remarkable speed, he was able to present his proposals to the Executive before the end of September, to secure provisional approval, and to spend considerable time during the next few months rallying support around the country, especially in the mining districts and Lancashire where residual loyalty to the Liberals was strong. These were the areas in which Labour candidates had to make strides if the party were to increase its number of seats. He directed his appeal to the unions, emphasizing their growth in size and importance, and stressing the need for an expanded party organization to cope with the mass of new voters. Sensitive to the predilections of his audiences, he spoke of political power, not of socialist goals.

As McKibbin has shown, the new rules in general formalized what had already been the practice in many constituencies before 1914.[44] The new constituency parties were established on the basis of older ward associations, which had been composed of members of affiliated societies and local residents. That individual membership became an essential component of the new constitution was less an innovation than a natural evolution from the organization Henderson had long espoused.

Although Henderson had no direct affiliation with a socialist body prior to joining the Fabian Society, he had become converted to the view that a distinctive ideological commitment was essential. The fragility of the moderate left in Russia had testified to the value of a strong parliamentary, socialist alternative to Bolshevism and a revivified socialist International. Labour, he contended, desired to make a 'swift and smooth transition to the new order', in which it would 'establish democratic control over all the machinery of State'. But this would be done peacefully and, in contrast to Russia, 'without a violent break with the past'. To achieve social liberty and end the domination of one class by another 'it will not be necessary to spill blood'.[45] It was under the guidance of Sidney Webb that Henderson approved the inclusion of the socialist creed familiarly known as Clause 4 in the new party constitution. While he would have advocated public ownership of monopolies and essential raw materials, his direct experience of state control in wartime and his antipathy to Bolshevism made him receptive to Webb's broader compromise committing the party to the common ownership of the means of production, a formulation sufficiently moderate to win union allegiance without sacrificing that of socialist militants. What Henderson had in mind was neither state capitalism, nor state socialism, but rather 'industrial democracy', which, in fact, seemed to mean an expansion of 'nationalized' control to railways, shipping, mines, and to the purchase and distribution of raw materials.[46] Despite initial apprehension, the unions had come to realize that state-controlled industries had managed resources more efficiently and equitably than had the free market before the war. Henderson was able to exploit a new awareness of their own growing power. Trade unions had shared, albeit in a limited way, in the schemes of regulation; now they might look forward to playing a dominant role in the post-war economy. A national party, rooted in the mass of organized workers, was essential if the movement was to consolidate the economic gains of wartime and to influence the course of reconstruction. Furthermore, Fabians, like Webb and Cole, had persuaded Henderson that a socialist objective was electorally appealing to the middle-class professionals he hoped to attach to the Labour Party.

Victory did not come easily. Henderson feared that the big unions would employ their bloc votes to eviscerate the constitution. At the Nottingham conference the proposals were referred back for the purpose of introducing amendments calculated to win over recalcitrant trade unionists. Beatrice Webb, striking a somewhat alarmist note, maintained that the constitution would have been rejected outright had it not been for Henderson's appeal to workers not to forfeit the chance to forge a great national party out of fear of infiltration of left-wing intellectuals.[47] Concessions were made to appease the big battalions: the number of seats on the N.E.C. allotted to affiliated societies was increased, and the Parliamentary party, which was expected to include a majority of unionists, was given a share in policy making. With these modifications, the new constitution won a solid majority at a reconvened conference in February 1918 over the objections of the I.L.P.

Thus Labour emerged from the war with a new image, a new

structure, and a new organizational apparatus. Credit for all of these belongs chiefly to Henderson. That he was compelled to make major concessions to win trade union support, thereby determining the course of the party's history for the next half century, does not detract from his personal success. Although these changes may well have been inevitable, a reaction to the experience of the war and the opportunity created by the enlarged electorate, it was Henderson who acted as the necessary catalyst. And it was his exposure to Russia, his dismissal from the War Cabinet, his rekindled ambition that triggered his response. He was the architect of these developments far more than MacDonald, whose relative isolation at the time diminished his effectiveness within the party and whose opposition to the war alienated him from the jingoistic trade unions. If Henderson deserves credit for exploiting the opportunities generated by the war, it should be remembered that part of the stimulus was the humiliation inflicted on him by Lloyd George. Had the Prime Minister moved to outflank the Labour ministers in his Government by articulating war aims in Wilsonian fashion and seeking to broaden his support by means of concrete proposals for social reconstruction, the occasion for Labour to strike out on its own might have been missed. Henderson seized that opportunity, but he was prompted to do so in part because the Coalition Government misjudged his character and his determination to avenge his peremptory dismissal. He had endured the contempt of politicians like Lloyd George because he felt impelled to sacrifice his pride in the national interest. But he never forgot the injuries inflicted on him. His experience in the wartime ministry turned him not only against Lloyd George but against the notion of any coalition in which Labour would be relegated to a subordinate role, a resolve that would influence his conduct during the 1931 crisis. Ultimately it was Henderson, rather than the Welsh wizard, who had the last word.

4 Uncle Arthur

By 1918 Henderson had secured a dominant position within the Labour Party. Although he had relinquished Parliamentary leadership the previous year to the lacklustre Adamson, he clung to the office of Secretary, which continued to be the foundation of his power after the war. If he had ceased to be Labour's public spokesman and most visible representative, a burden he had shouldered through most of the war, he relished his role as Uncle Arthur, expert wire-puller and reconciler of disputing factions. It was his control over the electoral machine, deriving from close links with the unions and constituency activists, that made his authority unassailable at least until he willingly conceded center stage to MacDonald in 1922. Yet it would scarcely do him justice to suggest that his power was merely functional. He had been the principal architect of the new constitution, the mastermind of that precarious balance between a democratic, constituency-based mass organization and a union-financed oligarchic structure. No one else in Labour circles at the time could have engineered the transformation from a loose alliance of interest groups into an embryonic national party, competing electorally with the traditional parties. Moreover it was Henderson who saw the need not merely to devise a bargain with the trade unions, but to appeal to a broader constituency, including women as well as men, intellectuals no less than manual labourers. A cautious man, he was sufficiently enterprising to seize the historic opportunity, and his responsibility for the structural and programatic changes of 1918 cannot simply be ascribed to diligence as Secretary.

His pre-war career and his abdication to MacDonald's authority after 1922 tend to overshadow his commanding position in the intervening years. With the death of Keir Hardie and MacDonald's retreat into the political wilderness, there was a power vacuum that Henderson adroitly filled. While his complicity in unpopular wartime policies temporarily alienated him from the more radical currents in the movement, his resignation from the Cabinet refurbished his image, enabling him to forge a viable party out of organized labour's dissatisfaction with the Lloyd George Coalition. What seems remarkable is not that he was able to concentrate so much authority in his own person, but that he was prepared to surrender it, provided, of course, that the party machine remained in his capable and experienced hands. It is all the more so in that Henderson totally lacked those charismatic qualities that served Hardie and MacDonald. Beatrice Webb contended that although he lacked 'graciousness and is apt to be sullen and rude' to his colleagues, he was, in contrast to some of his vain and self-important contemporaries, 'a veritable rock of bourgeois respectability and self-control'. She added tellingly, 'I have never known a man of undoubted power with so little personal charm or magnetism.'[1]

What was it that made this blunt and artless politician so adept at wielding power, at getting his own way in party affairs? It is true that he would occasionally bully subordinates and bludgeon the Executive into complying with his wishes, but their willingness to obey suggests more formidable talents. Nor was it rhetorical gifts that enabled him to persuade: Henderson's speeches were invariably dismissed as dull and rather pedestrian efforts. He eschewed the evangelical style of a Snowden or the ideological vagaries of a MacDonald in favor of plain speaking and was no match for the likes of Lloyd George on the floor of the House. Two American observers who witnessed his performance at the Nottingham conference quickly revised their initially negative estimate of him as a colorless bureaucrat:

> If one object of oratory is to persuade and convince, then in attaining his object Henderson is a powerful orator. He speaks without grace or beauty. But he speaks to the primary sense of justice, with a weight of fact and reason, and directness, in a strong one-toned voice of mastery. In a convention of many voices and wide divergences among the extremists, he bears down and conquers opposition and welds the welter into coherence and unity... He doesn't intervene until there is a rough-house. Unlike some men who compromise differences, he doesn't do it by soft soap and gentle conciliation. He uses a cast-iron voice and a bull vitality to pound in the sensible central interpretation of a plain man, and he does it with all the energy and noise of an exhorter of the extreme left.
>
> Henderson is one of the most deceptive men we have met. Like Ulysses, when he is seated you would take him for nobody in particular. In conversation he is a little verbose, impersonal and oratorical. In a small group he is without salience. But when the herd cries of a thousand strong men pierce through to the layers of his stored vitality, hidden under a commonplace exterior, something awakens and he puts on power and rays it out on the mass till they obey him.[2]

The most consistent of politicians, he never wavered in his moderate principles or in his tenacious loyalty to the movement, and this unflagging dependability earned him the devotion even of those who disagreed with his views. One knew where one stood with Uncle Arthur, and the confidence he inspired more than made up for the brilliance he lacked.

As the quintessential insider, the politician who preferred to operate behind the scenes, Henderson had neither time for, nor interest in regular expositions of his views. He did write occasionally for the *Daily Herald* and the *Labour Magazine* in the 1920s, but his authorship even of those pamphlets issued under his name is sometimes questionable. Unlike MacDonald, he did not envisage his role as formulator of party doctrine, still less as a phrasemaker. Plain speaking connoted not merely his rhetorical style, but equally his ideological legacy. It is possible, nonetheless, to extract from the small corpus of his wartime and post-war writings the substance of his political ideas, much of which he was instrumental in translating into election platforms and conference resolutions.

Although he had begun his career as a Liberal whose views were indistinguishable from those of other social reformers and progressives, he had by 1918 readily embraced broadly socialist doctrines. To be sure, he was not casting his lot with the advocates of violent revolution or even of stringent state control, but he had moved, at least tentatively, towards a disavowal of capitalism. Personal experience of industrial poverty had revealed the defects of the inherited system, and the war had pointed the way to economic alternatives. It was necessary, therefore, to resist any attempt to return those industries that had come under government control to private capitalists. Indeed by 1919 he was urging Sidney Webb 'to draft a complete scheme for "socializing industry" – the whole of industry' on the grounds that it was important to show that 'the principle of socialization was applicable today to all industries'.[3] Espousing the doctrine of common ownership of the means of production, he was wary of worker control, distrusting what he perceived as anarchic tendencies among the more militant unions. His quarrel with the proponents of direct action, most intense during 1919-20, was not over the extent of change, but over the means employed to achieve it. The revolution to which Labour was committed would be 'as thoroughgoing in its results as any violent convulsion involving the use of armed force can possibly be'. Indeed he spoke of abolishing the economic system based on private ownership and the control of government by the propertied classes. He advocated a 'comprehensive plan for the reconstruction of society' through the direct taxation of large incomes to prevent the accumulation of private fortunes. At the core of his socialism was a conviction about the need for redistribution of wealth to achieve a more egalitarian society.

Capitalism had hitherto failed to provide a national minimum standard of life, but there was now an irresistible impetus towards social transformation. The only question was whether the propertied classes would oppose the changes. 'By peaceable methods, or by direct assault,' he asserted, 'society is going to be brought under democratic control.' His own preference was obviously for peaceful change. No responsible person could contemplate violent revolution without horror; indeed the very notion of insurrection was alien to the British character. It was the task of Labour to demonstrate the efficacy of democratic methods, ensuring a smooth transition to the new social order and thus countering the appeal of anti-parliamentary propaganda. Its commitment to constitutional procedures made it all the more imperative for Labour to impose democratic controls over the machinery of state. This meant not merely winning a Parliamentary majority, but overhauling the administrative structure to prevent sabotaging of its legislative program.[4]

Henderson strongly resisted initiatives towards industrial action for political ends. Without disavowing the strike weapon to protect the economic interest of workers, he repudiated direct action by a minority as a violation not only of 'the orderly peaceable procedure of our parliamentary constitution', but of 'the spiritual and social brotherhood of men'.[5] His observations of Russia had shown him how volatile the masses could be, and he warned that the revolutionary impulse was alive even in England:

> Until the profiteering element is eliminated, until we have substituted for the motive of private gain in industry, the motive of public

service, industrial unrest will continue and will grow ever more pronounced.[6]

Yet he never ceased to believe that the mass of organized labour would reject social disorder as long as responsible leaders remained in control. Even when the party tacitly endorsed direct action at the 1919 Southport conference, he denounced such a policy as dangerous:

> To force upon the country by illegitimate means the policy of a section, perhaps the minority of the community, involves the abrogation of Parliamentary government, establishes the dictatorship of the minority, and might easily destroy eventually all our constitutional liberties... When we have elected a strong, capable, determined Labour Government, and it has failed us, then, and only then, could the workers find some ground for doubting the effectiveness of political and constitutional means.[7]

The other central theme in his articles and speeches at the end of the war was the need to rebuild a genuine People's International. He had never ceased to blame the war on Germany's aggressive rulers, bent on world domination, but their defeat opened the way to a victory for the forces of democracy. Distinguishing between the German people and their oppressive masters, he insisted that the war was being fought 'to destroy, not a great nation, but a militarist autocracy'. If Germany forsook militarism, there was no reason why world order could not be constituted under conditions of freedom, equality, and security.[8] Much as he disagreed with Lloyd George's determination to fight to the finish, he exonerated England from blame for causing or prolonging the conflict:

> We are not influenced by imperialist ambitions or selfish national interests. We seek a victory, but it must be a victory for international moral and spiritual forces, finding its expression in a peace based upon the inalienable rights of common humanity.[9]

He conceded that the post-war settlement would have to include restorations and reconstitutions. Belgium, in particular, must regain its independence and be compensated for German depradations, but other territorial questions could be resolved on the principle of self-determination. Although Germany deserved to be stripped of its colonies, these should be responsibly administered in the interest of the native populations, not annexed for profit by the Allies. Nor should there be any seizure of economic advantage by crippling Germany financially or by imposing revenue tariffs to enrich the victorious powers. The test of a democratic victory involved more than an even-handed treatment of Germany: the trust of the people would be betrayed if England sought territorial gains or if the discredited capitalist regime was simply restored. 'The hard, cruel, competitive system of production,' he asserted boldly, 'must be replaced by a system of cooperation under which the status of workers will be revolutionised.'[10]

The key to the realization of these goals would be the establishment of the League of Nations, which alone could 'guarantee peace and security for all peoples, and leave them free to develop their material and moral resources without the menace of recurrent wars'. But Henderson also saw the League as a corollary of the Socialist International, promoting unity among peoples. The establishment of the world organization would be 'a dramatic declaration of the fact that the peoples of the world form one family'. His hopes for the new body were limitless: an international legislature would foster democratic practices among its members, regulate freedom of trade and commercial intercourse, and abolish conscription and standing armaments. If the nations renounced 'vulgar imperialism' and submitted all disputes to arbitration by League courts, reinforced by economic and military sanctions, Western civilization might enjoy the benefits of peace and freedom instead of war and revolutionary conflict.[11] Thus the League had the potential for developing into a genuinely representative body, not just preventing war, but equally coping with political, economic, and industrial problems on an international scale. While many on the left distrusted a League dominated by the victorious powers, from which both Germany and the Soviet Union were excluded, Henderson waged a continuous campaign within the labour movement to mobilize support for the new organization.

Clearly more optimistic about League prospects than many in Labour circles, including MacDonald, he shared their misgiving about the peace terms. Despite lip service to Wilsonian idealism, the treaty was rooted in the punishment of Germany and the concession of economic and territorial advantages to the Allies. He was strongly critical of violations of self-determination that prohibited the union of Germany and Austria, that placed millions of Germans under Czech and Polish rule, and that consigned German territory to succession states. Instead of equality of treatment, Germany was denied access to essential raw materials and subjected to an economic blockade. The stringent terms imposed would play into the hands of militarists, while the deprivation caused by the blockade would wreak havoc for those least responsible for the war – children and the mass of labourers.[12] He urged Labour supporters to repudiate this 'unreal, undemocratic and unjust' treaty and to demand 'speedy and drastic revision'. The people, he continued, had to be taught that deliverance could not come through militarism, conscription, and secret diplomacy, but by strengthening the League and making it representative and democratic.[13]

II

Henderson had travelled up and down the country, explicating the new constitution and prodding constituencies to set up local

Uncle Arthur

parties in anticipation of the imminent general election. In the first heady moments he had envisaged as many as 500 Labour candidates, but reality bore down on him, and at the June party conference he announced a total of 301 candidates. Labour could not yet field a full national slate, and, as he told C. P. Scott, would try to run a candidate 'wherever there was a tolerable chance of carrying him'. In practice Labour's electoral aspirations were circumscribed by the rudimentary state of local organization. Slow progress had been made during the war, intensified somewhat in the early months of 1918, to establish constituency parties, but Henderson realized that in so far as Labour was equipped to fight an election it was 'because they had an existing trade union organization in every town'.[14] It was this recognition that had, at least in part, prompted his concessions to trade union opinion during the negotiations and resistance to MacDonald's bid to strengthen local parties earlier in the year. Although it was moving in the direction of a mass party, the transformation was still incomplete in 1918, and the party was compelled to rely on the same network of union branches and trades councils that had nominated and sustained candidates in the past.

A further problem was Labour's continued association with the Coalition. Local parties were attacking Labour ministers in their own constituencies, a situation that became more invidious once the annual conference resolved to abandon the electoral truce. Internecine squabbles over continued participation in the Coalition jeopardized the fragile unity that Henderson had sought to foster. Reluctant to fight an election while Labour ministers remained in office, he was apprehensive that an early election would hurt electoral prospects by casting Labour in an unpatriotic light, tarring even those who had loyally supported the war effort with the dissident brush. Sidney Webb confided to his wife that Uncle Arthur was 'in the depths of depression, doubtful whether he will win his seat or, if he does, whether he will have any Party to lead'.[15] When the N.E.C. discussed withdrawal from the Coalition, there was resistance from M.P.s who believed that resignation would undermine Labour's hopes of influencing the peace and reconstruction. J. R. Clynes foresaw that candidates who stood apart from Lloyd George would be swept away in the tide of popular jingoism, and even Henderson, whose reputation had risen as a result of his post-doormat resignation, was hesitant about what course to recommend. In the event the Executive voted to place a resolution before a conference calling upon the party to resume independence and to withdraw its members from the Government, a resolution ratified by the emergency gathering in London three days after the armistice.

The Coupon Election of December 1918 found Henderson's hastily improvised machine incapable of handling the heavy burdens imposed. Although Labour contested many more seats and was numerically far stronger than in 1910, the results constituted a major defeat. Out of 363 candidates, only fifty-seven were elected, and of those forty-nine were union nominees. The local parties had nominated 140 candidates, but only five were elected in addition to three I.L.P. successes. Henderson's own experience proved equally disastrous. He had abandoned Barnard Castle, no longer as safe since it had been divided under the redistribution provisions of the Representation of the People Act, for the untried waters of East Ham South. It was probably unwise to cut himself off from his regional base of power, even in order to contest a seat closer to party headquarters, but given the popular mood, he was likely to be defeated wherever he stood as a candidate. With his keen electoral sense, he was under no illusions about his prospects once the Coalition managers targeted him for defeat. His visit to Russia was misrepresented, and Churchill denounced him in the constituency as 'one of the Stockholm extremists'. It made no difference that Henderson had served in the War Cabinet or that Lloyd George had initially endorsed the Stockholm conference. Instead he was excoriated for associating with Lenin and Trotsky and for 'shaking hands with murder'. The result, duplicated almost everywhere Labour candidates repudiated a vindictive peace, found him at the bottom of the poll with only 27 per cent of the vote. Victory went to the National Democratic candidate, A. C. Edwards, who stood in the Coalition interest, with the Conservative capturing second place.

Facing the first of recurrent electoral misfortunes, Henderson had little time to nurse his wounds before leaving for Berne, where a reconstituted International was scheduled to confer at the same time as the peace conference. In February 1918 the inter-allied socialists meeting in London had appointed Henderson, Emile Vandervelde, and Albert Thomas as a three-man committee to convene a world conference, and as soon as the armistice was signed the Labour Party Executive authorized him in his capacity as Secretary to the British section of the International Bureau to cooperate with socialists of other countries to implement the London proposals. Henderson attended as a delegate of the majority socialists, composed of Labour and trade union representatives, but, eager to placate the I.L.P., he also saw to it that MacDonald and Ethel Snowden were included in the delegation.

Even before the conference formally opened he took advantage of the occasion to renew his acquaintance with German and Austrian socialists, like Karl Kautsky, Herman Müller, Hugo Haase, and Friedrich Adler, with whom links had been interrupted by the war. His was a steadying influence, mediating between hostile French and German delegates, the only figure whose stature matched that of the veteran neutral country socialists, Hjalmar Branting and Camille Huysmans. Although he spoke only English, he had no trouble in communicating with his fellow delegates and in gaining their respect. As Mrs Hamilton, who had occasion to observe him later in Geneva, wrote:

> Each, in his differing way, felt in him something rock-like: rock-like in its poise, and yet not hard. He was a person whose judgment and whose disinterestedness all trusted, and a person to whom they also went with their troubles, for counsel – always sane and commonsensical; and for a certain healing touch... he, more than any other, held the Conference together, and prevented it, on many an occasion, from going off the rails or losing itself in passionately felt detail.[16]

The conference elected Branting as President and Henderson as one of the four Vice-Presidents. In addition it nominated an Action Committee, composed of Branting, Henderson, and Huysmans, with instructions to take steps to re-establish the International without delay.

That such a step was fraught with difficulty became apparent in the initial debates on the issue of war responsibility, which the French insisted on raising. Albert Thomas introduced a resolution which alleged that the war had been unleashed by the governments of Central Europe and sought to proscribe socialists guilty of complicity. In deference to the sensibilities of the German majority socialists, the issue was referred to a special commission, which persuaded the reluctant German delegation to affirm that they had destroyed the old system responsible for the war and would work for the realization of socialism within the League of Nations. A second contentious issue, and the one which would ultimately shatter the International, was that provoked by the Bolshevik revolution. Branting's resolution, subsequently endorsed by a large majority of the delegates, reaffirmed that parliamentary government was the appropriate way to achieve socialism and insisted that revolutionary dictatorship was incompatible with social democracy. Without endorsing Bolshevism, the rival Adler–Longuet resolution disavowed the implicit criticism of the Soviet Union and denounced those patriots who had paralyzed socialism during the war. The minority, consisting mainly of French, Austrian, and minority German socialists, wanted to ensure that all tendencies were welcome within the reconstituted International at whatever cost to ideological coherence, a stance abhorrent to the moderates in England, Germany, and the neutral countries. Henderson had no doubts where his own sympathies lay, as a moderate and patriotic socialist, willing to embrace his wartime enemies, but not those doctrines he had found so repellent during his visit to Russia in the early days of the revolution. He proved as immovable on this issue as he was to be over the initiatives by the Communist Party for affiliation to Labour. On the other hand, he was cheered by the resolutely anti-militarist sentiment he encountered and was confirmed in his view that international cooperation was the key to world peace.

Despite the appearance of vitality within international socialism, the Berne Conference was a resounding failure. In contrast to the statesmen in Paris it had tactfully sidestepped the question of war guilt, but it had demonstrated that the conflict between parliamentary democracy and Leninist dictatorship was irreconcilable. Instead of proclaiming a reconstituted International, the delegates merely resolved to try again in 1920 in the hope that in the intervening months they might then find a basis for resolving differences. In the meantime a Permanent Commission was established to conduct business and oversee the peace negotiations. After the Draft Covenant was announced, Henderson was part of a delegation that presented the resolutions passed at Berne to Clemenceau. The Permanent Commission met in Amsterdam in April to consider the terms of the peace treaty, so clearly at odds with the sentiments of international socialism. Henderson's resolution criticizing the Draft Covenant and urging disarmament was revised to reflect the delegates' disapproval more explicitly. They expressed approval of the

Anschluss if the Austrians wished it; they condemned the surrender of German territory to Poland; and they denounced imperialist annexations. On a more positive note, they insisted that members submit disputes to international arbitration through the League of Nations and wanted to place armed forces under its authority until disarmament was implemented. The executive committee, which included Branting, Henderson, and Huysmans, and a Committee of Action were dispatched to Paris with instructions to plead their case, but the delegates were never received by the Big Four. In Paris Henderson was also able to do useful work in promoting the charter to establish the International Labour Office.

III

If the beginning of 1919 saw the forces of international socialism in disarray, there were also signs of a deep cleavage within the labour movement at home. Strikes in Belfast and on Clydeside, warnings of further unrest in the mines and on the railways, suggested to the impressionable that the tide of revolution might be sweeping across the English Channel. The threat of combined action by the Triple Alliance of miners, railwaymen, and transport workers prompted Lloyd George to take steps to placate disaffected workers. The Government sought to forestall a miners' strike by offering a commission of inquiry under Mr Justice Sankey which would look into demands over wages and hours and the issue of nationalization. In addition Lloyd George summoned a National Industrial Conference, comprising trade unionists, employers, and Whitley Councils, in late February to try to devise a charter of industrial relations which might alleviate the mounting unrest. Although most of the unions accepted the Government's invitation to take part, the Triple Alliance and the engineers withdrew early in the deliberations, thus ensuring that the voice of organized labour would be seriously weakened from the start. Many union leaders distrusted the Prime Minister's motives, but Henderson, despite his own painful experience of Lloyd George's duplicity, saw in the Conference the seed of an industrial parliament. While it is doubtful that Lloyd George had anything quite so visionary in mind, Henderson, then much under the influence of the Webbs, was willing to embrace any idea that implied functional representation for labour and that offered the hope of peaceful solutions to industrial disputes.

He not only accepted the personal invitation from Downing Street that he participate, but agreed to act as chairman of the workers' side. At the first session of 27 February he seized upon the vague suggestion that a committee investigate the causes of the present unrest by proposing specific terms of reference, which would include hours and wages, as well as the prevention of unemployment. A provisional committee of thirty from each side met between the end of February and the next plenary session on 4 April to debate a charter that would cover hours of labour, minimum wages, and the possibility of negotiating machinery for the resolution of disputes. Although Henderson was the key figure on the workers' side, it was his nominee, G. D. H. Cole, who drafted the trade union memorandum advocating a more democratic system of public ownership. It was an effective working partnership, all the more remarkable for its harnessing of two very disparate personalities. Cole was surprised to discover that despite Henderson's orthodox opinions, he had a keen appreciation of socialist intellectuals. Honest about his own limittations, he was eager to tap the talents of others, like Webb, Cole, Tawney, or Hugh Dalton, to draft reports or formulate programmes that he had neither the time, nor the inclination to tackle.

When the National Industrial Conference resumed in April, the joint committee was able to present a unanimous report proposing a forty-eight-hour week, to which Henderson and

Cole appended an analysis of the causes of industrial unrest. Henderson, who had just seen the Prime Minister in Paris, was able to transmit Lloyd George's endorsement of the report, making prospects for its implementation brighter. The real danger was that union criticism might impede the entire effort, and Henderson had to ply a devious course which pushed the Conference towards meaningful industrial reforms without sacrificing the more ambitious goals to which organized labour was committed. The final report recommended eight-hour legislation and the establishment of both a minimum wage commission and a National Industrial Council, with equal representation for workers and employers. It was to Henderson's credit that unanimity was preserved. With his usual negotiating skill, he had retained the confidence of his fellow workers while winning the trust of the other side, despite the inevitable conflict of interest. Deadlock was repeatedly averted, often by Henderson and his counterpart on the employers' side, Sir Alan Smith of the Engineering Employers' Federation, who conferred privately to reconcile differences. To appease recalcitrant workers, Henderson made sure that the report would be submitted to local organizations for approval once the Government decided to introduce legislation and to keep the provisional joint committee in being until the National Industrial Council had been constituted.

Heartened by his apparent success in holding the various elements together and in securing Lloyd George's blessing, he told Beatrice Webb that he had 'done better work in the last three weeks than I did in fifteen years in the House of Commons'. She attributed the happy outcome to 'Cole's ability and Henderson's wisdom in making use of him. Henderson is the only working class leader who understands making use of the brains of Socialist intellectuals.' She believed that if the arrangement could be institutionalized, the industrial conference would become the central authority within the labour movement on its industrial side, with Uncle Arthur emerging as the obvious chairman.[17] Although the Conference stirred public opinion and stimulated the Government to legislate a forty-eight hour week and a minimum wage commission, its more grandiose plans came to nought. Employer concessions, offered in a spirit of cooperation, were mostly withdrawn when the immediate crisis passed, whereas many of the unions continued to view the entire proceedings as a hoax perpetrated to shore up the employers' interest when it was seriously threatened. Amid the subsequent economic collapse the Government backed away from its pledges of protection for the workers, abandoning them to the exigencies of the market. His initial optimism rapidly dispelled, Henderson was obliged to concede that those leaders like Ernest Bevin and J. H. Thomas, who had refused to trust to Lloyd George's assurances, had been correct. He could only look on with dismay as Labour's inept Parliamentary leaders squandered opportunities to challenge the Government and trade unionists flirted with the nostrums of direct action. His convictions about the merits of democratic socialism never really extended to notions of worker control: responsible leaders, duly elected by the mass of working people, should exercise power. Authority must be delegated to those competent to wield it, which, in his view, seemed to mean state agencies in which workers would secure equal representation. To talk of seizing power, even in industries ripe for nationalization, played into the hands of those who equated socialism in England with Bolshevik tyranny.

With prospects for a generous peace settlement ebbing and labour militancy threatening to undo his efforts to bring about industrial conciliation, he became profoundly discouraged. The strain of the unceasing activity of the previous two years had sapped his energy and taken its toll on his health, which was never again as vigorous as it had been. Strongly antipathetic to the increasingly vocal radical currents within the movement, he was prone to petulant outbursts, even intimating to Sidney Webb that he might retire from politics altogether. His reflections on the Sankey Commission reveal an exaggerated sense of alarm, no doubt fed by nervous exhaustion:

> I feel that the charge of Bolshevism will find support if it is strengthened by a concrete example of confiscation... I came away from Paris with the feeling that there is one politician extremely anxious for the report to be in our direction. It would be a great misfortune if we failed owing to our overreaching ourselves and giving the impression that we were ready to act unjustly to any class of property.

Not for the first time had he misjudged Lloyd George's eagerness to conciliate Labour, nor was it the last time that he sought to restrain those eager to accelerate the momentum towards socialism. His caution stemmed in part from his realistic assessment of Labour's performance in the Commons, where its stolid leaders had made negligible political impact since the election.

> The Party in the House is doing so badly I sometimes think that the measure of solidarity necessary for success will never be forthcoming. What with the prospect of a revival of Asquithian Liberalism and so many of the Right of our own Party changing to the coalition, the prospects of the next election which may be in less than a year are not good. We appear to be Leaderless in the House and no better in the country and nobody in the Executive or out of it seems to care about this aspect of the case. I have felt strongly inclined to get out altogether.[18]

In the spring of 1919 the Triple Alliance, energized by the facade of industrial unity, extended their claim to the political realm by demanding action to secure the withdrawal of British troops from Russia. They also hoped to mobilize organized labour to secure the withdrawal of a conscription bill, to secure the release of conscientious objectors, and to lift the blockade against

Germany. To someone like Henderson, convinced that political and industrial activity belonged in separate spheres, such encroachment by unions was inappropriate, to say the least. To use industrial muscle to secure political objectives was a violation of democratic procedure, threatening the tenuous balance that he had striven to achieve in the 1918 constitution. It was, to be sure, Labour's ineffectual Parliamentary record that goaded powerful unions to overstep legitimate boundaries, but such intervention by trade unions placed in jeopardy all efforts to secure a broader electoral base for the party, especially among the unaffiliated. The refusal of the T.U.C.'s Parliamentary Committee to accede to pressure from the militants brought the conflict into the annual conferences. At the Southport conference in June 1919 Henderson warned that such policies involved serious risks for the movement:

> If the British Labour Movement is to institute a new precedent in our industrial history by initiating a general strike for the purpose of achieving not industrial but political objects, it is imperative that the Trade Unions, whose members are to fulfil the obligation implied in the new policy and whose finances are to be involved, should realise the responsibilities such a strike movement would entail and should themselves determine the plan of any such new campaign.[19]

He continued to believe that the mass of organized labour shared his own cautious values and would not follow the firebrands seeking to lead them down the revolutionary path.

The Ironfounders Union, of which he had been President since 1910, was having its own industrial problems during the course of 1919. Now merged into the National Union of Foundry Workers, its members believed that they had a justified grievance over rates of pay. Flat rate increases during the war had eroded the differentials secured earlier which had improved their pay relative to other engineering trades. In the conviction that their earnings were now eroding, the foundry workers put forward pay claims in early 1919 which were rejected by an interim Arbitration Court. Henderson arranged a conference with the employers in October to present the union's case, but all he could secure was the promise of a further review in four months if the men returned to work. Although the offer was rejected, the union lacked the funds to sustain lengthy industrial action, and by January 1920 strikers were obliged to return to work on the employers' terms.

Much of Henderson's frustration stemmed from his prolonged absence from the Commons, which he had come to regard as his natural platform, an essential complement to his role as Secretary. Labour's head office was disinclined to impose candidates on constituencies, especially at by-elections. Since unions still controlled the purse strings, party officials realized the difficulty in dictating how funds should be spent. While left-wing extremists could win I.L.P. endorsements, Henderson's tight rein at Head Office meant that prospective constituency party candidates were carefully vetted to exclude Communists and other suspicious elements. Whatever Head Office's reluctance to intervene, the Widnes by-election in August 1919 was too good an opportunity to miss. Although held by the Tory member Colonel Hall-Walker since the beginning of the century, this seat on the outskirts of Liverpool had amassed a decent Labour vote in 1918 and was the likeliest prospect for a victory since the general election. It was for that reason that Head Office decided to risk offending local activists by seeking to impose Henderson, whose return to the Commons was deemed an overriding consideration. When the seat had become vacant upon Hall-Walker's retirement, the local party turned again to Tom Williamson of the National Amalgamated Union of Labour, who had waged a creditable fight in 1918. In mid-August a deputation from the N.E.C. met delegates from Widnes in St Helens and pressured them to induce Williamson to withdraw and to accept Henderson.

Although the latter expressed hesitance about standing, the fact was that the local party yielded only after Head Office implored them to do so. Not that there were serious objections to him: as a prominent figure he would focus national attention on the by-election and might stand a better chance of capturing the seat for Labour than the more obscure Williamson. He was widely trusted, especially by trade unions, which made it relatively easy for him to overcome the misgivings of Williamson's supporters. Voters respected his willingness to take his chances in Widnes, a much riskier prospect than many Labour seats where vacancies might be anticipated. Despite his eagerness to return to the House, he had honorably refrained from claiming Chester-le-Street, an exceedingly safe Durham mining seat, on the grounds that the nomination should go to a miners' representative.

Henderson's intervention gave national significance to what would otherwise have been a routine by-election. From the outset he tried to stress the wider dimensions of the contest, noting that 'it would be a serious thing for the Labour Party in the constituency and for himself if he were defeated in the election'.[20] Henderson, fighting a 3,500 Coalition majority, was convinced from the outset that he could pull it off. As in 1918, his opponents made much of his mission to Russia, even implying that he had conspired with Lenin and Trotsky against the ministry of which he was a member. In one of his speeches he derided the charges, claiming that he had gone to Petrograd with Lloyd George's offer of the ambassadorship in his pocket. He invited the Prime Minister to publish his telegram insisting that to remove Sir George Buchanan from his post would be a mistake. More constructively, he tried to focus his speeches on the peace treaty, on repressive policies in Ireland, and on industrial conditions and found audiences far more receptive to his message than they had been eight months before.

No effort was spared in the campaign which coupled Henderson's organizing expertise with stringent efforts by Head Office. Hundreds of volunteers from Widnes and the surrounding region were used for canvassing, and prominent leaders were brought in to speak in his behalf. The candidate himself addressed as many as ten meetings a night, regaining some of his former energy on the stump. Local Liberals, who regarded him as a more palatable alternative than the Coalition nominee, decided not to contest the election, and Henderson did not hesitate to welcome their support. Even more blatantly than in pre-war Barnard Castle he was standing as the progressive candidate, despite the fact that he had been subjected to frequent reproaches for just such an alliance earlier in his career. But he could now afford to confound his critics: he was trying to convert Liberal voters to Labour, not seeking to blur the distinctions between the two. The Liberals at least gave the impression that they needed Henderson more than he needed them. The *Manchester Guardian,* the principal advocate of Lib–Lab *rapprochement,* expressed the 'hope that the Widnes fight may be the beginning of a new cooperation between Liberalism and Labour which will allow to each party its place in the forces of democratic progress'.[21] The local organ admitted that the Liberals 'without asking any pledges from him, threw themselves wholeheartedly into the fight, and had accomplished with Labour that which they had never accomplished themselves'.[22] The results confirmed the wisdom of Henderson's courtship of Liberal voters: his margin of victory was only 987 out of a poll of nearly 22,000.

If his Widnes victory propelled him back on to the Parliamentary stage, he continued to harbor serious misgivings about Labour's future and about his own part in it. Beatrice Webb recorded that he was 'inclined to shirk H. of C. work – hating to find himself subordinate to Adamson and in competition with Clynes and Thomas for the chairmanship of the Party'.[23] Perceiving his main task as completing the reorganization begun in 1917,

Uncle Arthur

he was more concerned to consolidate his power over party machinery than to try to displace Adamson. Successive chairmen found it convenient to rely on his expertise, and even MacDonald, rarely disposed to relinquish authority, regarded the office of Treasurer as a nominal one and left finances largely to Henderson. For that reason the years between 1918 and 1924 saw the administration of the Labour Party very much in his capable hands. At no other time in its history did a leading politician wield so much authority over its internal operations. Not until after he abandoned the secretaryship to his chosen deputy, Jim Middleton, did the position evolve into a purely functionary role. As long as Uncle Arthur was in charge, political and administrative power were directly linked, making him in many ways the linchpin of the party in the years before the first Labour Government. That stature could only be seriously challenged by MacDonald, who was out of the Commons until 1922 and whose authority would not become dominant until his accession as Prime Minister. Even later, Henderson's consummate knowledge of the party apparatus, and especially of local activists and constituency politics, made him indispensable. His long tenure in office meant that he had more names at his fingertips and was more familiar to all segments of the movement than anyone else. If he was manipulative and authoritarian, he was also tireless in his efforts to build Labour into a national party.

To a great extent his ascendancy was personal rather than simply a reflection of his administrative office. He toured the country regularly, speaking in most by-election contests and meeting local stalwarts, addressed annual party and T.U.C. conferences, and supervised every general election campaign up to 1929. In addition he was largely responsible for setting up the advisory committees, reorganizing the party into regions, building links with the T.U.C., overseeing the restructuring of the *Daily Herald*, and approving candidates. In no sense dictatorial – Labour was too refractory to conform to his directives – he nonetheless managed to have his way most of the time. Patient badgering and attention to detail generally secured compliance, although it was obviously easier to manage the N.E.C. and even the annual conference than to dictate to constituencies or to trade unions jealous of their autonomy. His very lack of charisma helped to consolidate his power by building confidence among the faithful: they felt his word could be trusted and that he was genuinely concerned with the welfare of the movement.

As early as September 1917 Henderson had begun to think about research and information. The idea of small committees of specialists advising the N.E.C. derived from Henderson's experience in the Cabinet and the War Emergency Workers' National Committee. Labour needed to inform itself about a whole range of issues if it was to stake its claim to govern the nation, if indeed its leaders were to be potential cabinet ministers. Tom Jones noted in January 1918 that Henderson was 'no longer unwilling or ashamed to depend partly on the help of intellectuals, having seen how dependent Cabinet Ministers were on such assistance'.[24] He hoped to combine the research functions of the N.E.C., the Fabian Society, and the T.U.C. Parliamentary Committee, but the unions were too suspicious of socialist intellectuals to agree to such a fusion. Henderson's own close ties with Fabians like Webb and Cole led him to support the formation of the Labour Research Department. Initially under the direction of Fabians, it was soon in financial difficulties and eventually became dominated by Communists. A far more fruitful initiative lay in the institution of advisory committees to investigate economic and international questions. Staffed mainly by middle-class intellectuals, these voluntary bodies became a kind of brains trust for the party after 1918, providing the expert knowledge Labour politicians so desperately needed in order to formulate credible policies. Henderson himself relied on their advice, especially in

Uncle Arthur

foreign affairs where his own personal experience was deficient. Indeed it was the memoranda and reports of the Advisory Committee on International Questions that shaped the perspective of the future Foreign Secretary. Without its guidance and the experience he gleaned in the International and during the 1924 Labour Government, Henderson's claim to the Foreign Office in 1929 would have been far more contestable.

Although keenly aware of Labour's dependence on trade unions both financially and electorally, he believed that the party could not compete effectively unless it gained the upper hand in the relationship. His attempts to propagate constituency organizations were not merely a device to improve electoral prospects, but also to displace trades councils locally, a goal only partially achieved by the early 1920s. His own candidacy at Widnes symbolized the party's resolve to challenge the assumption of trade unions that they could dictate the nominees. But, above all, Labour's viability as a party depended on his success in centralizing its organization. No longer a loose federation of autonomous bodies, it had to become professionalized, with full-time agents, an efficient head office, and clearly formulated programs. At the top of the pyramid was the N.E.C., which he dominated, at least until 1922, but it was no less important to develop reciprocal ties to the regions and to trade unions.

Between 1918 and 1922 regional conferences were devised to supplement the annual national gatherings. Addressed by Henderson, they were intended to be both inspirational and organizational, occasions to build party solidarity that would transcend the parochialism of the constituency. In 1920 regional organizers were appointed to strengthen the links with Head Office and within the next years a structure based on nine regions was devised. By 1922 delegates were meeting in regular conferences in each of the regions, providing an intermediate layer between constituency and party headquarters in London. Henderson clearly hoped that by creating alternative arenas of Labour activity he might wean activists from their attachment either to the I.L.P., Labour's principal rival for individual membership, or the union branch.

His efforts to co-opt trade unions and thereby to curb their power was largely doomed to failure. By the end of 1919 he had so far overcome union distrust of Labour that a Trade Union Coordination Committee was established, and by the end of the next year he presented the T.U.C. with a proposal for a National Joint Council of Labour with members drawn equally from the T.U.C. General Council, the N.E.C., and the Parliamentary Labour Party. Despite his keenness to demonstrate Labour's value to the unions, the T.U.C. repeatedly rebuffed proposals for closer partnership. The Council formalized a working relationship between the executives and staffs of the party and the unions, but this did little to ensure concerted action or seriously to infringe upon trade union autonomy. The trade unions diluted Henderson's proposals for a single joint research, information, and publicity department, although when the T.U.C. was reorganized in 1921, it did agree to the creation of joint departments accountable to the N.E.C. and the General Council. The advisory committees were now placed under joint authority, each having an M.P. as chairman. But while some progress was made, the National Joint Council was never empowered to formulate policy, nor was the N.E.C. able to induce the T.U.C. to coordinate the timing or location of its annual conferences with those of Labour.

Henderson presumed that after 1918 the unions and the party would move in tandem, but, although this was frequently the case, the unions insisted on retaining freedom of action. He was appalled by their propensity to disregard the party with impunity, underlining the inequality of the relationship. Whatever he did to placate them, there was no escaping the fact of Labour's dependence on the financial levy which the unions furnished.

Uncle Arthur

Union preponderance also ensured that the socialist content of Labour's programs would inevitably be toned down. The Secretary sometimes found these constraints useful: he could use trade union predominance on the N.E.C. to counter I.L.P. pretensions to dictate Labour policy. The unions were divided over many issues, but they tended to defer to Henderson over the direction the party should follow. Resistant to his centralizing plans, self-righteous I.L.P. leaders viewed his effort to achieve some kind of ideological accomodation with the trade unions as inimical to radical change. But the unions also hamstrung many of the initiatives of the advisory committees, which were closer to his heart than the obstreperous I.L.P. Mediating between these contending forces demanded not only the ability to conciliate, which Henderson had gained in years of industrial bargaining, but a determination to persist until he got his way. He could bring his incomparable knowledge of party activists and union leaders to bear in forging an agreed policy and foisting it on the N.E.C. or on conference delegates without much risk of being challenged.

During the 1920s Henderson sought to avoid creating a breach with the I.L.P., whose propagandist and electoral value he recognized. It was not only that the I.L.P. continued to nominate and sometimes to elect candidates, but also that its branches still performed a central role in electoral organization. During the war years he had maintained ties with that wing of the party, smoothing over antagonism and staying on good terms with MacDonald. He recognized that the I.L.P. had a value as both as a propagandist and an electioneering body that Labour could ill afford to sacrifice. Equally he made sure that divisions over the future of the International did not force things to a breaking point. He and MacDonald both believed that the radical fervor that seemed to possess the I.L.P. since the war was transitory and that eventually it would revert to its more moderate, gradualist approach to socialism.

Arthur Henderson

Such was not the case with the Communists, against whom Henderson waged continuous battle within the Labour Party and the International. To be sure, he reproached the Government for undermining the confidence of the Russian people in the good will of Britain by abetting those forces hostile to the revolutionary government. Upon returning to the Commons in 1919, Henderson appealed for greater tolerance toward a regime which he personally found ideologically repugnant:

> We should offer to the Russian people such moral and economic help as they need for the restoration of their country. Such help should be offered to them through the valuable machinery of the League of Nations. It is essential that Russia should have not only supplies, but machinery, credit, and the best advice that can be given to aid her in the restoration of her economic life.[25]

But international proletarian solidarity did not extend to internal subversion. In 1920 the Communists sought admission to the party as an affiliated socialist society, despite their ostensible adherence to the Third International and their denial that social revolution could be realized by means of parliamentary democracy. As Secretary Henderson voiced the prevailing view that the basis of affiliation must be the acceptance of Labour's constitution and principles, a condition inconsistent with the objectives of the Communist Party. After Lansbury endorsed the concept of an all-embracing International, Henderson, chastizing the *Daily Herald* for disseminating distorted information, warned against the danger of allowing their opponents an opportunity to implicate Labour with encouraging violent revolution. Complicity with Bolshevism, however well-intentioned, was a betrayal of those who had striven to prove that economic regeneration could be achieved without plunging British society into social upheaval.[26] When the issue of affiliation resurfaced at the 1921 annual conference Henderson rejected even a qualified acceptance of the

Communists if they conformed to the party constitution, a stance endorsed decisively by the assembled delegates. Replying to A. J. Cook of the Miners' Federation, who had harangued the delegates about the need for unity and brotherly love, he declared:

> If they were going to walk together, they must be agreed; there must be more than unity in name; there must be unity of purpose, unity of principle, unity of conception, and unity of method. No speaker had given a particle of evidence from the Communist Party that they were willing to change their position and to have the kind of unity that was essential to progress and success.[27]

It was, however, much easier to control party machinery than it was to reinvigorate the Parliamentary Labour Party. Even after his return to the Commons he was obliged to circulate a letter to his Labour colleagues suggesting how hard it was for him to refute press allegations about their ineffectual performance. This was one reason he tried, unsuccessfully, to have MacDonald appointed as a paid advisor to the P.L.P., which in turn complained that Henderson and the Executive disregarded their views in the making of policy.

Nor were individual trade union leaders any the more amenable to his cajoling. Despite his strictures against direct action, leaders like Robert Williams of the Transport Workers continued to advocate a general strike in order to bring industry to a standstill and to precipitate a general election that Labour could exploit favorably. Such a view, shared to some extent by industrial militants and Communists, was antithetical to Henderson's. He knew how precarious the trade union alliance was and doubted whether Labour was yet ready to face another costly general election with its electoral apparatus still incomplete. In his reply to Williams's initiative, the Secretary warned against an election in which Labour impetuosity would be the central issue rather than the failure of the Coalition. He felt that the inconveniences caused by the dislocation of industry would irritate just that segment of the electorate — women and white collar workers — which Labour needed to attract:

> I believe 'direct action' propaganda of the doctrinaire character has been definitely harmful and has had the effect of frightening away many voters who were inclined to support Labour. The failures of the Government both in its home policy and in its conduct of foreign affairs have thrown many new supporters into our ranks. This new aggregation of votes would have been even greater but for the stampeding of other disillusioned Coalitionists by the constant advocacy and repeated threats of direct action for political purposes . . . The coquetting with Bolshevism and the 'direct action' propaganda have prevented our reaping the full fruits of a promising strategical position.

He went on to warn that a general election fought in the context of a national stoppage over the miners' claim would prove disastrous to Labour. Not only would the miners' claim be defeated, but Labour would suffer a severe setback and the Lloyd George ministry would secure a new lease of life.[28]

If his selfless dedication to the advancement of the party in the early 1920s has been generally recognized, his accomplishments are less indisputable. Christopher Howard has argued that Labour's leaders, most notably Henderson, had created expectations of political and social advance which they could not realistically hope to fulfil. Sparked by an upsurge of idealism, the party had projected a new social order resting on the consent of workers by hand and by brain. Although progress was made in broadening the base of support, Labour proved too timid to initiate a moral crusade to implement its program. Henderson stressed the need for a great mass organization, but membership grew slowly, and little effort was made to reach out to rural areas or to progressive churchmen. In addition he and MacDonald disavowed direct action and ascribed the militancy of the Councils of Action to

Communist influence. With the extreme left <u>dis</u>affected and potential middle-class supporters alienated by trade union domination, the party dissipated opportunities to exploit common anti-Coalition sentiment. Hampered by financial stringency and dwindling activity, many of the constituency parties failed to develop into more than intermittent election agencies. Howard contends that Labour's opportunism in 1917 carried the party forward too quickly, without the necessary structural underpinning and with its leaders hesitant about how to extend its popular base. Henderson's constitutional reforms and Webb's program promised rapid transformation, but in fact it became clear by the early 1920s that Labour was structurally unprepared for the role it was supposed to play. Despite the reforms instituted, the party continued to resemble the pre-war alliance of trade unionists and I.L.P. socialists, with pockets of strength in the industrial areas, but little sign of growth at the periphery. At Eccleston Square too much authority was concentrated in the Secretary's hands, while in the regions apathy sapped the initial post-war fervor once the slump set in in 1920. Electoral victories, especially in municipal elections, diverted attention from the persistently low level of membership and political activity. The architects of the new constitution had faith in the inevitability of Labour's eventual triumph, but they lacked the resources necessary to achieve their goals – or at least to do so before the initial enthusiasm evaporated. Thus, Howard concludes, 'there was no real basis for expansion, no real basis for confidence, only a recipe for disappointment and bitterness ... The image of a vibrant, expanding new party was an illusion.'[29]

For this dilemma Henderson was more to blame than any of its other leaders. Its successes redounded to his credit, but its failures were at least in part the result of his inability to bring his organizational plans to fruition. He did build up a network of local parties, supported by district organizers and local secretaries, who acted as agents at election time. But he relied on voluntary effort and was constantly hamstrung by rank and file inertia, not to mention insufficient financial resources. Much as he tried to exhort, to stir up local activity, to encourage loyalty, the slow evolution of the party corresponded to his own cautious, unimaginative style. The very skills that made him effective as Secretary restrained the party from a more evangelical appeal that might have reoriented Labour from its trade unionist base into a national organization capable of outflanking both the Liberals and the Communists. Lacking the vision to recast the party, he helped to ensure that it remained largely the political arm of organized labour, not that moral crusade of progressives, transcending class lines, that encompassed the hopes of a 'Land Fit for Heroes'.

IV

Exhaustion and overwork brought on a complete physical collapse in the spring of 1920, and his recovery was delayed by an operation for gallstones in June. He missed the annual conference for the first time and was too ill to attend the International congress in July in Geneva. By now it had become clear that hopes for reunification expressed at Berne were misplaced, and at the Geneva meeting only British Labour, the German majority socialists, and the neutral parties were fully represented. The British, active in reconstruction efforts, were pressed to permit the transfer of its headquarters to London, which was only reluctantly conceded. Henderson, who thought prospects for unity more auspicious if the secretariat remained on the Continent, told Camille Huysmans that such a move would be inopportune. He urged the Congress to take no decision that would exacerbate differences within the international movement,[30] but in fact nothing could be done to dissuade the German independent socialists, the I.L.P., and the Austrians from breaking away and establishing the Vienna Union, which they hoped would provide a bridge between Berne and Moscow. However reluctant he was to confirm this fissure, Henderson emerged as President of the restored Second International when the Geneva delegates elected a new executive.

Impaired health thus brought no diminution of his responsibilities, either on the international scene or within the movement at home. Beatrice Webb's reaction was typical of those who had come to appreciate just how indispensable he was:

> Henderson's dangerous illness and doubtful recovery have made one realise his relative superiority to all the other men. He is really the only Labour man who considers the welfare of the Party as a whole and who is willing to work with any group within it without considering who is to be the leader.[31]

With his fingers in every pie, he found it difficult to delegate authority, which made party activity somewhat chaotic when he was indisposed. McKibbin has remarked that he had a 'tendency to accumulate responsibilities but a disinclination to shed them'.[32] Before the war he was involved in all the day-to-day details, but his functions became essentially executive after 1918, with his subordinates handling routine administration. Yet if he was relieved of some of the office chores, the expanded party bureaucracy demanded even more of his attention. No one else had his vast experience, his keen memory for names and faces, his reservoir of information. Whatever else he was doing, he continued to spend part of each day at the Eccleston Square headquarters. The excessive burdens made him irascible, but no less determined to retain power. Although willing to consult subordinates and to implement conference decisions faithfully, his temperament was autocratic. Fortunately he had a competent, if self-effacing deputy in Jim Middleton and a close ally in Egerton Wake, the National Agent from 1918. They accepted his bullying and pomposity because they realized that his loyalty to the party was absolute.

The fact that he was preoccupied with running the party made him less eager to compete for the Parliamentary leadership. He was willing to leave the burden to Adamson and later to Clynes, neither of whom generated much excitement, but he resumed his position as Chief Whip, recognizing the need to impose discipline on Labour's often fractious ranks. He was aware of his own shortcomings as a speaker and Parliamentary debater, although the lack of talent on the Labour benches compelled him to take a lead in certain issues. In October 1920 he penned a letter to *The Times* which suggested not only a heightened awareness of the Irish problem, but a willingness to sanction more radical solutions. No longer convinced that the concession of Dominion status would suffice, he asserted that 'the only step that can be taken with any hope of success is to leave the responsibility of determining the form of Government in Ireland to the Irish people themselves'. He went on to demand the convening of a constituent assembly and the withdrawal of British troops in Ireland.[33] He followed this outspoken letter with a ringing indictment of repression in Ireland coupled with a plea for an investigation into the causes and extent of official reprisals. He castigated the Government for inaugurating a policy of military terrorism which was

> not only a betrayal of democratic principles and not only a betrayal of the things for which we claimed to stand during the five years of the great world War, but is utterly opposed to the best traditions of the British people.

He recounted incidents of murder, armed assaults on unarmed civilians, raids on private dwellings, arrests, suppression of newspapers and public meetings, all of which constituted 'a deliberate policy of intensified coercion'. He concluded by insisting that no

Government should unleash such a policy unless its objects were 'to stamp out the legitimate aspirations of people who desire to be a free democracy'.[34] When Lloyd George refused to concede an independent inquiry, Henderson prevailed upon the N.E.C. to dispatch its own investigating team which he chaired. The eight-man group spent two weeks in Ireland, and upon returning Henderson addressed demonstrations around the country at which he continued to deplore official policy. At a special party conference in London on 29 December the commission reported its findings, documenting the connivance of the authorities at reprisals by the Black and Tans. On a motion by Henderson, the conference demanded the removal of British armed forces and the convocation of a constituent assembly, a gesture which may have helped to instigate a speedier resolution of the Irish crisis.

Despite recurrent strains in their relationship, Henderson and MacDonald found it expedient to remain on cordial terms. As long as MacDonald was outside the House, Henderson was clearly the dominant partner in the relationship, but he continued to regard MacDonald as 'the indispensable leader'.[35] Realistic about his own intellectual deficiencies, he deferred to MacDonald's informed knowledge and engaging platform style. Even his admirers concede that Henderson was drab, conveying the image of a 'dogged, stolid, rather domineering foreman'.[36] He was, as several commentators have noted,[37] invaluable in constructing the system, in organizing votes, finding candidates and money, and putting men into jobs. These were the practical duties of an administrative boss, but the party also required a leader who could provide the external glamor, the oratorical flair and literary style that he lacked. It was for that reason that he repressed his own ambitions in the 1920s and tried to facilitate MacDonald's return to the Commons and eventually to the leadership. Despite ambivalent personal feelings, he assured Beatrice Webb 'that if only J.R.M. could get into Parliament he would become a useful member of the Labour Party',[38] a comment which also implied that he found MacDonald an irritant outside the Commons.

In 1920 Henderson had been afraid that a sudden election on Lloyd George's terms would deal Labour a devastating setback. By the next year he was confident that the party, assuming it abstained from frivolous talk of direct action, would at least hold its own in electoral terms. While refusing to negotiate a policy of cooperation with the Liberals, he made it clear that if the Asquithian Liberals emerged from the next election as the main opposition party, some form of concerted action might be devised. He told C. P. Scott that the party might contest as many as 420 seats in the next election and be willing to take office with Liberal support but not to join a coalition. When Scott questioned Labour's competence to staff the great offices of state, Henderson told him that their resources were greater than commonly supposed, assuming, that is, that prominent figures, like MacDonald and Snowden, were able to regain their seats.[39]

In an article written for an American journal at the beginning of 1922 he asserted that Labour's policies in opposition were directed toward the prospect that the party might assume power. This explained its moderate tone and avoidance of violent pronouncements. He spoke, above all, of the need for greater efficiency in industry and agriculture, but insisted that the quality of public service in the coal mines and on the railways could not be enhanced unless they were owned by the state. In addition Labour would dedicate itself not merely to the avoidance of war, but to the positive organization of the peace of the world. This would involve opposing the exploitation of subject peoples and devising methods of cooperation to overcome disease and famine and to develop the world's resources for the common good.[40] In general Labour would seek to alter the course of foreign policy by relying upon the League of Nations 'as the guardian of world peace and the instrument of international cooperation'.[41]

If Labour was to win over uncommitted voters, it had to demonstrate a responsible attitude towards industrial unrest. Although the 1919 National Industrial Conference had proved abortive, Henderson resuscitated its proposals for a parliament of industry as a way to curb the strife. Although most workers had patiently endured privation, he doubted whether further sacrifices would be tolerated uncomplainingly. To avoid further conflict, he advocated an industrial truce under which employers and trade unions would pledge themselves to seek changes by mutual consent. Existing wage rates would be stabilized, and increases keyed to greater productivity. Grievances would be resolved by conciliation councils in each industry, and a permanent industrial parliament, equally representative of employers and trade unionists, would be convened to deliberate important issues.[42]

During the 1922 election Lloyd George, freed from his coalition moorings, cast himself as leader of the anti-revolutionary forces, but singled out Henderson, Thomas, and Clynes as reasonable Labour politicians with whom he was prepared to cooperate. Neither Liberal faction officially opposed Henderson at Widnes, but, with the ill fortune that dogged his Parliamentary career, he was defeated in a straight fight with the Conservative candidate, G. C. Clayton. Although he increased his poll by nearly 2,500, the Tory resurgence swept his opponent to victory by 1,782, almost double Henderson's margin of victory in the by-election. The result was not wholly surprising: Widnes had a long Conservative tradition, and the by-election victory had been something of an upset. Local Tories made sure that this time they were not caught napping, and their effort was strengthened by the adherence of those Liberals no longer inclined to cast an anti-Coalition protest vote as they had in 1919. Henderson could take pride, however, in the national figures. The party machine had been vindicated: Labour made major strides, winning 142 seats as compared with sixty in 1918. They forged ahead of the Liberals, both factions of which could only muster 116 seats. Such gains notwithstanding, it was clear that party reorganization had still some way to go. In 1918 fifty of the successful candidates were sponsored by trade unions; in 1922 the figures were eighty-eight out of 142. The I.L.P. managed to win thirty-one seats as compared with only three four years earlier. Thus Labour, despite the Secretary's efforts since the war, had not yet been completely transformed into a mass organization with active local constituency parties. The most significant outcome, however, was the return to the Commons of prominent anti-war leaders, including MacDonald, Snowden, Lansbury, and F. W. Jowett.

The I.L.P. gains seemed to symbolize an apparent leftward drift of the party. Breaking a recent tradition of electing their leader at the close of each session, the new M.P.s immediately raised the issue of a new election with the intention of replacing Clynes with MacDonald, whose I.L.P. associations and anti-war credentials gave the illusion of left-wing sentiments. At the first meeting of the P.L.P. Henderson, Chief Whip during the previous session, although not at this point an M.P., was voted into the chair. He took no part in the voting which gave MacDonald victory by a margin of four votes, but Snowden and Kirkwood both claimed later that Henderson favored Clynes, who was elected Deputy Leader. Misgivings on personal grounds may have made him more neutral in the contest than he had been in 1911. However, loyalty notwithstanding, Henderson certainly had a higher regard for MacDonald's talents than those of Clynes and believed that the outcome of the election was in Labour's interest. Although the votes of the Clydesiders had helped to secure the leadership for MacDonald, they soon became disenchanted. He was able to consolidate his leadership not because of I.L.P. backing, but rather because of the unflagging support of Henderson, his only possible rival, who ensured that the trade unions and the party machine remained loyal. Their rivalry, pronounced during the war, did not actively resurface until after 1929. The two had come to recognize each other's merits and had achieved a *modus vivendi* despite an undercurrent of animosity.

There was little doubt that Henderson would be returned to the House at the first opportunity. When J. N. Bell, who had won Newcastle East, died within a few weeks of the general election, Henderson was nominated. In a decisive swing to Labour he won the seat by 4,384 votes in the January 1923 by-election – considerably larger than Bell's majority – over both a Liberal and a Conservative.

If Labour had clearly emerged as the principal opposition party in Parliament, it had also become the protagonist in the International struggle against Communism. After 1918 Henderson had tried to rebuild a structure on the basis of the widest possible affiliation and to bring the Germans back into full partnership. The secession of the French socialists and divisions within the German S.P.D. had turned the Second International into a rightwing rump dominated by British Labour. It was the intransigence of the Soviet Union, the unwillingness of the Communists to sanction a pluralistic organization, that brought about a reconciliation between the moderates and the Vienna Union in 1923. The path to reunification in Hamburg in May 1923 was cleared by the healing of the breach between the two German socialist parties. In Hamburg all socialist tendencies except the Communists were represented in the newly constituted Labour and Socialist International. Henderson was elected Chairman of the secretariat, and London was chosen as its seat. The new body was, however, less under British control than its predecessor, with Henderson as the sole Englishman in the nine-member Bureau.

V

When in October 1923 Stanley Baldwin announced his intention of seeking a mandate to introduce tariffs, Henderson replied in a speech at Yeovil, 'Mr Baldwin throws down a challenge of protection as against Labour policy. That challenge we accept.' Mrs Hamilton contends that Henderson forced the election by translating the Prime Minister's bid as an immediate electoral gambit. Once Labour took up the challenge, Baldwin had no choice but to dissolve Parliament.[43] Such an analysis disregards the party's lack of preparedness. To be sure, free trade was a pillar of Labour doctrine, but an anti-protectionist vote might as easily serve the interests of the Liberals as those of Labour. Moreover, having recently fought an election, funds were alarmingly short, and it was necessary hastily to adopt 200 new candidates if Labour were to contest as many seats as in 1922. The party did manage to contest 428 seats as against 414 in 1922, but that still left one-third of all seats uncontested by Labour.

The results confirmed Labour's position as the dominant party of the left. Its vote rose only slightly, but it gained sixty-three seats, while losing sixteen to bring its total to 191. The Liberals, fighting as a reunited free trade party, polled nearly as many votes as Labour and won 158 seats. Hostility to Baldwin's tariff reform proposal did not prevent them from making advantageous electoral pacts with Conservatives. It was clear that the Liberals thought they could displace Labour as the main opposition party and refused to countenance even implicit collaboration. In Newcastle East the Tories allowed the Liberals a straight fight with Henderson, who lost the election by 1,124, although he actually increased his poll. With his keen sense of electoral realities, he predicted the outcome, telling his agent that there were houses that had displayed his picture in the previous election which were not doing so this time. Ironically, he had won the January election with 45.7 per cent in a three-cornered contest and now lost with nearly 48 per cent of the vote. He told C. P. Trevelyan, 'The combination of the two parties proved too strong for me, and as you know, they worked hard and consistently against me during the whole of the contest.'[44] He delighted, however, in the success of his two sons, both of whom were elected to Parliament for the first time.

There were several options for Labour at the end of 1923. Lacking a majority, they could refuse office entirely. Alternatively, they could take office as a minority Government with the tacit cooperation of the Liberals. Or they could court immediate defeat in the Commons by introducing radical legislative proposals. The third course was ruled out immediately, although it was endorsed by I.L.P. militants. None of the party's leaders believed a full-blooded socialist program politically expedient, and most of them were so nervous about the prospect of office that they could hardly contemplate doing much beyond demonstrating their capacity. Henderson, knowing that the party was in no shape financially to face another election in the near future, was certainly a voice for moderation. But equally he shared MacDonald's conviction that to refuse office would be tantamount to admitting incompetence. Sidney Webb told his wife that most of the leaders, except Henderson, had 'cold feet' at the thought of office. When lunching with the Webbs shortly after the election, he 'pressed for taking office at once' if MacDonald were sent for by the King. He felt that Labour should then concentrate on unemployment and inquire into the means for implementing a capital levy and nationalization.[45]

Labour's Big Five – MacDonald, Henderson, Snowden, Clynes, and Thomas – met at the Webbs to plan strategy. They agreed that MacDonald should not refuse to take power and decided that constitutional precedent dictated that the allocation of ministerial office should be left to the Prime Minister. After the meeting Henderson expressed misgivings about leaving the creation of the first Labour Cabinet entirely to MacDonald and hoped that the leader would consult fully before determining its composition. Both he and Snowden were dismayed that MacDonald chose to select his Cabinet while in seclusion at Lossiemouth, rather than from his London office, where he could remain in close contact with interested parties. Early indications of MacDonald's thinking seemed to suggest that the trade unions were being ignored in making appointments, presumably because he failed to detect much talent in their ranks.

Henderson's own situation posed a considerable dilemma for MacDonald. As the only Labour figure with Cabinet experience, aside from Clynes, he had an incontestable claim to major office. However, he had once again contrived to lose his seat. After the first meeting of party leaders MacDonald noted maliciously that Henderson was 'evidently very sore at being out. Spoke of what he wd. sacrifice if he attended to the country & was not in & asked for a safe seat.'[46] It may not have been unreasonable, but it was certainly unpolitic for MacDonald to imagine that Henderson, however selfless, would be content with supervising the party machine and remaining outside the Cabinet indefinitely. Yet the latter tried to convince himself that he would be better employed in gearing up for the next election than in running a government department. A week after his initial grumbling to MacDonald, Mrs Webb reported him in a very different frame of mind:

> I had a talk with Henderson this afternoon. Considering that he has lost his seat and has no immediate prospect of getting back in time to be included in the Cabinet he is amazingly cheerful, good-tempered, and determined to do his level best in organizing for the next general election.

She could not help admiring his disinterestedness but added that

Uncle Arthur

his views were those of an 'old Liberal who does not himself want any considerable change in social structure and is contented with a very moderate measure of social reform'.[47]

Invariably secretive and even more so now with the accretion of authority, MacDonald refused to take Henderson into his confidence, and his disregard for Henderson's stature and experience were deeply wounding to his steadfastly loyal colleague. MacDonald's provisional lists of Cabinet appointments oscillated between including Henderson and leaving him out entirely on the assumption that he would simply continue as Secretary, devoting himself to party organization and serving as its liaison with the Cabinet. The projected offices, which presupposed his re-election to the Commons, seem to have included Colonial Secretary, the Ministry of Health, and the wildly inappropriate role of Chairman of Ways and Means. MacDonald's flattering tone did little to allay indignation:

> I have tried a list of Ministers without you, and with you as Chairman of Ways and Means, and I must admit that it enormously increases my difficulties. The only reason why I would ever think of a list without is that I am terribly impressed with the importance of Eccleston Square . . . We ought to have some smart and very much alive man in Eccleston Square driving with his own energy the whole machinery of the country, getting candidates fixed up and arranging for organization and propaganda.[48]

Even if Henderson had been willing to acquiesce for the sake of the party, he was soon persuaded by family and friends that his exclusion was an intolerable insult. His sense of pique was heightened when MacDonald, upon returning to London, offered him the War Office, hardly a logical portfolio for a trade unionist and staunch advocate of disarmament. Instead he held out for the Home Office, to which MacDonald grudgingly consented.

The most favorable interpretation of this maladroit exercise is that MacDonald genuinely regarded the improvement of the party machine as of the highest priority. Clearly it had been overtaxed in the previous two elections, and if Labour was going to bid to become the majority party the fullest attention of Head Office was needed. This was particulary vital if, as MacDonald believed, Labour's term in office would be brief. On the other hand, it was undeniable that he underrated Henderson's ministerial abilities and doubted his capacity to handle a departmental brief in the Commons very effectively. But it was absurd for him to imagine that he could simply discount Henderson's claims to high office, especially once he managed to find himself a seat. If MacDonald was not obliged to consider himself merely the first among equals, he was still only the most important of the Big Five, each of whose claims needed to be acknowledged in the interests of harmony at the top. To offer Henderson the Chairmanship of Ways and Means – or even the Colonial Office or the War Office, both of which were possibilities – was demeaning, a denial of his standing in the movement as well as a flagrant disregard for his considerable ministerial experience. This was hardly the way to repay a trusted lieutenant who had helped to pave the way for MacDonald's return to the leadership, and it revealed his deficiencies as a political manager.

His appointment was a victory worth savoring. Two weeks later Beatrice Webb found 'Uncle Arthur bursting with childish joy over his H.O. seals in the red leather box which he handed round the company'.[49] Having beaten MacDonald at his game, he now had to devote himself to getting back into the House. He informed the Newcastle constituency organization that he would not stand there again[50] and when veteran socialist Dan Irving, who had held Burnley for Labour since 1918, died, Henderson was unanimously adopted to succeed him. Burnley was a moderately safe Lancashire seat, but the popularity that Irving enjoyed was partly personal. A member of the Social Democratic

Uncle Arthur

Federation, he had been an ally of H. M. Hyndman and was something of a maverick. In 1923 he won the election with a majority of 2,651 in a three-cornered contest, with the Liberals coming a strong third. Since Henderson had been defeated at Newcastle East as a result of a tacit Conservative–Liberal pact, any repetition of such tactics would diminish his chances. Local Liberals were keen to contest the seat, believing their prospects favorable in view of Burnley's free trade traditions. But Lloyd George, who now envisaged Labour–Liberal cooperation as his ticket to future power, could hardly look with equanimity on a a Liberal challenge to Henderson. In Newcastle East the pact was posited on the Tory standing down, but in Burnley the Tories had come in second in the general election and were unlikely to give way in the by-election. Liberal headquarters prevailed upon the constituency organization to refrain from putting forward a candidate, and the local executive, with ill-concealed reluctance, proclaimed its neutrality, leaving Henderson and H. E. J. Camps, the Conservative candidate, to compete for Liberal votes.

In most respects Henderson merely reiterated the party platform, but there were some differences. Much as he had done in Barnard Castle, he presented himself as a Nonconformist in terms as calculated to win traditional Liberals as it was to attract working-class Methodists. His election address was enlivened by quotations from the *Methodist Recorder* and the *Wesleyan Recorder,* and his studiedly moderate stance prompted *The Times* correspondent to observe that there was little in his campaign speeches that could not be endorsed by followers of Mr Asquith.[51] Despite this, the Tories waged a strident anti-socialist attack, linking Henderson with the Red Peril and the 'Socialist Arbeiter Internationale'. Winston Churchill's letter of support for Camps, denying any serious difference of principle between Conservatives and Liberals must have made many of the latter rush headlong into the arms of Labour.

Henderson himself caused a minor stir in one speech when he argued that revision of the Versailles Treaty was 'not only essential, but is very much overdue'. Although he was merely harping on a theme continually raised in his Newcastle East contest, reflecting successive conference resolutions, he had failed to consult MacDonald before making the statement. There was a difference between election pronouncements by opposition candidates, however, and one made by a Cabinet member. Three days before the Burnley polling Lloyd George himself raised a Private Notice Question, asking whether Henderson's speech meant that the Government was committed to revise the Versailles Treaty. MacDonald denied knowledge of the speech, and the press had a field day in deriding Labour for getting its signals crossed. Embarrassing to the Prime Minister, who faced the uncomfortable choice of disavowing his Home Secretary or torpedoeing hopes of an agreement with Poincaré, it did nothing to increase his confidence in Henderson. As Prime Minister and Foreign Secretary he was determined to be the architect of Labour's foreign policy and resented efforts by others in the party – or even in his Cabinet – to tie his hands. He had already taken the initiative by writing to the French Premier expressing regret that there were still outstanding differences between Britain and France, which he hoped could be resolved by mutual goodwill. The issue was not merely one of timing and consultation: Henderson invariably regarded conference decisions, most of which he had helped to formulate, as binding upon the leadership; MacDonald, by contrast, saw them as little more than soundings of party sentiment which, as Prime Minister, he could ignore with impunity.

Neither Churchill's intervention nor Henderson's inopportune declaration affected the outcome. The results showed that a moderate Labour candidate could win over Liberal supporters, many of whom probably felt that the new Government should be given a chance to prove itself. Henderson won with 24,571 to Camps's 17,534, a majority of 7,037 with a 5.4 per cent swing to Labour. But if the dimensions of Labour's victory were enlarged because there was no Liberal candidate, it convinced Labour's leaders that the Liberals were the real obstacle to a Parliamentary majority. Rather than promote closer ties between the two parties, the diagnosis made Labour's leaders more reluctant than ever to countenance a deal with the Liberals; Lloyd George, the wolf in goat's clothing, was not their ally, but their rival for the radical vote. After Burnley, Labour began more actively to adopt candidates in rural and middle-class constituencies in the hope at least of displacing the Liberals from second place in the polls.

The initial disagreement over Henderson's speech about treaty revision was a harbinger of things to come. Although there was an inner circle of the Cabinet which the Prime Minister consulted on major issues, he was loath to confide in colleagues. Distrusting their judgment, he preferred to take his own counsel, associating, many of them felt, with friends whose political allegiance was highly suspect. By March the early euphoria had passed, and Beatrice Webb, whose husband was one of the inner circle, noted,

> The relations between the leading Ministers on the Treasury Bench either do not exist or are far from cordial. The P.M. is unapproachable by Henderson, who is responsible for the Labour Party organisation in the country; and apparently by Clynes, the Leader of the House. 'No. 10 and No. 11 see no more of each other,' said Henderson to me, 'than if they slept and ate a hundred miles apart.'[52]

As a leading member of the Cabinet and the manager of the party machine, he was particularly distressed by MacDonald's failure to consult, his tendency to make decisions in solitude. The implications of Cabinet decisions on the party were always uppermost in Henderson's mind, if not in MacDonald's, although as Home Secretary he had been obliged to surrender day-to-day control over Head Office to Middleton. Unwilling to relax the reins of his power, he continued, as Honorary Secretary, to attend meetings of the N.E.C. and to supervise the administration of the party.

Henderson's tenure at the Home Office was entirely unremarkable. Although he was pleased to preside over one of the great offices of state, the routine administrative problems of prisons and the treatment of aliens did not greatly engage his interest. He relied heavily on the judgment of his able Permanent Secretary, Sir John Anderson, in handling the delicate questions of a police strike inquiry and the application of capital punishment. The only important piece of legislation he promoted, a factories bill, never reached the floor of the Commons. He tried to be conscientious in responding to Parliamentary questions, but his brief term in office made little impact. It did, however, provide valuable ministerial experience, especially in dealing with civil servants, that stood him in good stead when he assumed control of the more challenging Foreign Office in 1929.

It was as a senior statesman within the Cabinet that Henderson made his impact on the first Labour Government. The Prime Minister appointed him a member of the British delegation to the July London conference. MacDonald was committed to implementing the Dawes plan, which linked a realistic schedule for the payment of reparations to the ending of the French occupation of the Ruhr. He believed that Labour could make a distinctive contribution to European reconciliation without acquiescing in the French demands for greater security. It took Henderson's skills as a reconciler to mollify the testy Snowden, who threatened resignation over what he regarded as exorbitant French demands and supported the German insistence on a loan as a precondition to new obligations. Once the former allies concluded an agreement, German officials were invited into the discussions, and the cordial relations established between Henderson and Stresemann helped to pave the way towards a ratification of the Dawes Plan.

An economic settlement that met German needs without alienating the French was a considerable achievement for the fledgling government, but it did not entirely allay French fears regarding mutual security. In 1923 the League Assembly had debated a Draft Treaty of Mutual Assistance, but the measure had been coolly received by the Labour Party and the Dominions. The projected regional pacts were seen as likely to increase national armaments and to incur further military obligations. Addressing the Fifth Assembly in September 1924, MacDonald reiterated the British view that security could not be achieved through a military alliance. Instead he suggested the imposition of compulsory arbitration of disputes; those refusing to comply would be deemed guilty of aggression, against which collective action by League members would be warranted. Britain was represented at the Assembly by MacDonald, Henderson, and Lord Parmoor, a pacifist lawyer brought into the Cabinet with special responsibility for League questions. Since there was still wide divergence between the British and French, the latter contending that arbitration was not sufficient to ensure security, the issue was referred to relevant commissions of the League. With MacDonald having returned to London, the main burden of piloting the British proposals through the Political Commission fell to Henderson.

During the weeks of sub-committee deliberations he acquired an intimate knowledge of the League Covenant and the internal machinery of the organization. He established warm contacts among the Secretariat and delegates of member countries, some of whom had been acquaintances from meetings of the International. His long experience of industrial bargaining as a trade union leader proved invaluable, knowing on which issues to compromise and on which to remain inflexible. Gilbert Murray, another member of the British delegation in 1924, recalled the differences between the British, who wanted to retain a free hand over support for the Covenant, and the French, who called for automatic military sanctions. Henderson helped to devise a formula binding members to cooperate loyally and effectively in resisting acts of aggression. When the French demurred, querying the precise meaning of 'loyally and effectively', Henderson banged his fist on the table and said, 'It means he will knock the fellow on the head.' Whether amused or startled by his undiplomatic, but characteristic bluntness, it seemed to reassure the French sufficiently.[53]

The document that emerged from the weeks of negotiation, familiarly known as the Geneva Protocol, was promptly endorsed by the Assembly, but that was no guarantee that the leading powers would subscribe to its provisions. Although it was clearly in the spirit of the League Covenant, it sought to reinforce it by defining an aggressor nation as one who refused arbitration. By institutionalizing the peaceful resolution of disputes, it hoped to make war an international crime. Nations which refused to submit disputes to obligatory arbitration would render themselves liable to sanctions, initially of an economic and financial nature, but ultimately including military measures as well. These proposals would only become operative after signatory nations reduced their armaments to the level of an international police force. The key element in the plan was that pooled security would only come into effect after general disarmament. This would remove the prevailing sense of insecurity and encourage nations to rely on the League, rather than their own weapons, to resolve disputes. By providing a test of aggression, the architects of the Geneva Protocol hoped that they had taken a giant step toward the total elimination of war.

Henderson was genuinely convinced not only of the merits of the plan, but that Labour would ultimately ratify it. But although

France and nine other countries appended their signatures before the close of the Assembly, MacDonald had reservations and would not permit the British delegation to sign. There was opposition from the service chiefs, who feared a sacrifice of naval autonomy and imperial interests, as well as from Snowden and Haldane. Furthermore, on the Labour side, adherence to the Protocol would have required a dramatic shift in attitude. Few in the party were prepared to subscribe to the notion of collective security or even to trust fully in a League of Nations still dominated by the victorious Western powers. In this Henderson was certainly in the forefront of party thinking. His experience at Geneva reinforced his conviction that the League was the last best hope for humanity, but he also recognized the implications of the Protocol as few on the left were prone to do. In a speech to his constituents at Burnley, shortly after his return from Geneva, he warned that the nation would have to face up to the possible use of force in order to maintain the international order, a prospect abhorrent to Labour anti-war sentiment. To be sure, he emphasized the arbitration and conciliation aspects of the Protocol, so akin to his own industrial ideals, but he did not shy away from recognizing that military sanctions might have to be employed.[54] His admission, according to Henry Winkler, came as close to enunciating a doctrine of collective security as any responsible British leader would do in the 1920s.[55] It was his greatest contribution to the transformation of Labour thinking about foreign affairs, a crucial link between the memoranda of the Advisory Committee on International Affairs in the first years after the war and the policies he sought to implement in the Foreign Office between 1929 and 1931. Never as wedded to francophobe, pacifist attitudes as many in the movement, he had achieved a more realistic appraisal of League prospects by the mid-twenties. The League, he believed, could be an effective force for peace, if there were teeth put into the Covenant. Unlike

MacDonald, he was not only willing to trust to the international body to safeguard the world from recurrent war, but to permit it to impose sanctions to deter aggression. In the course of the 1924 negotiations his vague internationalist sympathies had been given a clear programatic focus, and his advocacy of the Geneva Protocol was in no way diminished by Labour's fall from power.

As Honorary Secretary and effective manager of the party's electoral strategy, Henderson was appalled by the circumstances surrounding the defeat of the Government. He had consented to remain in Geneva during the tortuous negotiations on the condition that there should be no electoral challenge without consulting him. Without preparation, he was now saddled with the task of mobilizing the machinery to fight a general election under adverse conditions. He thought the Campbell inquiry was the wrong issue on which to resign, since it would provide the Opposition with anti-Communist ammunition and suggest abuses of executive authority. Fresh from triumphs in Geneva, he was reluctant to see MacDonald forfeit opportunities for an international breakthrough over the Russian treaties and the Protocol. The actual election showed that his misgivings were warranted: the Campbell case and the Zinoviev letter put Labour on the defensive, and the main lines of its policies were obscured by the inflammatory electioneering tactics of the Conservatives and Liberals, once again making common cause against the Red menace. Although Labour's vote rose by more than a million, this was partly a consequence of contesting nearly ninety additional seats. With a net loss of forty seats, Labour re-emerged with 151 M.P.s instead of 191. Most of its leaders retained their seats with reduced majorities: Henderson was returned for Burnley, but his vote had fallen by 4,000. More ominously, he won with only 45.4 per cent in a three-cornered race, with the Liberal candidate evidently capturing many erstwhile Labour votes.

The election defeat inevitably prompted recriminations over MacDonald's leadership among leading figures in the party. Snowden, Bevin, John Wheatley, and H. N. Brailsford all urged Henderson to challenge MacDonald, but he rebuffed the overtures. He deliberately chose to chair a dinner given in MacDonald's honor by the General Council and the N.E.C. in order to disprove rumors that a palace revolution was in the offing. Nothing could dissuade him from the conviction that, whatever his failings, MacDonald retained an unassailable hold on the devotion of the rank and file. All the factors that had prompted his own encouragement of MacDonald to become leader were still valid. Despite the defects of his leadership style, especially his failure to consult associates, he remained their strongest candidate for the Prime Ministership, the one figure who commanded national prestige. Much of the criticism emanated from I.L.P. socialists, who felt that MacDonald had betrayed them, but Henderson also knew that these malcontents did not represent majority opinion within the party. Not that he, despite the assurances of Snowden, was any more popular among I.L.P. members, who regarded him as a stern disciplinarian and an unregenerate Liberal. Nor was there much evidence that he commanded wide backbench support for a challenge, even if he could have rallied his Cabinet colleagues. In the elections for the Shadow Cabinet after the fall of the Government, Henderson came out tenth out of twelve, securing only thirty-eight votes. The very idea of discarding a leader at the behest of the militants offended Henderson's moderate instincts and trade unionist roots. Mrs Webb, a MacDonald detractor, but equally unsympathetic to Clydeside radicalism, recorded:

> Henderson and Clynes and all the older and saner members of the Party are determined to keep J.R.M. as leader, feeling that once the Party acquires the habit of casting out leaders when they dis-

please the Left, rot has set in ... If he is saved it will be by the loyalty of Henderson, Clynes, and Sidney and other members of the right wing.[56]

Yet it would be a mistake to exaggerate loyalty as a factor in Henderson's behavior. There is little reason to doubt that had he regarded his own prospects more favorably, he would have challenged MacDonald. But his sense of his own limitations was reinforced by a shrewd sense of the practicable. He might have hesitated in 1918 or 1922, but he would probably have forged ahead in 1924 if he believed that he could win and that such a victory would not prove divisive. Unity within the party always meant more to him than personal power, and he never had much ambition for the Prime Ministership. It was for that reason that he resumed the office of Chief Whip in 1925, a post not usually held by a politician of such seniority. Within a year he was confiding to the Webbs that MacDonald's influence was waning and that a growing band of disgruntled members were resolved to turn him out of the leadership. He prophecied that they would succeed in replacing him with Snowden, whom he, somewhat surprisingly in view of past enmity, also favored.[57]

VI

Between 1925 and 1929 Labour could do little more than bide its time in the hope of regaining the confidence of the electorate. Concerned, above all, to maintain a responsible image for the party, Henderson shared MacDonald's dismay at the General Strike and the I.L.P.'s Living Wage policy. But in contrast to the leader, he saw little to be gained in antagonizing dissident elements within the movement and hoped to prevent pushing the I.L.P. to a final confrontation. When MacDonald and Bevin clashed over the T.U.C.'s handling of the General Strike, it was left to Henderson to patch things up. Instead of placing Bevin's denunciation of MacDonald before the N.E.C. as the pugnacious union leader demanded, he brought the two men together and succeeded in reconciling them. Equally he sought to dissolve internal revolts against the leadership, pleading again and again for unity against the Tory enemy. 'Henderson's great superiority,' Beatrice Webb noted, was the fact that he was 'a first-rate manager of men – the only one in the front rank of the Labour Movement.'[58] Invariably present on the platform, frequently intervening in debates to press home a resolution, he had no equal as a manipulator of party conferences. It was not his use of language, but his sense of identity with the party – 'this great Movement', as he called it – that evoked a sense of rapport with the rank and file. They knew him to be unyielding in promoting the views of the Executive, yet they also appreciated his unswerving loyalty to conference decisions. What counted, Mrs Hamilton observed, was that 'everybody felt him as, in a special sense, the incarnation of the Party as a Party'.[59] But Beatrice Webb also contended that he was 'not a first class statesman with a policy of his own to carry out'.[60]

The policy he did try to promote after Labour left office was that embodied in the Geneva Protocol. Speaking as President of the Labour and Socialist International, he urged delegates at the 1925 Marseilles Congress to work for its adoption as the only practical method for conserving the peace of the world. He tried to suggest that the spirit behind it was that of the international working-class movement, prodding the League of Nations to tame the aggressive instincts of the capitalist powers in the interests of universal brotherhood. By 1925, however, he realized that he could no longer pledge British Labour's adherence to the Protocol, even though it incorporated so much of his own effort. Three years later in Brussels he claimed that the preliminary focus of international socialist activity was the outlawing of war. Although reactionary governments had destroyed the Protocol, he found cause for optimism in the Kellogg Pact and in projected machinery for arbitration. While concrete results never even approximated his aspirations, Henderson clung to the ideal of peaceful settlement of disputes through the League, and by 1929 he was no less determined in that course than he had been five years earlier.

It was very largely the result of Henderson's pressure that Labour espoused arbitration and the collective renunciation of war as an instrument of policy and incorporated it in *Labour and the Nation,* the program promulgated in 1928. He had argued forcefully at the 1925 Liverpool annual conference that a program was indispensable to safeguard the party from misrepresentation and to provide candidates with a common platform. MacDonald, resistant to any constraints on his autonomy, initially disparaged authorized programs as ropes around the necks of leaders, but by 1927 Henderson's view prevailed. At Blackpool that year the delegates authorized the Executive to draw up proposals that would constitute a program of action for the next Labour Government. Henderson told MacDonald that it was essential to secure agreement with representative sections, such as the General Council of the T.U.C. and the National Administrative Council of the I.L.P., before presenting a document to the annual conference in order to preclude serious divisions before the next general election.[61]

Labour and the Nation, largely written by R. H. Tawney, was a moderate statement of party objectives, exactly in tune with Henderson's own views. In reformist essentials it differed little from the post-war *Labour and the New Social Order.* Despite references to transforming capitalism into socialism, it stressed the need to avoid violence and to secure for all citizens the largest measure of economic welfare and personal freedom. It aimed to convert industry into a cooperative undertaking by nationalizing land ownership, coal and power, transportation, but not banking.

Uncle Arthur

Labour promised a National Economic Committee under the Prime Minister to counsel him on questions involving economic development and employment. A greater emphasis was placed on direct taxation and inheritance taxes as means to finance social services. The document skirted the contentious issue of worker control by vaguely affirming the right of the nation to control its economic destinies and of workers to participate in the governing of their professions. Beyond this the proposals committed Labour to political and economic cooperation through the League, to the furtherance of trade with the Soviet Union, and to ending the economic exploitation of colonial peoples. It was a compromise between those who sought a clear exposition of party dogma and MacDonald, who refused to sanction any program that would bind the action of a future Labour Government. Nothing in it diverged from familiar Labour policies, but these were now reformulated for popular consumption. The whole process bore the imprint of Henderson's personality: the noncontroversial content of the program; the balance between domestic and international concerns; the acknowledged need to provide guideposts for the movement without imposing rigid doctrinal constraints; the optimism about the efficacy of democratic socialism. It reflected not only his tactical wisdom, but also his ideological perspective. If Henderson had no doubt by 1928 that he was a socialist, the nature of that commitment was perfectly defined by the parameters of *Labour and the Nation*. Furthermore, he was convinced that in promulgating the document, the party had paved the way to the democratic revolution he had sketched out a decade before. As an enlightened piece of political propaganda, it would so galvanize workers by hand and by brain and men of good will throughout the community as to make a Labour majority unstoppable. Although there was nothing very novel about *Labour and the Nation,* it represented for Henderson his 'book of the words'. It acquired for him the sanctity of a religious text, a secular bible to replenish his socialist faith. He had fought to impose it against the instincts of MacDonald; it encapsulated what seemed to him the collective wisdom of the movement, and it remained the key to his political outlook for the rest of his career.

5 Foreign secretary

Until 1929 Henderson's standing in the labour movement derived largely from his role as party manager, the man who, arguably, did more than any other individual to transform Labour from a sectional interest group into a party contending for national power. As the mastermind of electoral strategy, he had prepared the way for its emergence in 1929 as the largest party, lacking a Parliamentary majority, but with an indubitable claim to a second term in office. With a substantially increased electorate, including those young women excluded in 1918, Labour's poll rose by nearly three million to confound those who forecast a comeback by Lloyd George's Liberals that year. Thanks in part to Henderson's oversight of constituency organization, the party was able to field fifty-five more candidates than in the previous general election and emerged with 289 seats, a gain of 138. With a much larger turnout his own vote at Burnley rose by nearly 8,000 in a three-cornered contest, and his majority of 7,954 surpassed his by-election victory five years earlier when the Liberals had given him tacit support against the Tory candidate.

In 1924 MacDonald had taken advantage of Henderson's temporary electoral embarrassment to try to exclude him from the Cabinet, a tactless and ultimately futile gesture towards the man responsible for the party's organizational vitality, as well as for MacDonald's easy return to the leadership after his years of exile. Even before the election, when the senior figures discussed the future disposition of offices, Henderson promptly asserted his claim to the Foreign Office and declined to consider returning to the Home Secretaryship, a job he had not particularly enjoyed. Although agreeing to consult his colleagues, MacDonald insisted that ultimately he alone would be responsible for the appointment of ministers.[1] Yet Henderson's successful push for a major office in 1924 was clear evidence that the Prime Minister's authority in cabinet-making was not unlimited. In the early days of the new Government MacDonald met with the other members of Labour's Big Five, all of whom counselled against attempting to combine the Prime Ministership with the Foreign Office as he had during the first Labour Government. If he reluctantly yielded to their advice, he nonetheless resolved to be the architect of foreign policy and therefore wanted the Foreign Office in the hands of someone who would not challenge his authority. Since he found the genial Jimmy Thomas compatible and got on badly with Henderson, his suggestion of the former for the Foreign Secretaryship and the latter as Lord Privy Seal in charge of unemployment seemed plausible. MacDonald and Henderson had divergent views on the potential of the League of Nations and had disagreed over the merits of the Geneva Protocol. It was however a ludicrous choice, since Thomas lacked either the international experience or the *gravitas* to shoulder the burdens of the Foreign Office, whereas Henderson refused to be fobbed off with a lesser job.

There is some evidence that he might have relented had the position offered carried with it the Deputy Leadership, but Snowden, no less mindful of his own prerogative, objected on the grounds that the Deputy Leadership belonged to the Chancellor of the Exchequer.[2] With Snowden proving equally obdurate, Henderson threatened to refuse to serve in any ministerial capacity, which would have proved embarrassing given his stature within the movement. On the mistaken assumption that MacDonald would juggle both offices that he had held in 1924, Thomas at first agreed to accept the Dominions Office, but when

Foreign secretary

Henderson proved immovable, he consented to become Lord Privy Seal. Once again MacDonald's intentions were thwarted, and with ill grace he offered Henderson the position he had pursued with such stubborn pertinacity.

Vain and self-regarding, MacDonald was often insensitive to the feelings of colleagues, and nowhere more so than in his contemptuous treatment of Henderson. His maladroit handling of his erstwhile ally in 1924 taught him nothing except to distrust him further. The entire episode exacerbated tensions within the inner circle of the second Labour Government with dire consequences in the crisis of 1931. Henderson and MacDonald harbored new grievances against one another; the former because the Prime Minister had tried to deny him the only office to which he aspired, the latter because his hand had been forced by a colleague whose qualifications he was loath to concede. MacDonald, jealous of any success achieved by the new Foreign Secretary, became convinced that he was untrustworthy and frequently went behind his back, conferring privately with Foreign Office officials. He was determined to keep exclusive control of Anglo-American relations, rarely bothering to inform Henderson of his initiatives. Time and again, Henderson was deliberately kept in the background in flagrant disregard of the need for coordination in the making of foreign policy. Right from the start he was subjected to what one journalist described as 'a steady stream of criticism, disparagement and, what was far more galling to the new Foreign Secretary, of contemptuous indifference from No. 10 Downing Street'.[3]

The situation was not improved by MacDonald's tendency to make public statements without consulting his Foreign Secretary. Thus within days of taking office he authorized publication of a *Sunday Times* article which reproached other European countries for their treatment of minorities. Since he targeted Alsace and the Saar as significant examples, he was in effect beginning his ministry with an implicit criticism of the French at a time when the Foreign Office was doing its best to avoid ruffling the Gallic feathers. Several months later, after Henderson embraced the Convention for Financial Assistance at Geneva, MacDonald bowed to Tory press criticism and wrote him an intemperate letter disavowing the Foreign Office endorsement. Since his officials had assured Henderson that the Convention did not implicate the Government in new commitments, he found MacDonald's outburst alarming and replied scathingly:

> Such attacks we expect, but what we do not expect, and what we resent, is the leakage which enables the Press to get busy with huge headlines about a split in the Cabinet ... Surely, we shall stultify our whole attitude, if, on being confronted by the first issue that gives an opportunity of giving some effect to our policy, we turn back because a few hostile and ill-informed critics elect to make a fuss ... I write strongly, because ... there is not that confidence that when working in the international sphere one is entitled to expect.[4]

In this instance the Prime Minister yielded, but confidence between the two, so essential to the formulation of foreign policy, never developed. At best, a dubious *modus vivendi* was achieved: Henderson left dealings with the Americans to the Prime Minister, who in turn reined in his tendency to criticize the Foreign Secretary more or less openly.

Even so, relations were anything but harmonious. MacDonald's repeated interference in the delicate negotiations with the Egyptians caused an exasperated Henderson to grumble that 'if he is to be pulled about much more, he will suggest that JRM should become Foreign Secretary and be done with it'.[5] Emanuel Shinwell even suggested that the Prime Minister inspired articles hostile to Henderson's Egyptian policy which the Foreign Secretary believed could be misconstrued abroad.[6] But when, frustrated by the attempts to sabotage his efforts, he threatened to resign, MacDonald backed down. Continuing the reforms initiated by his predecessor, Henderson made it clear that 'interference in internal administration is utterly incompatible with our recognition of Egypt as an independent sovereign state'.[7] He succeeded in obtaining Cabinet support for a draft proposal to restore relations with Egypt to the situation that existed before 1924, to end the occupation of Cairo and Alexandria, and to withdraw British troops to the vicinity of the Suez Canal. The Egyptians, facing pressure from nationalist militants, kept escalating their demands, especially over their right to send troops to the Sudan. MacDonald, echoing the King's view that the Sudan should be a British colony, demurred at Henderson's willingness to make concessions, making it difficult for him to 'fight such a combination'. He told Dalton that if it were only the Palace which opposed his policy, he was confident that he could prevail 'especially with our own people. After all, we are a constitutional monarchy'. Royal displeasure was less alarming than intimations that MacDonald was 'disowning him behind his back'.[8] His persistence, coupled with threats of resignation, defeated MacDonald, who confessed to Lord Stamfordham, the King's Secretary, that he 'had been beaten by the Foreign Office and that the alternative would be the resignation of Mr Henderson'.[9] Despite his intention of conciliating the Egyptians without forsaking British imperial interests, the Foreign Secretary was eventually compelled to recognize that an impasse had been reached. All that he achieved was a friendlier atmosphere, but his hopes for a lasting settlement came to nought. Ultimately, it proved impossible not only to satisfy Egyptian nationalists, but to concede the substance of Egyptian sovereignty without sacrificing British strategic interests.

In addition to interference from 10 Downing Street Henderson also had to contend with royal hostility. King George V, alarmed by the reformist initiatives in Egypt, was even more offended by Labour's restoration of diplomatic relations with the Russians. To receive the Soviet Ambassador at Court would be tantamount to shaking hands with one of the murderers of his cousin the Tsar. As Henderson recounted his conversation at Sandringham, 'I just let him run on and then I said, "Well, Your Majesty, that's the Cabinet's decision".'[10] The task of persuasion was rendered more difficult since the Prime Minister obviously shared the royal compunctions. As a constitutional monarch, George V had to accept the democratic verdict of the electorate, but he made it clear that Labour policies – and several of its leaders – strained the limits of his fidelity to constitutional propriety.

Nor did Henderson hesitate to challenge an imperial pro-consul. Shortly after taking office he came to the conclusion that Lord Lloyd, the Egyptian High Commissioner, had not only proved insubordinate to his predecessor, Sir Austen Chamberlain, but remained unalterably opposed to the kind of reforms he hoped to implement. To the dismay of imperialist sentiment, the Foreign Secretary demanded and secured Lloyd's resignation. In contrast to his predecessor, he would brook no opposition and had curtly informed Lloyd that the divergence of outlook appeared to be 'so wide as to be unbridgeable'.[11] Since there was no likelihood that the High Commissioner would mend his ways, there was no alternative to his removal. Winston Churchill's efforts to discredit the dismissal of a pro-consul with close links to the Conservative Party as politically motivated backfired. In response to Parliamentary queries Henderson documented recurrent clashes between Lloyd and Chamberlain, who was overruled by Lloyd's allies in the Cabinet. Uncle, as Dalton recorded it, was 'quite splendid' in standing up to Tory backbenchers 'howling with fury'. It was an 'overwhelming triumph' for the Government, with Henderson 'direct, frank, and self-assured' in refuting the allegations to the resounding cheers of his supporters. At the next Cabinet meeting Henderson received a warm reception from his colleagues but only stony silence from the Prime Minister. 'He has never thanked me,' Henderson complained bitterly to Dalton, 'for anything I have done these six and twenty years.'[12]

It was not only his Parliamentary colleagues who hailed his performance. When he surveyed the first months of his stewardship at the Brighton party conference in a speech on 2 October, he received a standing ovation. The delegates were 'not carried away by rhetoric or sobstuff, but conscious of honest, big achievement all along the line'.[13] Although hampered by MacDonald's unreliability, Henderson admitted to the Webbs in December that he was enjoying his Foreign Office duties more than any work he had ever done. He blamed the Prime Minister for

> meddling in the details of the Foreign Office instead of keeping himself for general management of the whole business of government. He says that MacDonald sends for the officials of the Foreign Office even for his private secretary, and discusses affairs with them without communicating with the Foreign Secretary.

The growing mutual antipathy did not, however, turn him against the leadership of MacDonald, who, he still contended, was 'absolutely irreplaceable'.[14] It would, however, make him more susceptible to the appeals of others, a rallying point for the increasing number of disaffected politicians, a role he had deliberately eschewed before 1929. Not that he could be convicted of conspiring against his leader, but only that the growing antagonism eroded whatever residual loyalty he felt.

II

It is not surprising that established opinion greeted Henderson's appointment with derision. He lacked the ordinary accoutrements of the traditional Foreign Secretary: he spoke no foreign language and lacked the formal education and social graces that counted in a milieu still touched by the unbought grace of the aristocracy. His predecessor Austen Chamberlain, in a characteristic Tory misjudgment, noted his preference for Thomas 'because he is by far the abler man and is sound in essentials. Henderson I have always thought very stupid and rather afraid of responsibility.'[15] He was soon to confound his critics by revealing not merely his grasp of foreign affairs, but his intention of taking full responsibility for the actions undertaken during his tenure. What struck observers, at home and abroad, was his sincerity and his integrity, virtues all too rare in diplomatic circles where time-servers and posturing chauvinists held sway.

Despite Chamberlain's skepticism, Henderson had better qualifications for the Foreign Secretaryship than any prominent Labour politician, save MacDonald. Years of experience in industrial bargaining were an excellent preparation for diplomatic negotiation, as Ernest Bevin too would later discover. Furthermore, Henderson had not only undertaken a hazardous wartime mission to Russia, but had accompanied Lord Parmoor to the League Assembly in 1924, where he had been instrumental in formulating the ill-fated Geneva Protocol. In addition, his links with the Socialist International had brought him into regular contact with foreign politicians, albeit socialist ones, so that by 1929 he was widely known in European capitals and in Geneva. Two decades of exposure to international problems had transformed him from the provincial trade unionist he had been before the war to a leader who moved comfortably on the world stage. At home he had long been a stalwart advocate of the League of Nations and bore primary responsibility for the inclusion of a strong pro-League stance in *Labour and the Nation* in 1928.

Henderson wanted the Foreign Office not only because it would crown his public career, but also because he had a clear conception of what he wanted to accomplish. He did not assume his duties either empty-handed or open-minded. As the architect of Labour's international program, he sought to use his position to implement concrete policies approved by Labour conferences and by the voters. He was intimidated neither by hoary tradition, nor by the presumption of continuity in the direction of foreign policy. Believing, indeed, that there could be 'too much continuity in foreign policy', he was not afraid to politicize its objectives. Within a few days of his arrival in Whitehall, he gave orders that copies of *Labour and the Nation* be circulated among heads of Foreign Office departments. In his first meeting with the Permanent Under-Secretary, he announced that 'our view is diametrically opposed to that of the late Government's on the Optional Clause and on recognition of Russia to which we are definitely committed'. The following week he told his top officials that since the Government was determined to sign the Clause 'with the least possible delay', he 'did not wish to hear a lot of legal arguments about reservations'. When some of the civil servants balked at such impetuosity, Henderson exclaimed to Dalton, 'Don't these chaps know what our policy is?'[16]

Nor was he simply a visionary idealist, well-intentioned, but inept where practical considerations were concerned. It is true that he had little use for Whitehall mandarins and striped trousered diplomats, but he eschewed rhetoric in favor of a reasonable approach to what was practicable in foreign policy. Few British Foreign Secretaries ever took office with such clear-sighted objectives. In accepting congratulations on his appointment from Gilbert Murray, he affirmed the view that it 'offers wonderful opportunities for useful work' and hoped that he would 'be able to do much towards the advancement of international peace'.[17] He was able to earn the approbation of large segments of the British public because he articulated the desire of ordinary citizens to reconcile the divergent interests of European nations in order to build a foundation for peace. In that sense he advocated a democratic foreign policy, knowing that 'the public opinion of nations has always been ahead of what the Governments were prepared to do'.[18]

The task before him was to resolve the conflicts stemming from the Versailles settlement and to strengthen the mechanisms that would guarantee peace. He attributed the outbreak of the First World War, first of all, to the distrust and suspicion engendered by competing alliances and armaments, and, secondly, to the defective machinery of the Concert of Europe. If a stable European structure was to be achieved, a genuine balance of power needed to be restored, based on the common interest of nations. Only through the control of armaments by international agreement and the containment of aggression could such a balance be sustained. To guarantee its stability, permanent machinery would have to be devised which would ensure constructive cooperation among the powers and protection for the smaller nations. It was his emphasis on permanent institutions that led him to champion the League and to persuade the Labour Party that, however flawed, it represented their best hope for peace. In the immediate post-war years it seemed more urgent to reduce the tension in Europe by reducing Germany's reparations burden and securing her admission to the League. But the prevention of future conflict transcended the issue of treaty revision. Nations must work through the League of Nations to achieve a progressive reduction in armaments. It was with that objective that he proposed to the World Peace Congress in 1922 that the Covenant be amended to require states to submit disputes to the Permanent Court or to other League bodies for arbitration. Yet Henderson was also aware, indeed far more than many in the Labour Party, that ultimately the peaceful resolution of disputes through League arbitration depended on a commitment by the powers to enforce a settlement. He was able to reconcile his belief in disarmament with support for sanctions only by recognizing that coercive action by the League was compatible with the reduction of national armaments.

It was the need to reinforce the Covenant that led Henderson to espouse the Geneva Protocol, which would have required signatory nations to submit justiciable disputes to League arbitration. Its failure to win general assent did not deter him from pressing for Labour to endorse the Optional Clause, which bound nations to submit disputes to the Permanent Court at The Hague. He also advocated British adherence to the General Act, extending the principle implicit in the Geneva Protocol and the Optional Clause to all disputes, whatever their nature. Were Britain to assume the lead, as the Conservatives had been notably reluctant to do, in renouncing war as an instrument of national policy, Henderson saw the promise of a day near at hand 'when it should be unthinkable that a nation should refuse to submit its quarrels either to the Council or to the arbitration of the Permanent Court'.[19] Once nations began automatically to submit disputes to arbitration, recourse to military action would gradually disappear. If the peaceful resolution of disputes was the aim of his policy, its necessary corollary was the reduction of armaments by general agreement, not merely to appease German grievances, but to prevent that chimerical search for security through increased weapons. The Covenant had pledged signatory nations to work for disarmament, yet little had been accomplished by 1929 aside from vague promises. Security, Henderson believed, could only be achieved within the framework of the League, reliance on whose institutions would obviate the need for costly national arsenals. His views were made explicit in *Labour and the Nation* and also in the party's 1929 election manifesto, *Labour's Appeal to the Nation,* which proclaimed the commitment to arbitration and disarmament, as well as full and cordial support for the League. His own statements suggest a more realistic attitude towards collective security than that of many in the party, who saw disarmament as an alternative to military preparation. This made him more responsive to French demands than the Labour left, but also than MacDonald, who had been wary of the international obligations implicit in the Geneva Protocol. These were the policies that Henderson would try to bring to fruition during his two years as Foreign Secretary and which inspired him during his later tenure as President of the Disarmament Conference. As so often in his career, he saw himself as a spokesman for the labour movement and for the ideals of international socialism, even where these seemed to contradict Foreign Office experts or champions of imperial interests.

Resolute though he was in promoting these objectives, he recognized his own personal limitations as Foreign Secretary. Just as in devising a constitution for the party in 1918, he did not hesitate to rely on better minds and more experienced men in the day-to-day operations of the Foreign Office. Henderson selected an impressive team to assist him, strong in the intellectual realm where he was admittedly weakest. At his insistence the Prime Minister agreed to appoint Hugh Dalton, an academic economist and rising Labour politician, as Under-Secretary, thus gaining the latter's instantaneous and abiding devotion. Despite their differences in background, Dalton came to admire Henderson for his common sense approach and his genuine commitment to the twin goals of arbitration and security. Indeed his relations with his chief were much warmer than with fellow Old Etonians in the Foreign Office. Since Henderson was frequently abroad or preoccupied with other Cabinet business, much of the responsibility for managing the Foreign Office fell to the abrasive and boisterous Dalton, content to play Sancho Panza to Uncle Arthur's Don Quixote. Ambitious and conspiratorial, Dalton, who disliked MacDonald, was unflaggingly loyal to his chief, never seeking to upstage him or personally to take credit for Foreign Office successes. As his Parliamentary Private Secretary

Henderson chose the young Philip Noel-Baker, a Quaker and expert in international law, and brought back to the Foreign Office the renegade Tory, Lord Robert Cecil, by now Viscount Cecil of Chelwood, as advisor on League of Nations questions, defending him even after he incurred MacDonald's displeasure. Noel-Baker and Cecil both had previous Geneva experience, vital in view of the renewed emphasis on the efficacy of the League. These three men had considerable influence on the Foreign Secretary, perhaps because they shared his convictions more than his permanent officials did. That the calibre of these appointments was remarkable is borne out by the fact that three out of the four appointees were in due course to be awarded Nobel Peace Prizes, a record unmatched by any other Foreign Office team.[20]

With his permanent officials Henderson's relationships were less cordial. He was irritated by the efforts of Sir Ronald Lindsay, the Permanent Under-Secretary, to rush him into approving dispatches that he had no time adequately to consider. At the same time Lindsay proved too cautious in those areas, notably the Optional Clause and the recognition of the Soviet Union, where Henderson sought prompt action. Nor did the new Foreign Secretary hesitate to overrule the considered opinion of his subordinates. When it was suggested that he congratulate Mussolini and the Pope on the conclusion of the Lateran Treaty, he refused on the grounds that the Prime Minister was a Presbyterian and he a Wesleyan and that, moreover, he had already denounced Mussolini publicly as the murderer of Matteotti. When urged to deny Trotsky's application for residence in England, he insisted on referring the matter to the Cabinet, reminding his officials that there was such a thing as the right of asylum. A more serious complaint against Lindsay was his propensity to sabotage Henderson's initiatives through direct communications with the Prime Minister, always prone to distrust his Foreign Secretary. There was antagonism between Dalton and Lindsay over the Optional

Clause, to which the latter raised repeated objections. Dalton protested to his chief Lindsay's practice of plying the Prime Minister 'with tendentious advice, which we know is contrary to Secretary of State's point of view'.[21] It must have been with considerable relief to all parties concerned that Henderson soon had the opportunity to dispatch Lindsay to the Washington Embassy, replacing him early in 1930 with the altogether more pliant Sir Robert Vansittart, although he too occasionally communicated with the Prime Minister behind his superior's back as Lindsay had done. Even Vansittart, more resilient than his predecessor, was not immune to Henderson's petulant outbursts when he raised unwelcome difficulties in the course of negotiations. Henderson could inspire affection, and even awe, in subordinates, as Dalton and Molly Hamilton exemplified. Dalton, with his inverse snobbery, admired Uncle Arthur's solid virtues, but had only contempt for the narrow-minded, socially-exclusive diplomatic corps. Mrs Hamilton, appointed to the 1929 League delegation, had been startled when fellow M.P. Susan Lawrence had contended earlier that Henderson was 'the biggest man in the Labour Party'. After working with him at Geneva, she could only concur with that assessment: 'there was a largeness in him that was rock-like'.[22] But others on his staff found him obstinate and cantankerous, insensitive to the feelings of those more accustomed to diplomatic courtesies. Schooled in the rougher arena of the trade union branch and the party conference, he could be rude and abrupt when confronted by obstacles or bureaucratic red tape. Furthermore, he came from a different social milieu – working class, chapel, teetotal – which was never essentially compatible with the public school, clubbable atmosphere of the Foreign Office.

Dalton was initially fearful that his chief might become embroiled in detail, and Lord Cecil warned that permanent officials might overwhelm him with minutiae so that he would not 'have time to do any mischief'.[23] In fact, the opposite was true: his retention of the party Secretaryship and his continued preoccupation with election strategy did mean that he had less time for foreign affairs than was probably desirable, but in any event he preferred to leave details to others to carry out. Chamberlain, offering a somewhat jaundiced view, complained that 'the Government use him so much for Party and Home politics that he has not time for foreign affairs'.[24] This was certainly an exaggeration, but Henderson's tendency to wear several hats simultaneously meant that too many spheres competed for his attention. Although there were fewer distractions when he was abroad, he was often obliged when in London to reconcile conflicts in the Cabinet or to pour oil on troubled backbench waters. Many people in the party and in the movement at large automatically turned to him when problems arose, depending on his sound judgment and knowledge of men. It was often said that 'there is always some trouble when Uncle is away'.

Since he generally spent mornings at Head Office, he had neither the time, nor the inclination to read long memoranda, preferring to listen to the explication of a problem and to ask questions before making up his mind. Instead of writing frequently to ambassadors, as Lord Curzon had done, he would outline his position in discussions with his staff, leaving it to them to draft the necessary communiqués. In contrast to his interventionist practice as party Secretary, he became adept at delegating responsibility to others, especially to Dalton. His Private Secretary, Walford Selby, spoke of him as 'the most expert decentralizer' he had ever encountered. Yet, although willing to seek expert advice, in the final analysis Henderson made up his own mind. He relied on his officials to brief him for Parliamentary questions, but his strong convictions and general grasp of foreign affairs meant he was rarely at a loss when confronted by Opposition attacks. Usually too busy to write his own Parliamentary speeches, he would revise those drafted for him to suit his own somewhat pedestrian debating style. After nearly a quarter of a century in the Commons he made up for his lack of oratorical gifts with a keen sense of the mood of the House, and never was he heard with more respect than during his two years as Foreign Secretary.

III

In his first speech in the Commons on 5 July in his new office Henderson set forth three immediate goals. He announced that the Government was pledged to sign the Optional Clause, to evacuate troops from the Rhineland promptly, and to restore diplomatic relations with the Soviet Union. Reconciliation with Germany and improved relations with Russia were long-standing aims of the Labour Party, but the Foreign Secretary regarded them as the necessary preconditions to the consolidation of peace in Europe. These were the objectives that occupied his first months in office, and their rapid implementation boosted his own and the Government's popularity. If this series of 'bold strokes' did not, as Dalton later suggested, change 'the whole face of world politics',[25] it gave a welcome impression of decisiveness and restored British prestige.

Labour's opposition to the Versailles Treaty had engendered a strong current of Francophobia which made the new Government particularly responsive to German grievances. A decade of propaganda in the left-wing press from men like H. N. Brailsford, E. D. Morel, and Norman Angell had created a climate of distrust of the French and sympathy for the maligned former enemy. Whereas the Tory policy had, under Lord Curzon and Chamberlain, been directed towards cooperation with Paris, Labour veered towards applying pressure to the French to make concessions, especially over reparations. Henderson, considered better disposed towards the French than many of his colleagues, realized that while England could forego its claim to reparations, the key to a solution lay in the reconciliation of France and Germany. Thus at the Hague Conference in August 1929 the Foreign Secretary sought to establish a relationship of mutual confidence with his French counterpart, Aristide Briand, which was to serve him in good stead during these and other negotiations.

The Young Report, which had been issued in May, proposed to reduce German financial obligations by twenty per cent and to limit the schedule of payments to fifty-nine years. Foreign controls in Germany were to be abolished, and a new method of payment was instituted with the creation of a Bank for International Settlements. The British delegation at The Hague was actually headed by Snowden as Chancellor of the Exchequer, who nearly undermined Henderson's conciliatory approach to the French by insisting upon a greater share of reparations annuities for Great Britain than the Young Plan projected. While Henderson was an influence for moderation as Chairman of the Political Committee, Snowden's intransigence over the percentages of the British share of reparations imperilled the chances for a settlement. Since Henderson was willing to accept the provisions of the report, he and Snowden were soon at loggerheads, with the Prime Minister tilting somewhat uneasily towards his Chancellor. The Foreign Secretary's main concern was not some trifling increase in England's share in reparations but the prospect of European pacification. Dalton, who thought Henderson 'sound on the principles' but 'a bit afraid' of Snowden, shared the Foreign Office view that 'a few millions are dust in the balance, compared with the gains of the early and complete evacuation'.[26] An impasse was reached over the financial negotiations, with the British delegation in the invidious position of seeming to defy the report of the experts. Although his inflexible stance won unaccustomed praise in the jingoistic press, the former I.L.P. internationalist outraged erstwhile supporters on the left in England, as well as the American bankers, eager to win consent to the Young Plan. The German delegation, convinced that a stalemate was unavoidable, was ready to leave The Hague, but Henderson persuaded them to accept any settlement devised by the creditor powers. During the last days of August continuous sessions were held, first jointly and then with the British and Continental negotiating teams meeting separately. Henderson patiently refused to admit failure, telling the British delegates that they must remain at their task until the issue was settled. Finally, Snowden relented and agreed to accept 83 per cent of what he had originally demanded.

The Chancellor's belated compromise may be viewed as a victory for Henderson, since it paved the way for a resolution of the central issue. Stresemann had made it clear that evacuation was a precondition for German agreement to the Young Plan, but the French initially balked at accelerating the evacuation timetable. That a settlement was reached was largely the result of Henderson's personal diplomacy. Starting from the position that Britain would not consider a unilateral withdrawal of troops, he soon reversed himself and issued an ultimatum that British soldiers would begin to be withdrawn by mid-September regardless of whether financial terms had been concluded. In plain words he stated that 'the British Tommies on the Rhine shall eat their Christmas dinners at home'. Yet if Britain were to withdraw its forces from the Rhineland unilaterally as some on the left advocated, it would only serve to alienate France and Belgium and heighten European tensions. By a quiet show of firmness, with none of Snowden's nationalistic histrionics, Henderson managed to force Briand's hand. After several days of hard bargaining he and Stresemann hammered out a formula under which the French stipulated June 1930 as the date when all remaining troops would be evacuated. To satisfy the Germans, Henderson tried in private meetings at his hotel to wrest further concessions from the French, but Briand, having yielded on certain French demands, refused any further surrender. Although the financial provisions had still to be ratified, the agreement over the Rhineland occupation marked a significant breakthrough in Franco-German relations for which the British Foreign Secretary deserved the lion's share of credit. By advancing the evacuation date specified in the Treaty by five years and by substantially reducing Germany's reparations burden, the Hague Conference was hailed as a major success for the Labour Government. Snowden safeguarded British interests, but it was Henderson's persistence that removed the spectre of renewed international conflict. As J. L. Garvin, no friend to Labour policies, later conceded,

> Mr Arthur Henderson, insisting on the speedy evacuation of the foreign garrisons, accomplished the best single stroke for peace that any Foreign Minister has achieved since the armistice.[27]

That he had managed to do this while fostering mutual trust between England and the two Continental powers promised further successes at Geneva in the coming months.

When Labour returned to power in 1929, relations with the Soviet Union were at a low ebb. The Tories had abandoned the draft treaty devised during the first Labour Government and in 1927 expelled the Soviet trading mission. Although Comintern propaganda had continued unabated, the party was pledged to restore diplomatic and commercial ties with the Russian government. Henderson was convinced that only by placing relations between the two countries on a solid footing could the causes of the tension be dissolved. He had long recognized the inadvisability of isolating the Soviet Union in the international arena and hoped to prepare the way for her eventual admission to the League of Nations. Despite his antipathy towards Communism, he maintained, as he had ever since the revolution, that

> Russia, with its vast population, cannot be permanently ignored;

only by diplomatic and other intercourse with her will it be possible to bring her once more into the family of nations.[28]

Once in office, MacDonald and Henderson proceeded cautiously, indeed more cautiously than many of their left-wing supporters would have liked. They sought assurances that propaganda would be suspended, but the Russians refused to accept responsibility for the activities of the Third International. With customary disregard of his Foreign Secretary's plans, the Prime Minister, without consulting the Foreign Office, further promised that the Government would not permit the exchange of ambassadors to take place unless Parliament gave its approval. Although this provoked a storm of opposition from the Labour back benches, Henderson recognized that little could be done to alter the situation without risking an outcry in the press. He told Dalton, 'Russia has brought us down once. We can't afford to let it happen twice.'[29] When dissident M.P.s threatened to put down a motion demanding the immediate resumption of normal relations, he tried to calm the inflamed spirits by reminding them that Russia was 'not the only pebble on the beach'.

The appearance of firmness in London may have convinced the Soviet leaders that they would have to make concessions if they were to secure the normalization of relations. Henderson, who took charge of the negotiations, had earlier stated that Soviet undertakings to restrict propaganda were an essential precondition for the exchange of ambassadors. He also informed the Commons that since diplomatic relations had been suspended, rather than abrogated, the question of renewed recognition of the Soviet Union did not arise. Yet when Valerian Dovgalevsky, the Soviet Ambassador in Paris, met Henderson at the Foreign Office at the end of July, little progress was made. The Russian envoy was told that the restoration of relations could not take place until after Parliament reconvened in the autumn, although

Foreign secretary

Henderson assured him that plenty of work could be done in the meantime in resolving disputed issues. The Soviets misconstrued this tactic as a sign that the British were insisting that the substance of outstanding questions, such as the claims of bondholders, be settled prior to the resumption of relations. Henderson also approved left-wing M.P. E. F. Wise's mission to Moscow as a sympathetic intermediary, although he warned that there were limits to the Government's flexibility. 'I adhered firmly to the position,' he told Dalton,

> I had taken up with Dovgalevsky and told him that, in my opinion he was not likely to help in securing the object he had in view if he gave the Russians the impression that we were always ready to modify our attitude whenever they presented a difficulty real or unreal.[30]

Negotiations remained stalled until Henderson announced at Geneva in September that he would welcome a Soviet representative in London.

When Dovgalevsky returned to England for a resumption of talks, Henderson put forward a list of issues to be discussed, including pledges in regard to propaganda, the revival of the 1923 provisional agreement on fishing rights, and the establishment of consulates. Discussion of debts was to be postponed until after the exchange of ambassadors. Even these fundamental questions provoked disagreement, and Henderson abandoned the attempt to resolve any issue except that of propaganda, the *sine qua non* of a settlement. The final discussion took place in an informal setting at the White Hart Inn at Lewes, where Henderson, taking time out from the party conference at Brighton, informed the Soviet representative that the Government inferred that any guarantees regarding propaganda would extend to the Third International. By papering over their differences the Foreign Office could appear to snatch a modest victory without the Soviet authorities agreeing to specific references in the formal protocol that admitted their responsibility for the actions of the Comintern.

The successful conclusion to the talks was welcomed by the delegates at Brighton but denounced by the opposition press, always ready to accuse Labour of capitulation to the Soviets. In a debate in the Commons on 5 November Henderson defended his actions, reminding M.P.s that the Government had compelled the Russians to provide assurances about propaganda. Supported by the Liberals, the Russian agreement was approved by a vote of 324 to 199. Henderson did, however, bow to Conservative demands that no Government-guaranteed loan be made to the Soviet Union, a political concession that probably jeopardized further progress on outstanding debt claims.

When agreement was reached, it fell to the Foreign Secretary to appoint a British ambassador. He believed that a professional diplomat would be most appropriate for the Moscow post and discounted the claims of Labour M.P.s, like Arthur Ponsonby, and Sir Daniel Stevenson, a prominent Union of Democratic Control figure, as too controversial. Instead he chose Sir Esmond Ovey, who at least spoke Russian, but was otherwise in the traditional ambassadorial mold. Despite the King's protestations, he was obliged, under pressure from Henderson, to receive the Russian envoy, Gregory Sokolnikov, at a royal *levée* in March 1930.

Despite Labour's good intentions, there were meager results to show for the *rapprochement* with the Soviet Union. The persistence of anti-British propaganda was especially galling, since Henderson had, perhaps naively, trusted Russian pledges. Although it was engineered by the Comintern, complaints to the Soviet authorities were to no avail, since they continued to disclaim responsibility.

> I can claim [he wrote to Ovey] to have done more than any other

to bring about resumption of relations with the Soviet Government in the teeth of strong and formidable opposition, and my desire to develop and improve those relations continues; nevertheless my difficulties have been immensely increased by reason of the fact that far from campaign of propaganda and abuse undergoing some diminution as a result of action of His Majesty's Government in exchanging Ambassadors, campaign would seem to all appearances to have been increased in intensity since exchange has taken place.[31]

Challenged in Parliament, the Foreign Secretary admitted that the problem had not been alleviated, but suggested that normal relations at least provided a framework for discussion. To sever ties on the grounds that the Russians had not fulfilled their part of the bargain would set back hopes for expanded trade and for peace. Unless Russia were included, there was little chance that pacification would be realized in Europe. Even Dalton admitted in the end that all the Government accomplished was to make Anglo-Soviet relations 'less unsatisfactory than they would otherwise have been'.[32]

Henderson arrived in Geneva in September 1929 for the Tenth Assembly of the League with a clear sense of purpose. Convinced that the future of the world depended on the efficacy of the League's operations, he aimed to undo the legacy of indifference to internationalist sensibilities left by his predecessor, whose greatest success, the Locarno agreement, marked a return to traditional power diplomacy. He carried the additional burden of MacDonald's known lack of enthusiasm for the organization, barely concealed during the Prime Minister's coolly-received speech at the opening of the session. Less concerned with details than with general objectives, he sought to foster a spirit of cooperation and trust among the European powers. For once his own parochial, trade unionist perspective was ideally matched to the occasion. Henderson saw the League as something akin to an enlarged T.U.C., where bluntness and accessibility were valued more than oratorical flourishes. He seemed to possess an instinctive negotiating sense and knew when to intervene forcefully and when to make concessions. At the same time he was not a particularly imaginative improviser and tended to stick close to his brief lest he overstep the limits imposed by his generally unsupportive Prime Minister. He was already on amicable terms with Briand and Stresemann and hoped that personal contact with delegates would allay their suspicion of British motives.

It would not be an exaggeration to suggest that Henderson personally transformed the mood of the Tenth Assembly and restored British leadership. His genuine commitment to making the League work and his conciliatory manner in dealing with officials and foreign statesmen earned him high marks. His biographer quotes one typical reaction: 'Mr Henderson was the one statesman who made a tremendous impression at Geneva – and we never expected it.'[33] His unaffected manner and patent ignorance of foreign languages encouraged plain-dealing and unambiguous statements. But foreign delegates were soon disabused if they imagined that his simplicity was a sign of weakness. One League official remarked that Henderson was 'rather slow to move, but, when he gets going, he is like an elephant crashing through jungle – there is no stopping him'.[34]

What made the Tenth Assembly significant was the acceptance by Great Britain and the Dominions of the Optional Clause prescribing compulsory arbitration for all justiciable disputes. Before the League convened MacDonald had argued against signing unless the Dominions concurred, although Labour's election promise had not implied that Dominion support was a prerequisite. As in the case of the earlier Geneva Protocol, Henderson encountered obstruction from the service chiefs, who advocated the inclusion of as many as nine reservations, casting considerable doubt as to the credibility of British adherence. The Foreign Office succeeded in devising a compromise that would satisfy

Dominion politicians who feared that the Optional Clause would implicate them in European conflicts or permit foreign intervention in intra-Imperial affairs. By reserving certain questions, notably disputes exclusively between members of the British Empire, from arbitral procedures, he was able to win over all the Dominions. Although the Optional Clause was signed by Great Britain on 19 September, Henderson still had to face Opposition objections to the abandonment of any reservation over the law of the sea, but a Tory amendment was easily defeated in the Commons.

In his speech to the Assembly on 6 September Henderson had assured the delegates that his Government believed that arbitration was the best method of resolving disputes. Once nations became accustomed to submitting disputes to an impartial judge, they would cease to rely on armed force to protect their interests. But he added that the Optional Clause, symptomatic of a new cooperative spirit, was merely the initial step towards peace. Finally, it was vital to cap their efforts by formulating a general treaty of disarmament. The British delegates became increasingly active in the so-called Third Committee, which met in 1929 to consider the progress being made by the Preparatory Commission for the general Disarmament Conference. Henderson was eager to ensure that the British 'should be free in the Preparatory Commission to raise any element of importance for the limitation of national armaments',[35] but at the same time he realized that French sensibilities had to be taken into account. It was clear that nothing useful could be achieved in opposition to the French, whose concern with security made them unwilling to accept restrictions on reserve forces or budgetary limitations. He also publicly endorsed the Convention for Financial Assistance to States in Danger of Aggression, with the proviso that the British would lend support only to those nations who subscribed to a general disarmament treaty not yet even on the drawing board. Even so, Henderson's pledge evoked the angry outburst from the isolationist press that so alarmed the Prime Minister and led to the exchange of mutual recriminations.

Although personally very active during his two months at Geneva, the Foreign Secretary relied, as he did in London, on his subordinates. He trusted them and made them feel that their contributions were significant. His own main function was in the public occasions – the plenary sessions and social gatherings – while other members of the delegation attended the interminable committee meetings. But he conveyed to them his conviction that only by strengthening the machinery of the League could a more effective means of keeping the peace be realized. This was also the motive behind his proposals for a reform of the League Secretariat: only by developing a genuine international civil service would the organization become efficient, less vulnerable to the uncertain loyalties of member states. His greatest success was to inspire other delegates with his own optimism about rebuilding the political stability of Europe. While the actual shifts in British policy under the Labour Government may have been marginal, Henderson was able to impart a new spirit of cooperation that contrasted sharply not just with his Tory predecessor, but with MacDonald and Snowden as well. That he was able to implement his program in the face of obstruction by the Opposition and, on occasion, by his own Cabinet was a testimony to his tenacity of purpose. Little wonder that the Tenth Assembly witnessed a restoration of British prestige at Geneva and widespread approval of Henderson's performance, all the more impressive in that neither result could have been predicted.

It was at the same session that Briand broached the subject of a European Federal Union, initially as an economic community, although subsequently more as an alternative arena for the solution of political problems. Because of their friendship, Henderson felt constrained to receive the proposals with interest, but by May 1930 the Foreign Office expressed serious misgivings. The projected federation ran the risk of arousing the displeasure of the United States and the Dominions, but, more ominously from the Foreign Secretary's perspective, it threatened to diminish the League's prestige by erecting rival international institutions. Furthermore, although it suggested that the French were forsaking a narrow nationalism in favor of a European consciousness, the plan did little to mitigate the growing tension with Germany. Henderson's delicate task was to torpedo the proposals without offending Briand. At the Eleventh Assembly, taking place amid increasingly unstable conditions, there was little enthusiasm for new initiatives, and the Briand plan was referred to a special commission which consigned it to oblivion.

Henderson was no less popular at the 1930 Assembly meeting, but agreement on crucial issues turned out to be far more elusive than in the previous year. His own Assembly address focused attention once again on the disarmament question, insisting on a general agreement as a precondition for British adherence to effective sanctions. As he told the delegates on 11 September,

> Security is impossible if competitive military preparations continue as they are going on to-day . . . We can never fulfil the purpose for which the League has been created unless we are prepared to carry through a scheme of general disarmament by international agreement . . . The pace is slow, and the peoples of the world are growing impatient and doubtful, in many cases, of our good faith.[36]

Henderson's plea, however moving, fell on stony ground. The growing electoral strength of right-wing parties in Germany alarmed the French, who were, in any event, reluctant to weaken their defences without international guarantees. In the face of intransigence in Paris, the British had little option but to acquiesce to French military superiority, hoping that the Germans might settle for less than genuine equality. Although he had shown himself sympathetic to German grievances, he offered no encouragement to strident revisionists. There were limits to what England could do as an intermediary, he warned Sir Horace Rumbold, the Ambassador in Berlin:

> We shall continue to exert all our influence in Paris to strengthen the hand of those statesmen such as Briand who are in my belief sincerely desirous of pursuing a policy of pacification, but Germany must be made to realise that there are limits to the extent of our influence and that without the wholehearted co-operation of her leaders of opinion we cannot be held responsible for a hardening of French opinion against her.[37]

More successful were his efforts to reinforce the procedures for the peaceful settlement of disputes. The Convention for Financial Assistance was signed by twenty-five nations, including Great Britain and France. Henderson was also able to announce to the Assembly British intentions to sign the General Act of Arbitration, Conciliation and Judicial Settlement once the Dominions had agreed. This would extend the arbitration procedures under the Optional Clause to non-justiciable disputes, eliminating the right of a nation to judge its own case. With the exception of South Africa, the Dominions were prevailed upon to sign, although with the same reservations as in the Optional Clause, and in May 1931 Great Britain acceded to the General Act. These measures were, in Henderson's view, an essential prelude to a general agreement on disarmament. Upon returning to London, he told the Commons that

> nations will be prepared to reduce and limit their national forces in proportion to the measure of their confidence in the constructive machinery of peace. If they are convinced that Governments have renounced war, not in name only, but in real intention, as shown by their willingness to support the League proposals for peace, they will be more ready to dispense with the machinery of war.[38]

He further hoped to persuade the League to amend its Covenant in order to close the supposed 'gap' that appeared to sanction private war under certain circumstances. Since the Kellogg–Briand Pact had outlawed war and the General Act had guaranteed that disputes would be resolved by arbitration, there should have been no impediment, but his proposals were never implemented. This setback notwithstanding, League members had, under British leadership, accepted formal restraints on their right to make war, but these would only be effective if national armaments were reduced. Henderson exhorted the Preparatory Commission to announce a date for the convening of the World Disarmament Conference, and in January 1931 the League Council settled on February 1932.

IV

What seems in some ways remarkable, given his earlier career, is that Henderson was much more successful on the international scene than within the Cabinet. MacDonald was at best indifferent to the League and largely left his Foreign Secretary to his own devices at Geneva. The Prime Minister did not deign to attend the 1930 session, enabling Henderson to assume an even more prominent position than in the previous year. Bored by the proceedings in Geneva, MacDonald never made the League the center of his foreign policy, preferring to rely on traditional methods of personal diplomacy to cement relations with the United States. He viewed it as a quarrelsome, ineffective forum, whereas Henderson embraced the League as the cornerstone of an embryonic world community. The 1930 London Naval Conference did not take place under its aegis, and it was here and in his private negotiations in Washington that MacDonald shone.

The latent conflict between Henderson and MacDonald flared up during the London Naval Conference, where the Prime Minister, acting under the influence of Sir Maurice Hankey, overruled the Foreign Secretary's brief on behalf of French demands for greater military security. Henderson saw little possibility of securing disarmament concessions from the French unless these were accompanied by a British commitment to international security. He also waged a campaign against the retention of battleships, which the Admiralty claimed were essential, although he was vindicated when the British agreed to a truce in the building of battleships until 1936. His role was more significant once the conference ended when he struggled valiantly to mediate between French and Italian demands. Since the Prime Minister ceased to concern himself with naval disarmament after the conference, the Foreign Secretary was left in charge of the negotiations. The Italians were willing to impose a moratorium on naval construction while discussions ensued, but the French refused to halt their building plans, despite Henderson's pleas to Briand at Geneva. The Foreign Secretary journeyed to Paris in February 1931 and reached a tentative agreement with the French at the cost of British abandonment of the two-power standard. In Rome Mussolini at first refused to grant an audience to Henderson, who had denounced him as a murderer at a meeting of the International. When the two men finally met, Henderson was able to prevail upon the Italian dictator to limit his building, and it looked as though his efforts would be capped with success. But the agreement then fell apart when the French decided that the conditions allowed them to lay down cruisers as early as 1935. This put an end to any hope of a definitive settlement among the three powers, and nothing could be done by Henderson or anyone else to salvage the situation. He conveyed his regrets to Beatrice Webb, blaming the collapse of the negotiations on 'the intolerable untrustworthiness and greed for armaments of the French Parliamentary Committee'.[39]

The failure to achieve a substantive naval agreement did little to improve relations between MacDonald and Henderson. The former blamed the latter for his willingness to yield to French demands and was suspicious of his undeniably cordial relations with Briand. MacDonald tended to view Henderson's Geneva initiatives either as gestures of self-promotion or capitulation to the French. Although Henderson was never immune to ambition, there is nothing to suggest that he deliberate tried to supplant his chief. As early as January 1930 he told Dalton that if MacDonald were to resign, there would be a close contest between Snowden and himself, but the leadership would not be worth having if he were chosen by a narrow majority. He observed that his best opportunity would have been in 1922 if MacDonald had not returned, adding that 'my chance of that is gone now'.[40] Yet Henderson's visibility only intensified MacDonald's premonition that Henderson was conspiring against him, possibly with Mosley. As the most popular of the leading ministers, the one whose successes had been indubitable, the Foreign Secretary might become a rallying point for backbench malcontents. 'Sunday papers make it plainer,' he recorded, 'that the plots are against me as well as Snowden & they are right. Henderson wants the job.'[41] In fact there is not a shred of evidence to implicate him in any conspiracy. At the end of the year rumors were rife that MacDonald might resign the Prime Ministership to become Viceroy of India, but Henderson told Dalton that

> he wouldn't take the succession if it were offered him. There would be a great rivalry between his supporters and Snowden's. And some would push for Clynes, who might come in as the compromise third. If the chance had come to him ten years ago, it would have been different or even a year ago before all the splits in the Party. But those shouting for JRM to go now would be shouting for him to go a year hence.[42]

Although immersed in Foreign Office business, Henderson kept his finger on the pulse of the party. He attended conferences faithfully and made sure that he never lost touch with backbench sentiment. He and Clynes served as Cabinet representatives on the Consultative Committee, the body which acted as liaison between the Cabinet and rank and file members. Yet he remained not only the indulgent uncle, willing to receive confidences, but the stern party disciplinarian. When the question of discipline arose at a meeting of the P.L.P. in March 1930, it was Henderson who defended the Government against its critics. He and his colleagues were doing their best in the difficult circumstances of economic crisis and their minority status, and their task was only rendered more difficult by attacks from dissidents on the left and M.P.s who castigated them in the press. He urged that criticism be confined to the privacy of P.L.P. meetings, but his efforts to curb dissent fell on deaf ears. Ministerial obligations forced him to turn over his secretarial duties to Jim Middleton, but he would not relinquish ultimate authority and continued to make daily visits to headquarters when he was in London.

Oswald Mosley's resignation as minister in May 1930 revealed once again Henderson's special role in the party, the single figure capable of reconciling factions and binding up wounds. At the special party meeting on 22 May Mosley proposed what was virtually a motion of censure on his own party. When Uncle Arthur rose to reply, he tried to soothe the irate Mosley, assuring him that his concerns over unemployment were widely shared and acknowledging his contribution in ventilating the issue. Since the party was united on the need to take more energetic steps, surely it was unnecessary to press his motion and divide the ranks of Government supporters. Had Mosley withdrawn his motion, the dispute might have been resolved amicably, but he resisted Henderson's appeal and was resoundingly defeated. It was Uncle Arthur who ably exploited the reservoir of party loyalty, rallying the rank and file in an expression of near unanimity. Shortly thereafter, Mosley urged Henderson himself to challenge MacDonald for the leadership. Henderson listened patiently, as he generally did to those who threatened his cherished unity, and later remarked perceptively, 'He will be going for me in six months.'[43] Other members, bristling at MacDonald's aloofness, raised the Henderson balloon, but Uncle Arthur swiftly punctured it. Despite his faults, the Prime Minister possessed qualities that no rival could match, and he would not openly countenance expressions of disloyalty.

The constant in-fighting wore him down, making the idea of escape appealing. By 1931 Henderson was sixty-eight, and his unremitting toil for the labour movement had taken its toll. He was tired of the acrimony and eager to devote himself more fully to the promotion of disarmament. He intimated to MacDonald in April 1931 that he would be receptive to the offer of a peerage, as long as he could retain the Foreign Secretaryship, but the Prime Minister, never valuing Henderson more highly than when on the verge of losing his services, protested that if both he and Snowden went to the Lords, there would be no one to carry the burdens in the Commons.[44] Henderson elaborated similar concerns to the more sympathetic Dalton later on the same day. Since he expected to be abroad for an extended period at the forthcoming Disarmament Conference, he would welcome being relieved of the strain of the House of Commons and his constituency responsibilities. Vansittart and others believed that it would facilitate his work as Foreign Secretary if he were to accept a peerage, removing himself from the rough and tumble of daily Parliamentary combat. He had informed MacDonald that he was not disposed to contest Burnley again, possibly sensing, with his acute political antennae, that his prospects in the next election were doubtful at best.[45]

When the League Council at last fixed a date for opening the Disarmament Conference, it was assumed that its choice as President would be announced simultaneously. Eduard Beneš, the Czech statesman favored by the French, was opposed by Germany, Italy, and Russia, and a decision was therefore postponed. In May the League Council, having witnessed Henderson's adroit leadership of its recent session, unanimously invited him to assume the position. It was a deserved, if not entirely surprising honor, an acknowledgement of the high esteem with which he was universally regarded in Geneva. This was perhaps all the more remarkable in that during his chairmanship he rapped the Poles over the knuckles for election-rigging in Upper Silesia and openly refuted French claims that the changing political climate in Germany constituted a threat to European security. That Henderson had no inkling that he would be selected is clear from his letter to MacDonald in early May pressing the claims of Lord Cecil to be the principal British representative to the Disarmament Conference. MacDonald, always jealous that Henderson might outshine him, had tried to preclude the Foreign Secretary from assuming responsibility himself and suggested the replacement of Cecil, an obvious surrogate for the Foreign Secretary, by the ostensibly neutral General Smuts. While Henderson objected to the nomination, he also conceded that he personally would not 'be able with all my other work to give the required attention, apart from the difficulty of remaining at Geneva indefinitely'.[46]

Reflected glory was never MacDonald's game. It seems probable that he harbored thoughts of being offered – and presumably refusing – the Presidency himself and was infuriated when Henderson, without any hesitation, accepted the proffered crown later that month. What made matters worse was that he had done so, at least in principle, without consulting his Cabinet colleagues. Dalton and Vansittart were deputed to rally ministerial support for a strong endorsement, but the Prime Minister demurred, raising questions about who would run the Foreign Office if the Foreign Secretary were tied up in Geneva. Henderson's 'absence will be considerable & that will put more work

Foreign secretary

on others', he grumbled. By presenting his colleagues with a *fait accompli,* the 'wily' Uncle Arthur had made it impossible for the Cabinet to consider the matter objectively or to veto it.[47] Initially they sent a grudging message to Geneva which simply left the decision to Henderson's discretion, but the Foreign Secretary demanded a more enthusiastic response, congratulating him on the honor accorded. It was only with difficulty that Vansittart was able to elicit a sufficiently cordial statement from the Prime Minister, so that Henderson could make his public acceptance in suitable terms. Dalton attributed Cabinet churlishness to

> jealousy, ignorance of the probable conditions of the Conference & a desire that Uncle should always be on tap in London to take on everybody else's burden & get them out of the holes which they dig for themselves . . .[48]

In a conciliatory letter which tried to mollify the seething MacDonald, Henderson noted that he had at first tried to discourage overtures, replying to emissaries that he was not willing to be considered as a candidate. Despite his awareness of the difficulties such an appointment would impose at home, he felt unable to refuse when the Council ignored his wishes and, determined to choose a British President, unanimously offered him the Presidency. The somewhat belated endorsement of his action by the Cabinet was 'all that I could have desired' and his subsequent acceptance of the offer 'produced a very good effect' by indicating that the British Government concurred with the decision of the Council. Somewhat disingenuously, he tried to dispel the Prime Minister's misgivings by belittling them, seemingly oblivious to the essentially personal basis of MacDonald's anger:

> I can understand the considerations which must have arisen in your mind when the problem came to you for decision, I surmise that they were not very different from those which occurred to me when I first heard of the proposal. Nevertheless, I am satisfied in

171

> view of all that I have seen of the question of the Presidency, that if the Council could once be brought to make up its mind on a candidate it would have been a mistake for us to make difficulties.
>
> For the rest, I am not oblivious to the inconvenience involved in many respects by my appointment; nevertheless, I think and hope that with a little organisation they can be surmounted.[49]

Such conciliatory words could not heal the breach between them, which was to widen irreparably during the next few months with dire consequences for the future of the Labour Government.

Ever since the end of the Eleventh Assembly of the League Henderson had made the promotion of disarmament his primary goal. Once an agreement was concluded, the League would be empowered to enforce the peace. In the meantime it was essential to appease Germany: by granting concessions, the sensible elements would be strengthened and French fears allayed. Unfortunately, this was not to be. The French proved recalcitrant on the arms control front, and even the respectable Brüning Government would not relent in its demand for equality of status. Though Henderson's firmer line early in 1931 may have forestalled the Germans from declaring a moratorium on reparations payments, it did little to moderate German claims. An invitation to Brüning and Dr Curtius, the Foreign Minister, to visit England testified to British goodwill, but in February Henderson felt compelled to issue a warning to Curtius through Rumbold:

> The German Government must be aware that the ideal of complete, or anything like complete, disarmament, is not at the present moment within the sphere of practical politics ... The degree of actual disarmament, i.e., of the reduction of existing armaments, which can be attained at the first Disarmament Conference, will depend in large measure on the psychological atmosphere which can be created during the year which will intervene before the conference meets.[50]

For the moment he was willing to ignore indications that the

Germans were beginning to rearm rather than to jeopardize the efforts towards general pacification. His attitude hardened, however, in March 1931 when the idea of an Austro-German Customs Union was floated in flagrant defiance of the peace settlement. To the British, the German initiative seemed the height of irresponsibility, and Henderson feared the psychological impact the proposal might have on disarmanent negotiations. His aim was to kill the plan without humiliating the Germans. They had to be persuaded to abandon the scheme, something that was only possible if the French did not insist on forcing Berlin and Vienna to cease negotiating at once. Henderson urged the Austrians and Germans not to take precipitate action but instead to place the issue on the agenda of the next League Council meeting. When the Germans at first refused to accede, he explained that he did not intend for the Council to decide the merits of the case but only to seek an advisory opinion from the Permanent Court. This the Germans could accept, with the face-saving proviso that they reserved to themselves freedom of action. A further confrontation was forestalled by the failure of the Creditanstalt Bank in Vienna, which left Austrian finance hostage to French loans and led eventually to the renunciation of the Customs Union even before the Permanent Court rendered its negative judgment. The project was doubtlessly doomed from the start, but it was Henderson's skilful maneuvering which avoided a breach between Briand and Curtius. He had resented Germany's impetuous challenge to French sensibilities, especially because Briand's own political position was shaky. Yet he also recognized that the German government needed a diplomatic success if it were to fend off the militarist elements at home. Although the Customs Union proposal dealt a blow to pacification, it was resolved without either side losing face, an outcome for which the British Foreign Secretary could take credit.

As the financial crisis worsened in the summer of 1931, Henderson's ability to manoeuvre was severely curtailed, and tensions between him and the Prime Minister flared up once again. In June President Hoover had floated the idea of a one-year moratorium on inter-governmental debts, a proposal abhorrent to the French so soon after the Young Plan was put into effect. The Germans were under increased financial pressure, and without the prospect of foreign loans, major banks were facing the threat of collapse. In return for British hospitality at Chequers, MacDonald and Henderson were invited to visit Berlin on 18 July. In order to dispel the looming panic the Foreign Secretary decided on a stopover in Paris on his way to Berlin in the hope of negotiating some kind of settlement between the French and Germans. He seems to have believed that the Berlin visit could be used to persuade the Germans to make political concessions to the French in return for financial assistance.

The day after his arrival in Paris, the Americans endorsed the idea of an emergency conference in London with the object of finding a solution to the immediate German crisis. The British Cabinet was willing to take part if the French proved cooperative, and Henderson was instructed to discover what the French would do to stave off a crisis. In the meantime the Prime Minister told him to postpone the projected Berlin trip. Henderson conveyed MacDonald's message to the French, who proved resistant to negotiations in London and insisted on German concessions as a precondition for aid. In discussions on 16 July with Briand, Pierre Laval, and the American Secretary of State, Henry Stimson, Henderson took the initiative and proposed that he and MacDonald go to Berlin to find out what the Germans were willing to concede. The French, hoping that the British were tilting in their favor, jumped at the idea. In the account the Foreign Secretary sent back to London, he seems to have deliberately misled MacDonald, implying that it was the French who insisted on the Berlin meeting, but concealing that French participation in a

Foreign secretary

London conference was contingent upon a prior German visit to Paris. He explained to MacDonald that there was no intention of shifting the conference from London to Paris, but recognized that the London gathering would be seriously compromised were any attempt made to prevent the prior meeting between German and French ministers. MacDonald still refused to sanction the two-stage discussions, insisting instead on the necessity of an immediate conference in London because of the mounting pressure on the Bank of England. Now Henderson, with a show of obedience, secured French agreement to come to London provided German ministers went to Paris.

Not to be outwitted by his superior, Henderson at first decided to go to Berlin himself in order to escort a German delegation willing to negotiate a provisional agreement to Paris prior to their London visit. He hoped that by so doing he could soften their revisionist demands and smooth the way for an agreement without MacDonald's interference. This plan was thwarted by the Prime Minister who determined that he and Henderson should both go to Berlin and bring the ministers directly back to London, thus by-passing Paris. By now Henderson, sensing possible gains, threw caution and ministerial subordination to the wind. Unlike the Prime Minister, he perceived the atmosphere in Paris and knew that if the British proved implacable, the French would either opt out of the conference entirely or dictate untenable conditions. In defiance of MacDonald's directives, he summoned the German Ambassador in Paris to the British Embassy, informed him that the Berlin visit was scrapped, and invited German ministers to come to Paris at once. MacDonald was predictably furious:

> Henderson's vanity has overcome him. He is working to keep everybody 'off the grass' except himself. Telephones to Paris & Berlin reveal that he has cancelled the Berlin visit without consulting me

> or the Germans. He has assured me that the Germans have agreed whilst our Ambassador at Berlin says direct from Brüning that they have not & German ambassador has called to tell me that Brüning is in consternation & that cancellation will do harm. Henderson says proposal to cancel was made by German ambassador in Paris. Brüning says it was made to ambassador by Henderson. The Government has been doing everything it could to prevent Germans going to Paris & having an ultimatum presented by French. Henderson has thwarted us.[51]

MacDonald, undaunted, continued to try to sabotage the Foreign Secretary's initiative, ordering Rumbold to warn Brüning that a Paris meeting would not accomplish anything useful and forbidding Henderson to pressure the Germans to make concessions in Paris. Snowden also made it clear that a collective loan, including British banks, had been ruled out. There is some evidence that Henderson had been deliberately kept in the dark over Bank of England machinations, ostensibly because Montagu Norman was afraid that he might leak secrets to Briand.[52]

By the time the German ministers arrived in Paris on 18 July, Henderson, now apprised of the financial decisions, refrained from telling the French that Great Britain would not contribute to a new loan in order to guarantee their participation in the London conference. When the Germans discovered that the French would only provide a loan if they agreed to a docile acceptance of the peace terms for another ten years, the Paris meeting broke up without result.

Henderson's attempt to mastermind a Franco–German agreement had proved abortive. He had fulfilled his pledge to deliver the Germans to Paris and the French to London, but the Germans remained unwilling to make the requisite concessions and the British declined to share in a collective loan. Had his policies succeeded, it would have been the crowning triumph of his Foreign Secretaryship, and he had reason to believe that his record as an honest broker might have enabled him to mediate between the French and the Germans. But he failed to realize that political exigencies made it inopportune for the German government to make political concessions however compelling the financial crisis. The French, masters of the financial situation, had leverage to wield against Germany that made them intransigent in the face of German revisionism. With the British economic outlook deteriorating, the Treasury and the Bank of England were unwilling either to bail the Germans out or attempt to apply pressure to the French.

If MacDonald was outraged by Henderson's rank insubordination, he had only himself to blame. For nearly two years the Prime Minister had sniped at the Foreign Secretary's lack of competence, hamstrung his initiatives, and maligned him in the presence of politicians and trade union leaders. Henderson's early threats of resignation temporarily curbed his chief's tendency to intervene but did little to restore mutual confidence. At the time of the London conference he remarked bitterly to Dalton that 'whenever he went abroad he had the same experience: lack of confidence, suspicion and jealousy on the part of his leader and colleagues'.[53] By July 1931 his own diplomatic agenda took precedence over his loyalty to the Prime Minister, and he was willing to disregard instructions from Downing Street with impunity.

Once the delegates convened in London MacDonald regained the upper hand, and the Foreign Secretary's options were circumscribed. Henderson, tacitly supporting the French, was unable to wring any further concessions from Germany. In a private meeting with Curtius he pleaded for a German moratorium on further revisionist claims but, with no financial inducement to offer in return, he realized that it was futile to press too hard. When he and MacDonald made their belated visit to Berlin on 27-28 July, the subject of further political concessions was assiduously avoided. Henderson, however, remained optimistic. Even though the German leaders refused to renounce their right to seek treaty revisions, in practice they imposed self-restraint and avoided exacerbating tensions. He reported to Briand his gratification at the friendly reception he and MacDonald had been accorded, adding that he was convinced that Brüning's position had been strengthened as a result of his visits to Paris and London. While it was evident that the emergency measures instituted in Germany had brought about 'grave embarrassment to the whole economic life', he had the impression that 'nothing but good had resulted from our recent collaboration, and that a new spirit of hopefulness had begun to operate'.[54]

Although his achievements never matched his expectations, it is difficult to deny Henderson a generally favorable verdict for his tenure as Foreign Secretary. Alone among Labour Governments, the 1929-31 ministry commanded the virtually unanimous support of rank-and-file supporters for its international policies. Henderson's resolute support for the League of Nations, disarmament, and compulsory arbitration even satisfied left-wing critics who found little else in the Government's record to applaud. He succeeded in overcoming resistance to such measures as the Optional Clause and the General Act, although his efforts to close the Covenant 'gap' faltered not only at home, but abroad. Furthermore, he did more than any other figure in the party before the late 1930s to foster the idea of collective security as a concomitant to disarmament, indeed, as the only way to make the League an effective agency for peace. To be sure, he carried the idea of collective security further than many in his party were yet willing to go, but in so doing he added a necessary dose of realism to the anti-war idealism prevalent on the left in the inter-war period. A genuine internationalist, he invested his faith in the League as an alternative to unfettered national sovereignty and as an extension of the concept implicit in the Socialist International.

His greatest achievements were in capturing the imagination of the British public as no other Foreign Secretary had done since the war and in convincing other nations that Great Britain was genuinely committed to European pacification. He was far more successful in expounding his principles in Geneva or at party conferences than he was in pressing his views within the Cabinet or in wringing concessions from foreign statesmen. His burden was made heavier by the Prime Minister's ill-concealed hostility and by the crumbling world economy, neither of which left him much room for maneuver. He could be resourceful in dealing with men like Briand and Curtius and certainly helped to improve relations between France and Germany, even though ultimately he failed to bridge the chasm of distrust left by Versailles. Unlike some of his predecessors, he convinced both countries of his good will. He was able to assert the justice of German grievances without denying French claims for security, and during his first year in office had some measurable success in reconciling the two before the political and economic climate worsened. Without rigidly defending the Versailles settlement, he indicated from the outset that he would not condone unilateral action by Germany to alter the *status quo.* As much as possible he sought to encourage changes by mutual agreement, most successfully in the evacuation of foreign troops from the Rhineland and the scaling down of reparations payments. After 1930 German politicians, facing resurgent nationalism at home, were less conciliatory. Henderson demonstrated considerable firmness over the projected Austro-German Customs Union and adopted a more pro-French stance in the summer of 1931 in pushing for German concessions than he had previously.

In his relations with MacDonald he continued almost to the end of his term to swallow his chief's contempt in order to avoid splitting the Cabinet and jeopardizing the fragile morale of the movement. The Prime Minister pulled back early in the term after Henderson vigorously objected to unwarranted interference. Equally, Henderson did not press his views in those areas, such as relations with the United States, where MacDonald operated autonomously. Nor did their attitudes on international questions invariably diverge. Less of a jingoist and imperial champion than his superior, the Foreign Secretary showed himself capable of defending British interests forcefully in relation to the Soviet Union and in the negotiations with Egypt. It was only in the final months of the Government that Henderson undertook an independent foreign policy in the hope of reconciling France and Germany. Relations between the two men became openly hostile, and an open breach was only narrowly averted. His reckless defiance of the Prime Minister, David Carlton has argued in his study of foreign policy during the second Labour Government, is unparalleled in British history. It was probably only Henderson's popularity among Labour back-benchers and the gravity of the financial crisis during the summer of 1931 that saved him from retribution.[55]

What Henderson demonstrated was an integrity and a tenacity in his efforts for peace. These were the personal qualities that gained him popularity at home and abroad. He was also more committed to building a genuine structure of international guarantees through the League of Nations than any other British statesman in this period. Yet if he was a constructive statesman, he was not always either a realistic or an effective one. He was sometimes a pawn in the hands of more devious politicians, both domestic and foreign, and lacked the mastery of the European scene that might have enabled him to counter contrary Cabinet opinion. His weakness as a debater, his occasional bursts of petulance, his lack of experience made his task more difficult. It became fashionable to dismiss his devotion to the League as deluded utopianism and to forget that he had coupled his plea for disarmament with a recognition that military sanctions were an inevitable corollary. More than a decade after Henderson left office, Selby, his Private Secretary, admiringly recalled his stint in office:

> I always think the chief trouble came after 1931 when one and all of our chief pilots in the field of foreign affairs were discarded, including dear old Uncle Arthur of whom I was very fond and for whom I entertained a deep regard. I thought him a very good Foreign Secretary.[56]

6 Tribune of peace

During the summer of 1931 Henderson, preoccupied with Franco-German relations, had no premonition that Britain too would be engulfed by the financial crisis. That the problems were intertwined became apparent immediately after the fruitless London conference on payments when there was a precipitate flight from the pound. Although the French, resisting concessions to a crumbling German financial structure, were to blame, it was London, as the repository of reserve funds from abroad, that bore the brunt of the bankers' retribution. Foreign holders of sterling, seeing their assets frozen in Germany, sought to recoup their losses by withdrawing assets from London, creating a liquidity crisis and a drop in international confidence in British solvency. At the end of July the publication of the May Committee's report on the economy, predicting budgetary deficits and recommending drastic cuts, including reductions in expenditure on the unemployed, compounded the panic. While John Maynard Keynes advocated abandoning the gold standard and devaluing the currency, Snowden and MacDonald were predisposed to maintain orthodox deflationary policies, which had generally been supported within Labour circles.

There is no evidence that Henderson either anticipated the problems or had alternative solutions up his sleeve. Like most of his colleagues, he had little understanding of economics and regarded high finance 'as a dark and hieratic mystery, impenetrable to the ordinary uninstructed mind'.[1] He never questioned expert Treasury advice, except where it conflicted with his own

Foreign Office agenda, as it had during the 1929 Hague Conference. While frequently objecting to the Chancellor's narrow nationalism, he was diffident about challenging the basic tenets of the Treasury or the Bank of England. Fortunately for him, his views were neither solicited nor offered, a considerable advantage because, as the only front rank minister with no direct responsibility for economic policy, he could not be blamed for its failures. Since he got on badly with both Snowden and MacDonald and was distrusted by Montagu Norman, it was unlikely that he would have been privy to any confidential discussions before the end of July. To be sure, he was the catalyst in regularizing the intermittent political dialogue with Liberal leaders, in which economic differences must have surfaced, but this had been chiefly geared to electoral reform. In return for Parliamentary cooperation Labour was prepared to include the alternative vote in a projected reform bill. Nor was he initially receptive to appeals from Liberal converts, like Keynes and Hubert Henderson, for a revenue tariff. Both Snowden and Willie Graham at the Board of Trade were strict free traders, and Henderson shared their preconception, a part of the common heritage of the British left. In September 1930 he had strongly supported Graham's push for ratification of a League convention committing signatories not to increase tariffs, arguing that the Government had no intention of changing Labour's traditional free trade policy. The Prime Minister allowed the free traders in the Cabinet the upper hand instead of providing a lead, although he was certainly less unalterably opposed to protection than Snowden. Suspecting a conspiracy by Henderson's allies to supplant him as Leader, he wanted to avoid giving opponents a pretext by discarding so central a pillar of Labour orthodoxy.

MacDonald's immediate response to the publication of the May Report was to appoint an economic sub-committee, consisting of himself, Snowden, Henderson, Thomas, and Graham, which would review its conclusions and recommend proposals to the entire Cabinet. So impervious was he to its potential impact that the sub-committee was not scheduled to meet for nearly a month. Parliament was in recess, and there seemed at first no reason to recall it prematurely. Henderson, scheduled to return to Geneva at the end of August, was recuperating from the rigors of his 'shuttle diplomacy' at the country home of Lord Sankey, the Lord Chancellor. Published without official comment or explication of policy, the May Report sent financial circles into a tailspin that the Treasury was unable to avert. MacDonald hastened to London from Lossiemouth at the beginning of August to consult with Snowden and British bankers about action to stem the loss of confidence. Henderson and the other members of the sub-committee were summoned back to London to meet on 12 August, two weeks ahead of the scheduled date. The Treasury had already circulated papers to sub-committee members advocating 20 per cent cuts in unemployment benefit as a way to meet the expenditure targets, a suggestion that Henderson regarded as skeptically as he did the report's dire deficit forecast. Like most of his colleagues, he had trusted to Snowden to rectify the situation and could not comprehend that the policies he had loyally backed had misfired. Yet it was clear when the sub-committee convened on 12 August that the crisis was genuine. There was an accelerating flight from sterling that additional credits from the French and the Americans failed to halt.

The sub-committee met on four days between 12 and 18 August, when proposals were brought before the Cabinet. From the start there were sharp disagreements over the Treasury solutions. All of the participants came to accept the reality of the crisis and the urgency of a package of economies. MacDonald and Snowden found the remedy in reducing expenditure, while Henderson preferred to begin by looking at methods of raising revenue. Only by considering new taxation first would it be possible to ensure that economies were as small as possible. There was general agreement on the need to balance the budget but not over the notion that the unemployment insurance fund must be kept in the black as well. Henderson refused to embrace specific recommendations for cuts, indeed did not believe that anything more than general suggestions should be forwarded to the Cabinet for discussion. His instincts told him that the proposals were faulty and unfair, but he was too ignorant of finance to devise an alternate strategy. While he and Graham intimated their dislike of projected benefit cuts, they could do nothing at that stage but reserve their options on the economic package until there was a full airing of Cabinet opinion. MacDonald, keen to secure unanimity within the sub-committee, viewed such vacillation not merely as disloyal, but as cynically opportunistic. Graham, Henderson's sub-committee ally, insisted that they were only engaged in preliminary discussions; they could agree on a report to the Cabinet without specifying the extent of the economies to be made.

It was Henderson, concerned as usual with the maintenance of labour unity, who took the initiative in demanding discussions between the sub-committee and representative bodies. If the Government felt impelled to solicit the views of leaders of the Opposition parties and the banking community, they were no less obliged to confer with their own supporters. Thus a meeting of the N.E.C., the P.L.P. Consultative Committee, and the General Council was called for 20 August in order to marshal support for emergency decisions against the wishes of Snowden, who denied the General Council's right to be consulted on Government policies. Although MacDonald was later to accuse Henderson of changing his tune in deference to trade union sentiment, his dismay was evident almost at the outset, as MacDonald's own diary entry for 17 August reveals:

> When we began Henderson at once showed his hand. He ... objected to sacrifices being on one side – his reason alleged being that we were to discuss savings first. I said first or last we should have to discuss them. Then he launched out into eloquence on the inadequacy of the unempd. grants & what we had all said for 30 yrs. We pointed out that this was a special crisis & we hoped temporary: that if the income was not there, there could not be the expenditure. He could not reply but lapsed into sulky silence . . .[2]

The sub-committee report, presented to the Cabinet on 19 August, reflected the majority views in suggesting cuts in unemployment insurance expenditure. In deference to the dissidents, however, the amount was scaled down from the initial May proposals and the rate of benefit was to remain unaltered. Henderson was probably one of the Cabinet members whose support for projected economies was contingent on the implementation of additional direct taxation.[3] Sankey's account of the Cabinet meeting indicates an apparently unanimous sub-committee recommendation except over the issue of a revenue tariff, with Snowden as the free trade holdout.[4] Henderson said that if faced by a choice of a revenue tariff or cuts in unemployment relief, he would prefer a tariff as long as the revenue could be diverted to benefit the needy. He saw it as a temporary expedient to balance the budget and prevent devastating cuts in social services. What is significant, in view of subsequent recriminations, is that he neither voted against the report, nor insisted that his reservations be recorded, although he regarded it as provisional and made it clear that he was by no means wedded to its conclusions. While his willingness to allow it to go forward to the Cabinet may have been misleading, it was certainly not deceptive. He was not secure enough in the face of expert Treasury advice to block the proposals in the sub-committee, but he never indicated that he had signed on for the duration as MacDonald expected him to do.

Whatever the sense of common purpose binding the members of the sub-committee, Henderson envisaged his own role as that of mediator between the Cabinet and the movement at large, as he indicated to the 20 August gathering:

> You know who my colleagues are. You can imagine that I have had a tremendously hard fight. Mr. Asquith once said of me that I was always getting into situations in which I felt a double loyalty. I have been experiencing that again this week, loyalty to my Cabinet colleagues & loyalty to the movement outside.

After the meeting he remarked that he had never endured so tense a period as the previous five days, but he recognized that 'our position is extremely grave'. He had accepted a cut of £1,000 a year in his own salary and, more reluctantly, reductions in social services but had waged an apparently successful battle to protect the unemployed. The price had been apostasy to his free trade convictions, compelling him to endorse a revenue tariff of 10 per cent, even on food, as a desperate alternative to a cut in unemployment benefit.[5]

If Henderson mollified the N.E.C. with assurances that the rates of benefit would not be curtailed, he was left in no doubt about the General Council's stringent opposition to any tampering with unemployment benefits. As an alternative, it had suggested a tax on securities and a suspension of the Sinking Fund. He was able to persuade the N.E.C. to leave tactics to its members within the Cabinet, including himself, for preventing any cuts in wages or relief for the unemployed. He certainly came away from the meetings with a keen awareness that organized labour not only repudiated any suggestion that the unemployed should bear the burden of the economies, but that it would regard reductions in social services as a betrayal of trust by a Labour Government whatever the financial exigencies. The resounding negative response of the General Council cut through the confusion and contradictory views of the P.L.P., stiffening the resistance of Cabinet waverers, like Henderson. Had the T.U.C. been won over to the Treasury line, he would no doubt have adopted the same viewpoint. He sensed that MacDonald was making a mistake, but the discovery that trade union leaders were vociferous in their opposition had more effect on Henderson than on other party leaders. As an old trade unionist, albeit one who had moved some distance from his roots, he saw union support as an essential component in Labour's mandate, not as a convenience.

What needs to be clarified at this stage is whether Henderson was guilty, as subsequently alleged, of duplicity, sending contradictory signals to Cabinet colleagues and trade union delegates. According to Sankey, Henderson, confronted by a potential split in the party, 'began to change his position'.[6] By 21 August, the day after he met the N.E.C. and the General Council, he was ready to denounce the proposed cuts openly, claiming that it would only be legitimate to introduce a package of economies in Parliament if the prior agreement of the movement were secured. The appearance of reneging on a previous agreement infuriated the Prime Minister, who realized that without Henderson he would have a difficult time in carrying the Cabinet. After the 21 August meeting he recorded in his diary:

> Henderson once more told us what he had proposed days ago & how everything had been initiated by him – except the things opposed by the people. He surrendered. He proposed to balance the Budget with insignificant economies, keeping the unemployed assistance what it is now . . . suspending sinking funds . . . & putting on a revenue tariff . . . Henderson never showed his vanity & ignorance more painfully.[7]

Yet there was no real inconsistency in his position. Tom Johnston, a first-hand witness, reported that he, Arthur Greenwood, and George Lansbury had been against the cuts from the start. Uncle Arthur had deliberately held back but had never subscribed to any of the proposals, always reiterating that he must see the complete picture before making up his mind.[8] That did not, of course, mean that he had an open mind about the issues, but only that he would not commit himself until he had considered the views of Cabinet colleagues and the movement at large. From the outset he had indicated his opposition to balancing the budget with economies in the public sector rather than by increasing revenues and had belatedly espoused a revenue tariff as an alternative to a reduction in benefits. Until he realized the depth of T.U.C. resistance, he still hoped to devise a compromise, moderating the scale of the cuts while preserving the existing rate. But after the meetings on 20 August he realized that to consent to the Prime Minister's strategy would provoke profound dissension in the movement. Sankey suggested that Henderson had earlier concurred that there must be equality of sacrifice, including a cut in the dole, but that he retreated because of T.U.C. objections, 'partly influenced no doubt by his quarrel with the P.M. & his desire for the leadership'.[9] Yet it is abundantly clear, Sankey's statement notwithstanding, that Henderson did not believe that the proposals, hitting hardest at the victims of the slump, involved equality of sacrifice. The possibility of a clash between the unions and the party was probably the decisive consideration for him. He was, as David Marquand has observed, 'a man of the majority',[10] and he could no more defy the consensus of the movement in 1931 than in 1914, when he collaborated with the war effort. The contingencies of government never counted for as much in his thinking as the goal of maintaining unity. Once the T.U.C. had avowed its opposition to cuts, the need to save the movement took precedence over the need to balance the budget. He not only retracted his grudging support for MacDonald's economy plans, but assumed a leadership role in fighting them. For the Prime Minister to persist in a plan calculated to split the movement seemed to Henderson the height of arrogance, not a courageous resolve to save the country from bankruptcy.

If Henderson might have gone along reluctantly with the limited package of £56 million that the Cabinet accepted on 19 August, whatever doubts remained were dispelled once MacDonald and Snowden announced three days later that Opposition parties would withhold the support international bankers were demanding without additional economies of £25-30 million. This was more than Henderson could stomach, and he now called for the Cabinet to resign. He blamed the Prime Minister for continuing negotiations instead of standing up to the Opposition, stating just what the Government was prepared to do, and then resigning if that proved insufficient. The Cabinet met twice on 22 August and learned that the American banks refused to furnish assistance unless the Government reduced expenditure on the dole, an explicit attempt by foreign bankers to dictate the economies imposed. At that meeting seven ministers, led by Henderson, Graham, and A. V. Alexander, asserted their implacable opposition to the cuts.[11] The next day, after the Prime Minister's final appeal to the Cabinet, the revised package of economies was carried by a narrow majority of eleven to nine. If he had not realized it before, it was now evident to MacDonald that Henderson and a number of his supporters were prepared to resign rather than submit to a 10 per cent cut in unemployment benefit. It confirmed his low estimation of those who 'chose the easy path of irresponsibility'.[12] He then went off to Buckingham Palace to inform the King that several of his most influential colleagues, notably Henderson and Graham, refused to consent to the proposed economies. Should they resign, the Government would have to be reconstructed. The King asked whether MacDonald would advise him to summon Henderson, to which he replied in the negative, urging the King instead to send for the leaders of the other two parties.[13]

On the next day the National Government was formed, with MacDonald as Prime Minister and comprised mainly of Tory and Liberal ministers. Of the former Labour Cabinet, only Snowden, Thomas, and Sankey retained ministerial office. MacDonald's ex-colleagues were stupefied by his announcement. Despite their disenchantment with his leadership and despite speculation in the inner circle that he aimed at a coalition government to resolve national problems, few of them imagined that he would be able to pull it off. The most likely scenario would seem to have been a Conservative Government with Liberal support, not an amalgam of Opposition politicians headed by their own Labour leader. Even Snowden had assumed that, like the rest of his colleagues, his days in office were numbered. Mrs Hamilton reported that Henderson left the final Cabinet meeting 'too shattered to speak'.[14] It was not so much that MacDonald had survived as Prime Minister, but that he had readily jettisoned faithful associates to preside over a ministry composed of lifelong political opponents. If their own personal relations had reached the breaking point, Henderson had still presumed that an underlying mutual loyalty to the party they had both nurtured over the past quarter of a century would have ensured unity in this crisis. In the days before the Cabinet's resignation Henderson had gravitated towards dissidents, like Lansbury, but only as a way of concerting resistance to the projected cuts, not as a way of disavowing MacDonald's leadership. After the Prime Minister's announcement on 24 August Henderson, according to one witness,

> seemed shrivelled and bowed and his usually ruddy face was yellow. Disloyalty was a thing he could not understand. He had given his

most unswerving support to the handsome, eloquent leader who had helped him build up the movement; he had never allowed himself to be influenced by the fact that he had not in his heart liked MacDonald and had more than once received discourtesy from him. Now that man had deserted the people in its greatest misery. He could not understand, though he would try to forgive; he looked like a man who had been given a mortal wound.[15]

II

In retrospect it is clear that MacDonald's motives were less sordid than they appeared at first to shocked Labour supporters. He had sacrificed party solidarity to his conception of a higher national purpose, not to his own ambition. It may have been futile to try to salvage the gold standard, and it was certainly heartless to do so by inflicting further penalties on the unemployed, but the economic constraints imposed by the Treasury and international bankers left him few options. It would have been better for his reputation had he resigned office, but his sense of duty and messianic self-image would not allow him to refuse the King's commission to form a National Government. That he regarded it as a temporary expedient was clear from a letter to Lord Ponsonby,

> It may take a little time for people to understand what are the issues & the alternatives to what I have done with some colleagues, but the events of today have shown that, but for the step which has been taken, before this week had well begun we should have been in the midst of a crushing calamity . . . Having failed to meet the immediate situation we should have been swept away in ignominy before the end of the week by popular clamour, so that it can be proved later on, whatever offence we have caused at this moment, we have created the conditions under which the Party can continue as an opposition & allow the public, saved from panic, to consider a return to our general policy when things have become more normal.[16]

Neither MacDonald nor his ex-Labour colleagues regarded their separation from the Labour Party as permanent. The new Government was a team of individuals, rather than a conventional coalition. It was, MacDonald told Henderson, a combination for a specific purpose and limited period, after which presumably there would be a reversion to customary party arrangements.

In contrast to the trade union leaders who, Dalton reported, were 'full of fight', Henderson had no desire to make the split definitive. Labelling the crisis as merely an interlude in the party's history, he felt it was crucial to avoid isolating MacDonald or forcing him out of the party. He refrained from gratuitous personal attacks and, despite his bitterness, continued to acknowledge MacDonald's long service to the movement. Coupled with his age and fatigue, this sense of a temporary wound that needed to be healed made him reluctant to stand for the leadership once the executives of the party and the T.U.C. decided that Labour should oppose the National Government. Furthermore, with the prospect of an imminent general election in a mood of national anxiety, he was acutely aware of hazards facing the party organization in the country, a serious distraction from the duties of a leader. But the pressures on him were irresistible. In its moment of crisis the party turned to him to assume the leadership. 'There is a feeling in all our minds,' Dalton recorded, 'that Uncle is now the only possible leader.'[17]

MacDonald and others who suspected Henderson of conspiring for power would doubtlessly have dismissed his hesitation as hypocritical, but there is every reason to believe that he tried to resist the blandishments. Discouraged about prospects at the next election, he felt there was little he could do to boost the morale of the rank and file. Only a few months before, he had solicited the offer of a peerage, indicating his unwillingness to contest Burnley again, but the Prime Minister had refused to accede. Ironically, on 25 August he dispatched his Private Secretary to the Foreign Office with the offer of a peerage in the resignation Honours List, but this time it was Henderson who declined politely on the grounds that he could do more for the party by remaining where he was. This cynical attempt to deny his rival the succession backfired; Henderson countered with the reply that he was parting from the Prime Minister without anger or resentment and that the party would be ready to receive him back again as they had after the war when he (Henderson) had kept it together.[18] While he might have welcomed a draft in 1919 or in the early 1920s, he had lost all ambition for the leadership and refused to displace Clynes who, as the Deputy Leader, took precedence. Gradually he began to yield to pressure and at a meeting of ex-Cabinet ministers on 27 August agreed to accept the leadership.

The next day a meeting of the P.L.P. was held at Transport House, with members of the General Council invited to be present as a mark of unity. Neither MacDonald, nor Snowden attended, but Sankey turned up to assert that while MacDonald's act had saved the country, 'Uncle had saved the soul of the Labour Party'. Malcolm MacDonald, acting as surrogate for his father, reproached Henderson for going back on his undertakings to support the sub-committee report, which he immediately denied. Rebutting further charges that he had tried to supplant MacDonald, he reminded Labour M.P.s, many of whom continued to harbor warm feelings towards their errant chief, that it was he who had moved before the war that MacDonald should continue as permanent Leader, ending the pre-war pattern of rotating Chairman.[19] After angry recriminations were traded, Clynes moved that Henderson be elected Leader. There were no other nominees, and he was chosen with only five left-wing dissentients.

What should have been a triumphant moment was filled with misgivings. When he rose to make his first speech as Leader of the Opposition after Parliament reassembled on 8 September, he declared that he found himself 'in a position which I never sought'. He recalled that he and MacDonald had occupied the most important offices in the Labour movement. For thirty-one years they had been the only two Secretaries the party had known, and, despite the rancor that had arisen in recent weeks, he felt impelled to note that 'whether the withdrawal of our colleagues be long or short, whether it is temporary or permanent, it is a direct loss to the Labour movement'. Yet not all of his remarks were quite so magnanimous. He taunted the Prime Minister for failing to justify his policy to his supporters. Throughout the August crisis, refusing to recall Parliament or to attend a P.L.P. meeting, he had never once looked into 'the faces of those who made it possible for him to be Prime Minister'.[20] Several weeks later, visiting the Webbs in the country, Henderson seemed 'depressed and tired, sad at leaving the Foreign Office and not enjoying the worry and toil of leading the Labour Party'. He told them that before the crisis occurred he had hoped to continue as Foreign Secretary, while devoting himself to the party machine. He had never, he claimed, wanted to be Leader, but 'only the manager of the Party'.[21] Whether it was honest to assert that he had never sought the leadership is questionable; what was certain was that by August 1931 it had lost its savour.

The advent of a National Government did little to restore international confidence, and on 20 September Great Britain suspended the gold standard, which the Government had been formed to preserve. In the meantime both sides traded recriminations, with Labour denouncing MacDonald for treachery, and the new ministers, abetted by the right-wing press, blaming the financial extravagance which had unbalanced the budget on Labour ministers. That these problems stemmed from the policies undertaken by the Prime Minister and the Chancellor seemed to be forgotten in the search for scapegoats. Whatever concessions had been discussed by the sub-committee on a provisional basis before 23 August were trotted out as firm commitments made and then betrayed by craven politicians shirking their responsibilities. On 24 August MacDonald indicated that the National Government, established to resolve a crisis, was an emergency measure and that when an election came, it would be contested as usual by parties. Within a few weeks, however, it became evident that he was determined to fight the election as head of the National Government, defending his record as the savior of the country. The ending of convertibility immediately fanned the flames of election speculation, with newspapers like *The Times* extolling the National Government for having saved the country from uncontrollable inflation and calling for the perpetuation of its rule. 'The only way,' *The Times* declared, 'to counteract the evil wrought by the ever-present threat of a General Election is to have a General Election.'[22]

Henderson did not welcome the prospect of an appeal to the voters, especially one in which Labour might be targeted as the culprit in the financial collapse. He doubted whether the party could wage an effective campaign merely on the basis of resistance to cuts in unemployment benefits. During the weeks after the formation of the National Government he tried to ensure that the breach did not become irretrievable. Thus he came to Downing Street on 20 September to assure MacDonald that 'he was willing to cooperate in getting business through'.[23] The next day he made a conciliatory speech in the Commons, urging his supporters not to oppose the gold standard legislation. This appears to have enraged many Labour M.P.s, 112 of whom defied his instructions, and he was vigorously attacked by those seeking a more combative posture. His patience sorely tried, Henderson demanded a special meeting to determine whether he should continue as Leader. At a meeting of the P.L.P. executive he offered to resign but was prevailed upon to remain. Several of those close to MacDonald hinted that Henderson, plagued by dissension on the back benches, would be willing to make terms with the National Government in order to avoid an election. If MacDonald offered some concessions to the unemployed, he might consent to lend limited and presumably unofficial support to the Government.[24] Such speculation cannot be dismissed as groundless, but the evidence for possible collaboration is inconclusive. MacDonald had not formally left the Labour Party and, no more than Henderson, did he wish to make the split complete. Sir Clive Wigram told the King on 28 September that the Prime Minister 'does not like the idea of smashing up the Labour Party at the head of a Conservative association'. He still hoped that a judicious policy would attract a Labour following, making his Government a truly national combination.[25]

On the same day the N.E.C. voted that all members and supporters of the National Government should immediately cease to belong to the party. This action, not officially announced until 1 October, effectively expelled MacDonald, a dramatic gesture of contempt for the once beloved Leader. Henderson cast the single vote on the Executive in opposition to the motion. Whether or not the news of his expulsion contributed to MacDonald's decision to call an election, it certainly shattered whatever hope either of the leaders had that their differences might be patched up. After a week of consultation with his coalition partners, a formula was devised for an appeal to the country, and on 7 October Parliament was dissolved.

The Government's election manifesto deferred to Tory protectionists by raising the possibility of tariffs as part of the 'doctor's mandate' that it was seeking to heal the nation's woes. While MacDonald, appealing for national unity, eschewed personal attacks on his old associates, the ensuing campaign was sparked by Snowden's vicious condemnation of Labour's policy, virtually identical to the one he endorsed in 1929, as 'Bolshevism run mad'. Former Labour ministers were accused of having shirked their duty in the hour of national emergency, and MacDonald and National candidates recklessly encouraged fears that the value of the pound would plummet if Labour won. It was not MacDonald who had betrayed the trust vested in him, but Labour which could not be trusted to govern responsibly and must be disavowed by sensible voters. The scurrilous attacks recalled the Coupon Election of 1918, with the National Government claiming credit for having rescued the country from the impending disaster to which Labour had brought it. That these charges were made not by traditional enemies like Lloyd George or Winston Churchill, but by their former Leader, imparted a special acrimony to the campaign.

Henderson was certainly not sanguine about the outcome of the election. Labour was on the defensive, embittered, demoralized, and organizationally unprepared. Given the promise of continued cooperation with the Liberals, there had been little sign of an imminent election until the August crisis, and no one could have foreseen the circumstances in which it was to be waged. Although there was no formal alliance concluded with Liberals, Henderson did visit Lloyd George at Churt on 10 October, and a decision was reached that Labour would not contest seats in which anti-Government Liberals provided the main opposition to the Tory candidate. He told the annual conference at Scarborough, in session when the dissolution was announced, that the election had been called with the principal goal of inflicting a crushing defeat on the Labour Party. His closest advisors were now drawn from younger socialist intellectuals, like Harold Laski and Colin Clark, and from ex-ministerial colleagues, like Herbert Morrison, Johnston, and Dalton. Tired and discouraged though he was, he recognized the need for the injection of new ideas, hoping to rebuild an invigorated party out of the shattered pieces that he had inherited.

Tribune of peace

As usual, Uncle Arthur travelled all over the country speaking on behalf of candidates, oblivious to the fact that such efforts were probably futile. His opponent in Burnley, standing as a National Liberal, was Gordon Campbell, an Admiral notably lacking in political experience. Under most circumstances, Henderson could have overcome the challenge without difficulty, but he could not buck the patriotic tide in 1931. In his own adoption speech he was openly critical of MacDonald for 'permitting himself to be used by his life-long opponents to smite his life-long political friends'. He charged the Prime Minister with having planned a National Government for months, lending credence to the popular notion of a MacDonaldite plot. Although insisting that he was doing all he could to avoid recrimination, he blasted his opponents for their 'orgy of misrepresentation'. In reponse to charges against himself, he hit back forcefully:

> We are accused of deserting the sinking ship and leaving MacDonald and Snowden standing, like Casabianca, on the burning deck . . . We did not desert the captain. It was the captain who brought in the pirates and deliberately scuttled the ship. We were prepared to balance the budget without unemployment cuts.

But his heart was not really in the fight, and he was unwilling to inject the kind of venom into his speeches that Snowden, soon to be elevated to the Lords, seemed to relish. He was no longer up to the gruelling pace of nightly meetings and found it difficult to reconcile himself to MacDonald's desertion of the party. 'I was ready to play second fiddle all my life,' he was heard to say during the 1931 campaign, 'but he wouldn't have it.' Several days before polling he contracted severe influenza, from which he was not to recover for many weeks. As he told Sankey, 'At my time of life I suppose I cannot expect to be able to career all over the country and address huge meetings and demonstrations without feeling the effects.'[26] He was obliged to cancel a dozen election meetings and a final rally at the Mechanics' Institution and was absent when the results of the election were announced. His majority of 8,000 was transformed into a defeat by 8,200 votes. Although Campbell's vote somewhat exceeded the 1929 combined Conservative and Liberal poll, Henderson's vote remained relatively steady, declining by just over 1,000. It was scant consolation amid Labour's overwhelming defeat, which denuded its front bench of its most prominent figures. The number of Labour M.P.s fell from 289 in 1929 to 46 in 1931, and its poll fell by two million. It was not the defeat but its staggering dimensions that astounded Henderson. After two years in power and nearly fifteen of constituency organization Labour was left with virtually the same number of M.P.s that it had in 1918.

Henderson returned to London on 29 October, far from well, to begin the task of reconstruction. When the P.L.P. met five days later, Lansbury, who had retained his seat, was elected as Chairman of the Parliamentary Party, while Henderson was invited to continue as Leader. It was generally assumed that he would soon be returned at a by-election and that Lansbury was merely a temporary substitute. While still debilitated from the flu, Henderson suffered a recurrence of an old internal ailment which caused acute pain. His illness was diagnosed and treated without surgery, but the doctors seem to have been unable to cure him. He spent several weeks recuperating at Brighton and at a sanatorium at Tring and then accepted an invitation to spend part of December in Cannes before returning to the nursing home after Christmas. Whether he was in fact suffering from a kidney problem or from some malignancy is unclear from the sources, but the problem flared up again, and he was never fully to regain his health. His doctors considered it impossible for him to undertake the onerous burdens of chairing the Disarmament Conference, but, against their advice, he proceeded to Geneva, having arranged to place himself in the care of a Swiss specialist. His persistence was as much a testimony to his stubborn tenacity as it was to his commitment to the cause of disarmament, a cause in which he willingly sacrificed himself. It was sheer willpower that kept him going, despite the physical discomfort and mental anguish, but his diligence never faltered. Although he looked ghastly, he refused to complain, doggedly attending every plenary session and meeting of the General Commission and Bureau. Sir Eric Drummond, of the League Secretariat, later confessed that there were moments 'when we thought he might die in the chair'.[27] Mrs Henderson was supplied with a seat near him in case he suddenly collapsed. Several months later members of the British delegation in Geneva told MacDonald that Henderson was 'a very sick man' and 'not equal to his task'.[28] In fact, his health did revive somewhat, and more sympathetic observers believed that, although frail, he lost none of his mental acuity. There was little even a more robust President could have done to bring the conference to a successful conclusion, but the physical punishment inflicted by the gruelling sessions and the constant travel doubtlessly shortened his life.

III

His Presidency of the ill-fated Disarmament Conference has been aptly described as a 'tragic epilogue' to his career.[29] At the time he was selected he had the enormous prestige of being the British Foreign Secretary and a reputation as an impartial and passionate advocate of peace. Had the Conference taken place early in 1931, he might have translated that prestige into effective power. Alternatively, had he resigned from the Cabinet to devote himself fully to the Conference as President-elect, it would have been possible for him to explore a framework for agreement in preliminary discussions in European capitals. It would certainly have been difficult to combine both positions, not merely because of the quantity of work involved, but also because the role of President needed to be separated from the policies of any particular delegation. By the time the sessions commenced in Geneva in February 1932 Henderson was only a private citizen, his loss of office considerably diminishing his influence with foreign statesmen.

Even before he went to Geneva, he was subjected to politically-motivated abuse in the British press. In order to discredit him, it was suggested that, as leader of a defeated socialist party, he no longer merited the high office and, more appropriately, that he was not sufficiently fit to assume its burdens. These attacks ignored the fact that Henderson had been chosen in his own right, as an acknowledgement of his stature in the League, rather than because of his ministerial role. He was even more ludicrously criticized in the French Chamber of Deputies on the grounds that he was known to be partial towards disarmament. Moreover, the British delegation under Sir John Simon, his successor at the Foreign Office, brought the political animosities of Westminster with them to Geneva, deliberately maligning his credibility. British representatives excluded him from conversations with foreign statesmen and rarely bothered to inform him of the initiatives being pursued. It was MacDonald's revenge for what he regarded as Henderson's opportunistic grasping of the Presidency. When, for example, the Prime Minister returned to Geneva for the resumed meetings in March 1933 he went through the motions of asking the Foreign Office to arrange a meeting with Henderson, but added that 'any good work I can do will have to be done directly with the parties whose disagreements strike at the root of disarmament difficulties'.[30] Only after registering a strong protest was he able to extract a pledge from Simon and Thomas to refrain from diplomatic negotiations behind his back. Treated contemptuously by his fellow countrymen, Henderson was hard pressed to hold sway over other nations, and his authority became little more than nominal. Even if there had not been blatant antagonism between the President and the powerful British delegation, the need to maintain impartiality would seriously have compromised his ability to influence events. Moreover, the leaders with whom he had once collaborated so effectively – Briand, Stresemann, Curtius – were gone, replaced by intransigent men, like André Tardieu and Louis Barthou, determined to impose a literal interpretation of Versailles and obstructing any limitations on armaments unless security commitments were bolstered.

His presidential address on 2 February 1932 struck a note of compelling urgency. No previous conference had represented as many nations, and their obligation to satisfy the universal aspirations for peace could no longer be delayed. The swollen military arsenals had only bred insecurity, with tensions continuing to mount because of the grave situation in the Far East. The history of the previous generation had proven incontestably the fallacy of the notion that a nation's safety was in proportion to the strength of its armaments. Refusing to contemplate even the possibility of failure, he proclaimed to the assembled delegates:

> The world wants disarmament. The world needs disarmament. We have it in our power to help fashion the pattern of future history. Behind all the technical complexities regarding man power, gun power, tonnage, categories, and the like, is the well-being of mankind, the future of our developing civilisation ... If we succeed, we shall have made a decisive contribution to strengthening the bulwarks we have been patiently building against war.[31]

No one could fault his own courage, his indomitable resolve to allow nothing to deflect the Conference from its objectives. Yet if his patience and single-mindedness prevented disruption, it was not sufficient to galvanize the unwilling powers into an accord. He received frequent petitions and testimonials from all over the world, especially from peace organizations, but the failure of the Conference testified to the impotence of public opinion in dictating policies to statesmen.

When the delegates got down to business, Tardieu, heading the French delegation, presented a far-reaching plan for eliminating dangerous weapons, including battleships and bombers, and establishing a standing international police force. Audacious though it sounded, it made no provision for dealing with the German question and envisaged new security commitments that neither the British Commonwealth, nor the United States would have been prepared to undertake. While the British and Americans urged a more modest round of qualitative disarmament, reducing offensive rather than defensive weapons, they too offered little to appease the German insistence on equality. Nonetheless the reductions contemplated opened the prospect of modest success if France and her allies were prepared to budge over the issue of strict enforcement of the Versailles provisions concerning German rearmament.

Unfortunately, these deliberations did not take place in an international vacuum. They were overshadowed by the Far Eastern conflict, which the League could do nothing to contain, as well as the forthcoming German presidential election. When the delegates reassembled in April after several weeks' recess, they were treated to an American proposal to identify all tanks and large mobile guns to be aggressive weapons. Progress, however, was impeded by the French insistence that security arrangements would have to precede any actual reduction in armaments. The arrival of Secretary of State Stimson and MacDonald in Geneva several days later prompted Brüning to elucidate German proposals to reduce the period of service in the *Reichswehr* while increasing its size, which were accepted by England, the United States, and Italy as the basis of a settlement. Observers noted that MacDonald had to be prodded by British delegates even to shake Henderson's hand at a meeting of the General Commission. Tardieu declined to participate in the discussions that followed, left Geneva, and, after a political reversal, resigned from the Cabinet. France was without a Premier until June, preventing more general debate over the German plan. The impasse sealed Brüning's fate: at the end of May Hindenburg replaced him as Chancellor with the far more reactionary von Papen.

The Americans tried to break the deadlock in June by proposing the abolition of specified offensive weapons, like tanks, large mobile guns, and bombers, and the reduction of other weapons and land forces by a third. All aerial bombardment was to be forbidden unconditionally. Despite initial enthusiasm, especially among smaller powers, the British balked at eliminating tanks, bombers, and submarines, and the French resisted any reduction in armed strength without concomittant guarantees of collective security. Thus by July 1932, after five months of laborious haggling, all that had been accomplished was a general resolution affirming a commitment to substantial reductions in weapons without stipulating precise limits. Even those delegates who accepted the resolution as a basis for future negotiation viewed it as an admission of failure. Despite the lofty aspirations voiced by Henderson and others, nothing concrete had been achieved beyond agreeing to deliberate further. Since even the vague formula made no provision for equality of armaments, Germany, voting against it, announced her refusal to participate in the Conference until the principle of equality had been admitted.

Although he could hardly say so publicly, Henderson held his own Government responsible for the collapse of the talks. Bitterly disappointed, he could find only meager consolation in the thought that the resolution kept the door open, and his efforts to accelerate progress proceeded unabated. In November Simon announced in the Commons that Great Britain was willing to modify its stance by conceding Germany's claim to equality of status on the understanding that it would not rearm and would join other nations in renouncing the use of force to settle disputes. By 11 December the four European powers had devised a formula whereby Germany would be granted equality within a system that provided security for all nations. This gave Germany the requisite assurances, while acknowledging the French insistence on enforcement. With Germany's return to the Conference anticipated, the delegations agreed to adjourn the Conference until the end of January. Thus whatever limited progress had been achieved came through direct negotiation among the powers, excluding both the President and the majority of the delegations, who continued to press the view that Henderson should be directly involved in any future discussions.

IV

Abroad for more than half of 1932, Henderson found it difficult to fulfil his responsibilities as Secretary and Leader of the Labour Party very effectively. He recognized the need to restore its confidence and was not unsympathetic to younger, aggressive spokesmen, like Cole and Laski, who wanted to redefine its socialist basis. Never unreceptive to innovation, Uncle Arthur gave his blessing to the New Fabian Research Bureau, although he refused to sanction any overtures to the extreme left. It was difficult for him to change his spots so late in his career. A staunch advocate of the labour alliance, he looked to the unions to furnish voting strength and reinforce his own moderate stance. His hostility towards MacDonald had been personal, not ideological, although there was a wide gap in their views over the way to deal with the unemployed. His first obligation was to the movement; he was its servant and would not compromise its interests for the sake of some supposedly higher national duty. But many on the left, still indignant over the failure of the second

Labour Government, attributed the disaster of 1931 less to MacDonald's treachery than to the fundamental policy of gradualism, for which Henderson was equally culpable. Despite a general rallying to the new leader, James Maxton and others in the I.L.P., which was never prone to organizational loyalty, were scarcely less hostile to Uncle Arthur than to MacDonald.

When Lansbury met him some time after the 1931 debâcle, Henderson seemed 'a bit upset with the sort of forward policy we aim at'. He interpreted Labour's defeat not as an indication that a more radical policy was called for, but rather that it must bide its time until the electorate was ready to respond to its message. Lansbury was convinced that Uncle Arthur was

> terribly worried about the party, that he feels Labour is in the wilderness for a long period unless we can trim our sails so as to catch the wind of disgust which will blow Mac and his friends out and that he is not anxious for us to be too definite about Socialist measures as our first objectives. Put them in our programme but be sure when we come to power we keep on the line of least resistance ...[32]

His speech at the Leicester party conference in October 1932 nonetheless sounded uncharacteristically militant. He stressed the need for 'bold and drastic Socialist remedies' to transform the existing system completely and 'to substitute co-ordinated planning for the anarchy of individualistic and unorganized competition'. He also underscored the need for 'the closest collaboration' with the Trades Union Congress, an alliance which would become 'even more intimate in the future'.[33] Such sentiments did little to mollify those like Sir Charles Trevelyan, who moved a resolution committing the next Labour government to promulgate definite socialist legislation and to stand or fall on the basis of these principles. The Secretary, absent from the platform during Trevelyan's speech, was invited by the N.E.C. to give its reply and, for the first time since 1917, had considerable difficulty in obtaining a hearing. Despite his opposition to a resolution that tied the party's hands in the future, it was decisively carried.

Such defiance of Uncle Arthur's wishes had been rare before 1931, indicating not merely a changing temper within the party, but diminished authority. Dalton attributed it to his absence in Geneva for most of the year:

> He could not exercise influence from a distance, & when he came back it was clear that he had lost touch a little with the home situation and had also lost, not unnaturally, a good deal of his old ascendancy over the N.E.C.[34]

By the end of the Leicester conference he was sufficiently disgruntled to resign the leadership, although Mrs Hamilton refused to attribute his decision to the incident at the conference. No longer confident of soon finding a winnable seat, he felt that it was a liability for the party to continue to have its Leader outside Parliament. Writing to the P.L.P., he declared that interests would be served best 'if we reverted to the former practice of regarding the Chairman of the Parliamentary party as the actual leader'.[35] He continued, however, to serve as Secretary, although responsibility for managing day-to-day business had been largely delegated to Jim Middleton.

The resignation was, in many ways, a relief. His year as Leader had not been particularly successful, and there was little indication yet that the party's fortunes were reviving in the country. He was, moreover, too much a member of the old guard, linked in the popular mind with the first stage of party development and not perceived as the appropriate figure to oversee the necessary renewal. That Labour was able to recover from the defeat of 1931 was a consequence of the durable organization he had patiently built up during his years as Secretary, but he had no new answers to offer. It was not at all difficult for him to give up the leadership, he told Sankey, because he had never really wanted it:

> I was always ready to be the hewer of wood or the drawer of water to others, content to look after the machine for the benefit of the great movement which I loved so much and felt it an honour to serve in the capacity for which I am best suited.[36]

V

Although Germany briefly returned to the Disarmament Conference at the end of 1932, there was 'a vacuum of unreality'[37] surrounding its proceedings from then on. Conversations took place between representatives of the great powers from which Henderson continued to be excluded. Although these negotiations produced an affirmation of the principle of equality, it proved impossible to implement it. A French proposal, based on mutual guarantees, was contrived to postpone disarmament and to prolong French military superiority. Further discussions on the limitations of weapons proved inconclusive, and the President, in desperation, informed the delegates that if they were unable to act decisively, he would formulate a plan of his own. Without even notifying Henderson, MacDonald then submitted a draft Convention to break the stalemate over the problems of disarmament and security. However, since the British plan did not eliminate aerial bombing and delayed any resolution of naval armament until after 1935, it not only aroused French hostility, but failed to satisfy the German concern. An American initiative, enthusiastically welcomed by Henderson as a viable compromise, proved unable to revitalize the stalled talks, and by June 1933 it was clear to all participants that no real progress had been made.

With the World Monetary and Economic Conference opening in London, it was generally believed that the Geneva meetings should be adjourned. Perhaps if agreement was reached on financial issues, the impediments to disarmament would be removed. Henderson had been instructed by the Bureau to use the opportunity of the London meetings to initiate private negotiation, and he assumed there would be ample opportunities to discuss the problems that seemed so intractable in Geneva. Unfortunately, MacDonald, chairing the London Conference, did little to facilitate his assignment, and his overtures to the busy delegates were politely rebuffed. One eye-witness reported somewhat ruefully that

> there have been few more pathetic pictures than that of Mr. Henderson sitting alone on one of the lounges in the delegates' foyer and gazing enviously at the milling groups of representatives who surged up and down the floor and cast not a glance at the lonely, rubicund, kindly figure in the corner.[38]

Recognizing that he was getting nowhere, he prevailed upon the Bureau in late June to authorize him to undertake personal diplomacy in the principal European capitals and to adjourn the General Commission until the late autumn.

Accompanied by the Conference Secretary, Thanassis Aghnides, a Greek diplomat and former Director of the Disarmament Section of the League Secretariat, he visited Paris, where he had lengthy discussions with Premier Daladier and Foreign Minister Paul-Boncour. They suggested that disarmament should be stretched out over two four-year stages, during the first of which there would be no actual reduction of weapons and no increase in German armaments. Continuing on to Rome, he found an unexpectedly cooperative Mussolini eager to press any reasonable proposal on the Germans provided the French were prepared to make concessions. In Berlin he had discussions with Baron von Neurath and General von Blomberg and then travelled to Munich to see Hitler. He was encouraged by his interview with the Chancellor, who assured him that Germany did not seek to acquire offensive weapons and was willing to submit to any controls that the other powers accepted. Henderson was received with deliberate courtesy in Germany, after the Ministry of Propaganda issued a directive to the press to ensure that he was not derided as a pacifist social democrat. In his discussion with German officials he urged direct contact between Hitler and Daladier once a four-power pact was signed. Implicit in his arguments was the assumption that almost any concordat that included Germany was preferable to sacrificing the chance of genuine disarmament. When he met Daladier during a second visit to Paris, his encouraging report was received skeptically by the French, alarmed by rumors of troops drilling and the manufacture of prohibited weapons. Despite the stalemate over equality, still the major obstacle to improved Franco-German relations, he told Anthony Eden – MacDonald was too busy to see him upon his return to London – that there were several issues on which differences had narrowed. Only on the questions of the duration of a disarmament convention and the reduction of land-based weapons was there still no glimmer of hope. In reporting these discussions to the Cabinet, Eden concluded that if a Disarmament Convention was to be obtained 'it can only be as the outcome of persuading the French to make such an offer as can be reasonably forced down the German throat with an Italian spoon'.[39] Nor was it only the British Government which had abandoned hope that the Conference would reach an accord. Beatrice Webb felt that Japanese aggression and the rise of Hitler had reduced the search for disarmament to a 'dreary farce'. As for Henderson personally, his

> guileless and naive dragging out of the conference over two long years has increased his reputation for dogged devotion and honesty, but diminished trust in his judgement. The great powers have found it easier to let him go on as chairman than to combine together to close the conference.[40]

Arthur Henderson

Although his guarded optimism was clearly misplaced, Henderson informed the Bureau that agreement could be reached on most points 'without our encountering any insuperable difficulty'. Any further postponement of the General Commission session would only arouse suspicion, and it was decided to reconvene the body.[41] When Simon indicated several days later that the British had accepted the French proposal of a four-year trial period during which Germany would still be subject to the limitations imposed by the Peace Treaty, Hitler used this statement as a pretext for withdrawing from the Conference. Recent events, he declared, had demonstrated that the heavily-armed states did not intend either to disarm in the immediate future or to concede equality to Germany. Early in 1934 there was a revival of private negotiations among heads of governments, despairing that anything of value would now emerge from the Conference. Largely at Henderson's insistence, the Bureau continued to meet, its sessions in May and June 1934 notable only for the acrimonious exchanges between Barthou and the other delegates. When the French representative cast aspersions on the President's impartiality, he threatened to resign. For all that he was accomplishing, he might just as well have quit. He responded angrily to Barthou's allegations:

> I do not regard the Conference as a debating assembly; the Conference has the lives of the entire youth of the world in its keeping. That is how it has appeared to me for the two and a half years during which I have sat in the chair. I do not view the closing down of the Conference lightly but it is no use trying to delude the public too long. I believe that it already feels very impatient. It feels that the Conference can do nothing but make speeches, that it can never take practical decisions.[42]

For the moment the crisis was alleviated and the Conference continued. While it was obvious that nothing further could be accomplished, the Bureau was loath to admit failure by dissolving forever. Instead there were desultory talks about converting it into a Permanent Disarmament Commission, although by 1935 even its indefatigable President was incapable of maintaining the pretense of progress. The enormous increase in the German military budget and the 1935 British defense White Paper made a mockery of any hopes of further restraint. In his summary report he speculated about whether the Conference was doomed from the start. 'It may be questioned,' he commented, 'whether when the Conference met early in 1932, there existed a minimum of conditions, political and moral, indispensable for success.'[43] He could certainly not blame himself. Maxim Litvinov expressed a widely-held sentiment when he remarked at a League Council meeting in January 1936, 'If the Conference has failed, one may say it was in spite of the great effort accomplished by Mr. Henderson.'[44]

VI

His last years were clouded by deteriorating health and the sense that his peace mission had failed, but they were years of vindication as well. In the spring of 1933 he was awarded the Wateler Peace Prize for 'the energy, persistence, ability, and impartiality' with which he had conducted the business of the Conference. Although he had begun to disengage himself from party affairs, he still hoped to end his days as an M.P. Many felt that he might add an authoritative voice to Parliamentary debates on foreign policy, especially in view of Labour's renewed commitment to the League and to disarmament. The death of Charles Duncan, M.P. for the safe Derbyshire seat of Clay Cross created an ideal vacancy for Henderson, too venerable by now to undertake a hazardous contest. But, as happened so often in his career, even the most auspicious opportunities turned out to be fraught with complications. Duncan had been sponsored by the Transport

Arthur Henderson

Workers, who put forward another union candidate to succeed him. Under strong pressure from Head Office, the constituency party decided to nominate Henderson. Ernest Bevin, who had not been consulted, objected, prompting an inquiry and an eventual apology. Even so, the T. & G.W.U. withheld their affiliation fees for a number of months in protest against the imposition of Uncle Arthur. Almost as embarrassing was the decision of Conservative Central Office to contest the seat, even though the outcome in Clay Cross was a foregone conclusion. They prevailed upon MacDonald to send a message of support to the Tory candidate couched in terms of loyalty to the National Government, rather than as a personal attack on Henderson. His friends thought it unseemly for him to have been opposed, and many Liberals and even Conservatives wrote to tell him so.[45] He no longer had the stamina for a heated contest and needed to husband his strength for the autumn meetings of the Conference. In the end he romped home, winning nearly 70 per cent of the vote, with a majority of more than 15,000. He was also opposed in the three-cornered race by the Communist Harry Pollitt, who came third.

Although he had resigned the leadership ostensibly because of his absence from the Commons, he made no effort to regain it. At the Southport annual conference in 1934, the last he was to attend after a third of a century of continuous involvement, he received a huge ovation following his speech, and a presentation was made to him for his faithful service. Five months earlier he had, at long last, surrendered the Secretaryship, although with evident reluctance. Dalton observed that he had 'practically to be pushed out' despite grim medical reports on his health. He told party elders that he wanted to hold on until the next general election and resisted the idea that new blood would revitalize the party organization. Clynes finally told him that the changeover could no longer be delayed, though he could continue as Honorary

Treasurer. His tenacity astounded Dalton, ordinarily one of Uncle Arthur's unflagging admirers, who saw its persistence in 'his decline at the expense of dignity as well as wisdom'.[46]

At the end of 1934 he completed, with the assistance of Philip Noel-Baker and Konni Zilliacus, an exposition of Labour's foreign policy, published early the next year under the title *Labour's Way to Peace*. Its call for international cooperation struck a discordant note in a world menaced by militant nationalism and rearmament. Recognizing the growth of reactionary elements, he concluded this impassioned piece of propaganda with an encomium to socialism as 'the only force in the world strong enough and determined enough to break the powers of darkness and reaction and to win through to peace and the brotherhood of man'.[47] His words no longer carried much conviction; even Henderson now recognized that the outlook was bleak, with socialism everywhere beleaguered and divided.

In the autumn of 1934 his labours were crowned with the award of the Nobel Peace Prize, only the third Englishman to be so honored. Whereas Austen Chamberlain had been rewarded for the triumph of the Locarno Pact, Henderson's award was a more personal one. It was not as a representative of a great power, but rather as a world leader, a tribune of peace, that his efforts on behalf of disarmament were so appropriately acknowledged. It was all the more poignant in that his struggle had been so lamentably unsuccessful. In his Nobel Peace Lecture in Oslo in December he stressed the need to subordinate national sovereignty to world-wide institutions and obligations. He admitted that a durable peace could not be achieved until the linked questions of security and equality were resolved and looked to the creation of an eventual World Commonwealth as the only alternative to a relapse into a world war. The psychological obstacles were, he noted, formidable, but not insurmountable if the British Commonwealth, the United States, the Soviet Union, and the surviving European democracies joined together.[48]

The annual New Year's Eve party at Transport House at the end of 1934 was to be his last, and it was his farewell to the staff he had bullied and cajoled and exhorted for so long. The Disarmament Conference petered out after March 1935, and by the summer he was exhausted and extremely ill. He underwent surgery in September but then grew steadily weaker and died on 20 October. Tributes poured in from all over the world, from kings and presidents and heads of state. The League Secretariat sent his widow an illuminated testimonial signed by 300 officials of all nationalities. A simple Wesleyan funeral was followed by cremation, with the eulogy delivered by George Lansbury. On 25 October a memorial service was held at Westminster Abbey to commemorate the career of the man who had given his life to the labour movement and the cause of international peace.

7 Conclusion

By the time of his death in 1935 Henderson's stature was universally acknowledged. The *Manchester Guardian* commented that 'he was for many years the greatest single force in the Labour party. The tremendous influence he exerted at the annual conferences of the party was such as no other man ever wielded.'[1] Several years later, comparing him to MacDonald, Beatrice Webb had no hesitation in asserting that Henderson 'will stand out as the wisest and most disinterested of the labour leaders' of that generation.[2] And yet, by 1945, when Labour enjoyed its greatest electoral triumph, his contribution had been all but forgotten, and fifty years after his death he is little remembered. He had never been an idol of the rank and file as Keir Hardie, MacDonald, or even Lansbury had been, and his achievements were the sort that could all too easily be overlooked. Leader only briefly and never Prime Minister, he had devoted himself primarily to the party structure, which was largely his creation. Labour might never have come to power before the Second World War had it not been for MacDonald, but the organization that ensured the election of ever larger numbers of M.P.s between 1906 and 1929 was the result of Uncle Arthur's efforts. As he intimated to Lord Sankey, he had been content to be 'the hewer of wood or the drawer of water' for others, looking after the party machine rather than his own public image. As long as it worked, the MacDonald–Henderson partnership was effective because their personalities and ambitions were complementary. Henderson never really wanted to be more than the manager, working behind the scenes for the movement he loved. He found his rewards not in personal glory, but in election victories and in the expansion and improvement of the party organization.

More than any other leader Henderson epitomized the solid alliance between trade unions and party that was and has remained Labour's bedrock. Unlike others in its history, content to discard their trade union identity for the glittering prizes of Westminster, Henderson never forgot his origins. He could share the feelings of ordinary working people because he was one of them and did not aspire to rise above his class. His sensitivity to the temper of the movement stemmed from his close links with organized labour, which served him in good stead as its representative in the wartime coalition governments. He recognized that the party would flourish only if trade unionism were given a dominant role, not only at the executive level, but also in constituency parties. With his genius for organization, he built a powerful machine after 1918 based on the simple loyalties that had inspired his own career – loyalty to chapel, to union, and to the ideal of the economic and social betterment of the less fortunate. His socialist ideology, such as it was, was essentially a practical trade unionist view of incremental gains through parliamentary democracy, couched in labourist terms palatable to all elements in the movement. He was a man of consensus, believing above all in the need for unity, however much fundamental principles needed to be fudged in the process. As the heir to Victorian artisan and Nonconformist values, he sought to avoid social conflict, to advance the position of the working class through conciliation and compromise. It was the very success of organized labour in mobilizing support to promote its objectives in the late nineteenth century that convinced Henderson that peaceful persuasion was not only preferable, but possible.

In personal terms he embodied, much as Ernest Bevin did, traits typical of trade union leaders at the time – a dogged persistence, an impatience with impediments, a bullying manner towards subordinates, an explosive temper, but equally a sense of class solidarity and a selfless integrity in striving for the welfare of those in his charge, whether they were fellow ironfounders, Labour voters, or humanity at large. He saw politics as trade union activity writ large and conducted himself in the Parliamentary arena and at the League of Nations much as he would at T.U.C. meetings. Intellectuals belittled his lack of sophistication, his simple piety and old-fashioned respectability, but he was a persuasive spokesman, a shrewd judge of men and political situations, and an indomitable idealist. Many who scoffed at first came to praise his tenacity and courage, and by the end of his life his admirers included Whitehall mandarins and foreign statesmen no less than Labour politicians and party functionaries.

Even before he died, his accomplishments had begun to seem impermanent, as the tragic futility of the Disarmament Conference began to overshadow the accomplishments of his Foreign Secretaryship. His aspirations for a peace that would safeguard the next generation against the scourge of a war like the one which claimed his eldest son's life were thwarted by the advent of Hitler. Yet the subsequent failures should not diminish his substantial, if somewhat fleeting, success. He had managed to transform himself from an insular and ill-informed trade union official into a leader of European socialism and then into an international statesman. The very skills he brought to bear in industrial negotiation were applied to diplomacy at Geneva to remarkable advantage. Between 1929 and 1931 he helped to reinforce the peace-keeping machinery and to lessen, albeit temporarily, the tension between France and Germany. Throughout the 1920s he had been the leading internationalist on Labour's front bench, the politician most responsible for re-orienting Labour's foreign policy to an increasing reliance on the League of Nations. An unflagging advocate of disarmament, he nonetheless recognized that pooled security was the essential corollary to a reduction in weapons. Only through the collective enforcement of peace, using institutions of the League, including military sanctions if necessary, could aggression be curbed. Idealistic in his hopes for international accord, Henderson remained realistic about the necessity of machinery to consolidate the peace. His plea for disarmament was coupled with a commitment to compulsory arbitration and an international police force. He willingly assumed the Presidency of the Disarmament Conference not because he sought to exercise power, but because by 1931 he had come to regard himself as the guardian of the public con science, the tribune of peace for ordinary people throughout the world who were eager to end the competitive armaments struggle.

If Henderson's importance as the architect of Labour's interwar foreign policy has sometimes been underestimated, his significance as the builder of the party machine has been more readily admitted. He was involved in every aspect of its life, as local organizer, candidate, and M.P., as Secretary for a quarter of a century, as manipulator and choreographer of annual conferences, as mediator between the Executive and constituency parties. He had an intuitive understanding of party sentiment which he exploited at the annual conferences and in his dealings with agents and with back benchers in the House of Commons. He knew when to be tough and when to be emollient, when to force a policy through and when to give way. It was Uncle Arthur who had devised and implemented the structural reforms that solidified Labour's position after 1918 and who patiently cultivated constituency parties to provide a popular base that could be superimposed on the union-dominated machinery. While recognizing the need to broaden local support and to nurture constituency activity, he was a consistent centralizer, 'Labour's Bismarck', as Kenneth Morgan has aptly called him.[3] The weakness of trade unionism was its lack of central direction; the party had to emulate trade unionism's single-mindedness, to mobilize its funds and tap its reservoirs of loyalty, but to avoid its centrifugal tendencies. Hence he used his authority as Secretary to overpower local revolts in Scotland and Wales, among I.L.P. militants and *Daily Herald* syndicalists, and to keep constituency parties as subservient as possible to the dictates of the N.E.C. Where intimidation was inappropriate, as in the Mosley rebellion, it was Uncle Arthur who rallied the P.L.P. by an appeal to party solidarity. It was Henderson too who selected and trained the agents and organizers who built the party in the 1920s and rebuilt it in the 1930s. Whatever charisma he lacked he more than made up for by his consummate skills as organizer, committee chairman, and administrator, as manager in the fullest sense of that term. He knew that Labour's future depended not on a single election or manifesto, but on the continuous attention to detail and to cultivating a growing popular base, giving it a solidity that could withstand defeats and even betrayals by errant leaders. He was a 'safe custodian' for the movement who 'built to last', and for that reason his contribution to the growth of the party surpassed that of all its other founding fathers.[4]

Few commentators have ever tried to make a case for Henderson's greatness. He had a pedestrian mind, was an indifferent Parliamentary debater, and lacked a sense of vision. Authoritarian, stubborn, plodding, he inspired loyalty, respect, and sometimes affection rather than adoration. Yet his simple virtues were enduring ones: he was honest, dependable, and consistent. Constitutionally incapable of self-importance, he was willing to subordinate his own advancement to the good of the movement. He could be trusted to keep his word and never allowed his eminence to separate him from the ordinary working people for whom he spoke. Fame and fortune meant little to him, and although he could bear a grudge, he never conspired against his colleagues or abused his power. G. D. H. Cole, one of many left-wing intellectuals who was surprised to discover that familiarity with Uncle Arthur bred admiration, aptly summed up his personal strengths:

> Arthur Henderson was not a particularly clever man, or an inspiring speaker. He had neither the glamour of MacDonald, nor the incisiveness of Snowden, nor the human warmth of George Lansbury. But he had great qualities – honesty, absence of self-seeking, doggedness and patience in action, and an unshakable faith in the ethical ideals of justice and freedom . . . He never let a colleague down, or attempted to shift on to other men's shoulders the burdens of his own mistakes. Uncle Arthur, much more than any other man, made the Labour Party what it was . . . Whatever he made it, he made it for the common people, and not for himself.[5]

Notes

Chapter 1

1 Address at Browning Hall during Labour Week, 1910.
2 *Review of Reviews*, June 1906.
3 Quoted in Edwin A. Jenkins, *From Foundry to Foreign Office: The romantic life-story of the Rt. Hon. Arthur Henderson, M.P.* (London, 1933), p. 4.
4 R. I. McKibbin, 'Arthur Henderson as Labour Leader', *International Review of Social History*, XXIII (1978), Part I, p. 82.
5 Quoted in Mary Agnes Hamilton, *Arthur Henderson: A Biography* (London, 1938), p. 29.
6 *Justice*, 11 July 1903.
7 J. Bruce Glasier to Keir Hardie, 26 Jan. 1903, Glasier Papers.
8 H. H. Hughes to Ramsay MacDonald, 20 May 1903, L.R.C. Papers.
9 Arthur Henderson to Ramsay MacDonald, 25 May 1903, L.R.C. Papers.
10 Herbert Gladstone to Richard Rigg, 7 July 1903, quoted in Philip P. Poirier, *The Advent of the Labour Party* (London, 1958), p. 200.
11 Quoted in Poirier, p. 198.
12 *Leeds and Yorkshire Mercury*, 9 July 1903.
13 A. W. Purdue, 'Arthur Henderson and Liberal, Liberal–Labour and Labour Politics in the North-East of England, 1892-1903', *Northern History*, XI (1976), p. 209.

Chapter 2

1 Ross McKibbin, *The Evolution of the Labour Party 1910-1924* (Oxford, 1974), p. 4.
2 Speeches in Browning Hall, 1-2 May 1910.
3 *Christian Commonwealth*, 12 Feb. 1913.
4 Hardie to Glasier [July 1904], Glasier Papers.
5 Henderson to MacDonald, 6 June 1903, L.R.C. Papers.
6 Hardie to Glasier, July 1904, Glasier Papers.
7 Hamilton, p. 49.
8 Hamilton, p. 52.
9 Henderson to MacDonald, 3 Nov. 1905, L.R.C. Papers.

10 Hamilton, p. 71.
11 George N. Barnes and Arthur Henderson, *Unemployment in Germany* [1907].
12 *Hansard,* 29 April 1909.
13 Henderson to Hardie, 4 Feb. 1907, I.L.P./Francis Johnson Papers.
14 Glasier to MacDonald, 27 Oct. 1908, MacDonald Papers.
15 Hardie to Glasier, 23 Dec. 1908, Glasier Papers.
16 Henderson to W. C. Robinson, 5 Feb. 1910, Labour Party Archive.
17 Hugh Armstrong Clegg, *A History of British Trade Unions Since 1889: Volume II: 1911-1933* (Oxford, 1985), p. 21.
18 Henderson to James Middleton, 9 Aug. 1906, Labour Party Archive.
19 Labour Party, *Papers on Elections, Registration and Organization* [1908].
20 Henderson to MacDonald, 2 Jan. 1911, MacDonald Papers.
21 Hardie to Glasier, 13 Feb. 1911, Glasier Papers.
22 McKibbin, 'Arthur Henderson as Labour Leader', p. 94.
23 Henderson to James Middleton, 31 Oct. 1913, Labour Party Archive.
24 16 Oct. 1921, Norman and Jeanne MacKenzie, eds., *The Diary of Beatrice Webb, III: 1905-1924* (London, 1984), p. 389; 10 Jan. 1930, Dalton MS. Diary, Dalton Papers.
25 Henderson to MacDonald, 7 Oct. 1911, MacDonald Papers.
26 Henderson to MacDonald, 30 Sept. 1911, MacDonald Papers.
27 Henderson to MacDonald, 26 Aug. 1912, MacDonald Papers.
28 H. N. Brailsford to Henderson, 6 May [1912], Labour Party Archive.
29 Election Fighting Fund Minutes, 2 Aug. 1912, cited in Leslie Parker Hume, *The National Union of Women's Suffrage Societies 1897-1914* (New York, 1982), p. 164.
30 Henderson to MacDonald, 29 May 1914, Labour Party Archive.
31 Hamilton, p. 92.

Chapter 3

1 Hamilton, pp. 91-2.
2 Quoted in A. J. Anthony Morris, *Radicalism Against War 1906-1914* (London, 1972), p. 414.
3 David Marquand, *Ramsay MacDonald* (London, 1977), p. 180.
4 *British Finance and Prussian Militarism: Two Interviews* (London, 1917), pp. 14-22.
5 Henderson, 'A People's Peace' (London, 1917). Reprinted from *Daily News,* 28 Sept. 1917.
6 McKibbin, 'Arthur Henderson as Labour Leader', p. 86.

7 H. M. Hyndman to Algernon Simon, 12 Aug. 1917, Simon Papers.
8 Henderson to MacDonald, 19 Oct. 1914, MacDonald Papers.
9 Henderson to H. H. Asquith, 26 July 1916, Asquith Papers.
10 3 Sept. 1915, Trevor Wilson, ed., *The Political Diaries of C. P. Scott 1911-1928* (London, 1970), p. 134.
11 Henderson to H. H. Asquith, 10 Jan. 1916, Asquith Papers.
12 Marquand, p. 197.
13 Quoted in Keith Middlemas, *Politics in Industrial Society* (London, 1979), p. 97.
14 29 Jan., 6 Dec. 1916, MacDonald MS. Diary, MacDonald Papers.
15 *Glasgow Forward,* 16 Dec. 1916, quoted in Marquand, p. 201.
16 Henderson to David Lloyd George, 7 Dec. 1916, Lloyd George Papers.
17 *Labour Party Annual Conference Report, 1917,* pp. 106, 110.
18 Henderson to Noel Buxton, 2 Jan. 1917, Buxton Papers.
19 Quoted in Stephen White, 'Soviets in Britain: The Leeds Convention of 1917', *International Review of Social History,* XIX (1974), Part 2, p. 182.
20 Henderson to David Lloyd George, 13 Jan. 1917, Lloyd George Papers.
21 Henderson to David Lloyd George, 14 June 1917, Lloyd George Papers.
22 Henderson to R. W. Raine, 19 June 1917, Labour Party Archive.
23 Henderson to J. Gilbert Dale, 19 June 1917, Labour Party Archive.
24 Quoted in Keith Robbins, *The Abolition of War* (Cardiff, 1976), p. 139.
25 Henderson to David Lloyd George, 1 July 1917, Foreign Office Papers.
26 J. M. Winter, 'Arthur Henderson, the Russian Revolution, and the Reconstruction of the Labour Party', *Historical Journal,* XV, 4 (1972), p. 765.
27 29 Aug. 1917, Thomas Jones, *Whitehall Diary Vol. I: 1916-1925* (London, 1969), p. 36.
28 David Lloyd George to Henderson, 10 and 11 Aug. 1917, Lloyd George Papers.
29 Quoted in Hamilton, pp. 151-2.
30 11 Aug. 1917, Scott, *Diaries,* p. 299.
31 Henderson to David Lloyd George, 11 Aug. 1917, Lloyd George Papers.
32 Henderson to Walter Runciman, 17 Aug. 1917, Runciman Papers.
33 Arthur Ponsonby to C. P. Trevelyan, 13 Aug. 1917, Trevelyan Papers.
34 *Daily News,* 28 Sept. 1917. Reprinted as *A People's Peace* (1917).
35 *Labour and an After-War Economic Policy* (1917).
36 Henderson to MacDonald, 31 Jan. 1918, MacDonald Papers.
37 Henderson, 'The Outlook for Labour', *Contemporary Review,* Feb. 1918.
38 29 Aug. 1917 Jones, *Whitehall Diary,* p. 36.

Notes to pp. 73-100

39 11 Dec. 1911, Scott, *Diaries*, pp. 316-17.
40 Marquand, p. 221.
41 7 Jan. 1918, Scott, *Diaries*, p. 327.
42 21 Jan. 1918, *Diary of Beatrice Webb, III*, p. 294.
43 Marquand, p. 229. MacDonald had called Henderson's original memorandum 'very badly drafted in form & in spirit & grasp just an election agent's document. Certainly not the vision of a new democratic party.'
44 McKibbin, *Evolution of the Labour Party*, p. 95.
45 Henderson, *The Aims of Labour* (London, 1918), p. 63.
46 Henderson, 'The Outlook for Labour', *Contemporary Review*, Feb. 1918.
47 24 Jan. 1918. *Diary of Beatrice Webb, III*, p. 295.

Chapter 4

1   23 June 1918, *Beatrice Webb's Diaries 1912-1924*, p. 124.
2   Paul U. Kellogg and Arthur Gleason, *British Labor and the War* (New York, 1919), pp. 94-5.
3   24 Sept. 1919, *Diary of Beatrice Webb, III*, pp. 347-8.
4   *Aims of Labour*, pp. 24-5, 57-62.
5   'Democracy and Christianity', in *The Religion in the Labour Movement* (London, 1919), pp. 147-52.
6   'Brotherhood and the World's Unrest', in Basil J. Mathews, ed., *World Brotherhood* (London, 1920), p. 105.
7   *Daily Herald*, 14 July 1919.
8   *Aims of Labour*, pp. 29-42.
9   Speech at Inter-Allied Socialist Conference, February 1918.
10 *Aims of Labour*, pp. 43-51, 71-3.
11 *The League of Nations and Labour* (London, 1918), pp. 5-13.
12 *The Peace Terms* (11 May 1919).
13 *Daily Herald*, 30 June 1919.
14 11-12 Dec. 1917, Scott, *Diaries*, pp. 316-17.
15 4 Nov. 1918, *Beatrice Webb's Diaries 1912-1924*, p. 134.
16 Hamilton, p. 195.
17 27 March 1919, *Beatrice Webb's Diaries 1912-1924*, p. 157.
18 Henderson to Sidney Webb, 17 May 1919, Webb Collection.
19 *Labour Party Annual Conference Report, 1919*, p. 116.
20 *Manchester Guardian*, 20 Aug. 1919.
21 *Manchester Guardian*, 26 Aug. 1919.
22 *Widnes Guardian*, 2 Sept. 1919.

23 24 Sept. 1919, *Diary of Beatrice Webb, III*, pp. 347-8.
24 12 Jan. 1918, Jones, *Whitehall Diary*, p. 46.
25 *Hansard*, 17 Nov. 1919.
26 *Daily Herald*, 10 April 1920.
27 *Labour Party Annual Conference Report, 1921*.
28 Robert Williams to Henderson, 15 Sept. 1920; 'Notes on Mr. Williams' Letter by the Secretary', Sept. 1920, Labour Party Archive.
29 Christopher Howard, 'Expectations born to death: local Labour Party expansion in the 1920s', in J. Winter, ed., *The Working Class in Modern British History* (Cambridge, 1983), pp. 65-81.
30 Henderson to Camille Huysmans, 26 June 1920, Labour Party Archive.
31 18-25 June 1920, *Beatrice Webb's Diaries 1912-1924*, p. 182.
32 McKibbin, *Evolution of the Labour Party*, p. 125.
33 Letter to the Editor, *The Times*, 7 Oct. 1920.
34 *Hansard*, 20 Oct. 1920.
35 Hamilton, p. 229.
36 Hamilton, p. 219.
37 See, for example, McKibbin, 'Arthur Henderson as Labour Leader', *passim*.
38 16 Oct. 1921, *Beatrice Webb's Diaries 1912-1924*, p. 218.
39 28 Feb.2 March 1922, Scott, *Diaries,*, pp. 417-18.
40 'The Character and Policy of the British Labour Party', *International Journal of Ethics* (Jan. 1922), pp. 120-3.
41 *Labour Magazine*, Jan. 1923.
42 *Labour Magazine*, July 1922.
43 Hamilton, p. 233.
44 Henderson to C. P. Trevelyan, 11 Dec. 1923, Trevelyan Papers.
45 12 Dec. 1923, *Beatrice Webb's Diaries 1912-1924*, p. 255.
46 10 Dec. 1923, MacDonald MS. Diary, MacDonald Papers.
47 18 Dec. 1923, *Diary of Beatrice Webb, III*, p. 432.
48 MacDonald to Henderson, 22 Dec. 1923, MacDonald Papers.
49 8 Jan. 1924, *Beatrice Webb's Diaries 1924-1932*, p. 2.
50 Henderson to MacDonald, 20 Dec. 1923, MacDonald Papers.
51 *The Times*, 14 Feb. 1924.
52 15 March 1924, *Beatrice Webb's Diaries 1924-1932*, p. 13.
53 Gilbert Murray, 'Notes for M. A. Hamilton's life of Henderson', March 1937, Murray Papers.
54 Speech in Burnley, 12 Oct. 1924, published as *The New Peace Plan*.
55 Henry R. Winkler, 'The Emergence of a Labor Foreign Policy in Great

Britain, 1918-1929', *Journal of Modern History*, XXVIII, No. 3 (Sept. 1956), p. 256.
56　21 Nov. 1924, *Beatrice Webb's Diaries 1924-1932*, p. 51.
57　8 Aug. 1925, *Beatrice Webb's Diaries 1924-1932*, p. 67.
58　10 Sept. 1926, *Beatrice Webb's Diaries 1924-1932*, p. 119.
59　Hamilton, p. 266.
60　5 April 1927, *Beatrice Webb's Diaries 1924-1932*, p. 137.
61　Henderson to MacDonald, 14 Oct. 1927, MacDonald Papers.

Chapter 5

1　12 April 1929, MacDonald MS. Diary, MacDonald Papers.
2　6 June 1929, Dalton MS. Diary, Dalton Papers.
3　Quoted in Henry R. Winkler, 'Arthur Henderson', in Gordon A. Craig and Felix Gilbert, eds., *The Diplomats* (Princeton, 1953), p. 321.
4　Henderson to MacDonald, 12 Sept. 1929, quoted in Hamilton, pp. 327-8.
5　7 July 1929, Dalton MS. Diary, Dalton Papers.
6　Emanuel Shinwell, *The Labour Story* (London, 1963), pp. 135-6.
7　*Hansard*, 23 Dec. 1929.
8　30 July 1929, Dalton MS. Diary, Dalton Papers.
9　Harold Nicolson, *King George the Fifth: His Life and Reign* (London, 1952), pp. 443-4.
10　5 Nov. 1929, Dalton MS. Diary, Dalton Papers.
11　*Hansard*, 26 July 1929.
12　1 Aug. 1929, Dalton MS. Diary, Dalton Papers.
13　27 Sept.-4 Oct. 1929, Dalton MS. Diary, Dalton Papers.
14　2 Dec. 1929, *Diary of Beatrice Webb IV: 1924-1943* (London, 1985) pp. 202-3.
15　Quoted in David Carlton, *MacDonald versus Henderson: The Foreign Policy of the Second Labour Government* (New York, 1970), p. 16.
16　10 and 17 June 1929, Dalton MS. Diary, Dalton Papers.
17　Henderson to Gilbert Murray, 14 June 1929, Murray Papers.
18　Henderson, *Consolidating World Peace* (Oxford, 1931), p. 26. This is a reprint of the Burge Memorial Lecture, which Henderson delivered on 3 June 1931.
19　Henderson, *Consolidating World Peace*, p. 20.
20　Henderson, 1934; Viscount Cecil of Chelwood, 1937; Philip Noel-Baker, 1959.
21　Quoted in Ben Pimlott, *Hugh Dalton* (London, 1985), p. 193.
22　Mary Agnes Hamilton, *Remembering My Good Friends* (London, 1944), p. 252.

Notes to pp. 151-181

23 17 July 1929, Dalton MS. Diary, Dalton Papers.
24 Quoted in Carlton, p. 22.
25 Hugh Dalton, 'British Foreign Policy, 1929-1931', *Political Quarterly*, II, No. 4 (Oct.-Dec. 1931), p. 492.
26 17 June 1929, Dalton MS. Diary, Dalton Papers.
27 *Observer*, 31 May 1931.
28 Quoted in Hamilton, p. 309.
29 Hugh Dalton, *Call Back Yesterday* (London, 1953), p. 231.
30 Henderson to Dalton, 17 Aug. 1929, Foreign Office Papers.
31 Henderson to Sir Esmond Ovey, 26 Feb. 1930, in *Documents on British Foreign Policy*, 2nd Series, VII, No. 69, p. 105.
32 Dalton, 'British Foreign Policy', p. 500.
33 Quoted in Hamilton, p. 321.
34 Quoted in Hamilton, p. 331.
35 Henderson to Viscount Cecil, 27 Sept. 1929, Cecil of Chelwood Papers.
36 League of Nations, *Records of the Eleventh Assembly*, 11 Sept. 1930, pp. 39-42.
37 Henderson to Sir Horace Rumbold, 11 Nov. 1930, Foreign Office Papers.
38 *Hansard*, 9 March 1931.
39 18 April 1931, *Beatrice Webb's Diaries 1924-1932*, p. 270.
40 12 Jan. 1930, Dalton MS. Diary, Dalton Papers.
41 16 Nov. 1930, MacDonald MS. Diary, MacDonald Papers.
42 5 Dec. 1930, Dalton MS. Diary, Dalton Papers.
43 Quoted in Hamilton, p. 352.
44 16 April 1931, MacDonald MS. Diary, MacDonald Papers.
45 16 April 1931, Dalton MS. Diary, Dalton Papers.
46 Henderson to MacDonald, 6 May 1931, Foreign Office Papers.
47 19 and 20 May 1931, MacDonald MS. Diary, MacDonald Papers.
48 20 May 1931, Dalton MS. Diary, Dalton Papers.
49 Henderson to MacDonald, 23 May 1931, MacDonald Papers.
50 Henderson to Sir Horace Rumbold, 12 Feb. 1931, in *Documents on British Foreign Policy*, 2nd Series, I, No. 348, pp. 554-5.
51 16 July 1931, MacDonald MS. Diary, MacDonald Papers.
52 5 Nov. 1931, Dalton MS. Diary, Dalton Papers.
53 20 July 1931, Dalton MS. Diary, Dalton Papers.
54 Henderson to Aristide Briand, 30 July 1931, Foreign Office Papers.
55 Carlton, *MacDonald versus Henderson*, p. 222.
56 Sir Walford Selby to Viscount Cecil, 14 Sept. 1944, quoted in Carlton, p. 223.

Chapter 6

1 Hamilton, p. 377.
2 17 Aug. 1931, MacDonald MS. Diary, MacDonald Papers.
3 See Marquand, p. 617.
4 19 Aug. 1931, Sankey MS. Diary, Sankey Papers.
5 20 Aug. 1931, Dalton MS. Diary, Dalton Papers.
6 21 Aug. 1931, Sankey MS. Diary, Sankey Papers.
7 21 Aug. 1931, MacDonald MS. Diary, MacDonald Papers.
8 27 Aug. 1931, Dalton MS. Diary, Dalton Papers.
9 24 Aug. 1931, Sankey MS. Diary, Sankey Papers.
10 Marquand, p. 623.
11 22 Aug. 1931, Sankey MS. Diary, Sankey Papers.
12 24 Aug. 1931, MacDonald MS. Diary, MacDonald Papers.
13 23 Aug. 1931, MacDonald MS. Diary, MacDonald Papers. MacDonald noted that the King was 'relieved' when told he would not have to send for Henderson.
14 Hamilton, p. 385.
15 Raymond Postgate, *The Life of George Lansbury* (London, 1951), pp. 271-2.
16 MacDonald to Ponsonby, 24 Aug. 1931, Ponsonby Papers.
17 24 Aug. 1931, Dalton MS. Diary, Dalton Papers.
18 Marquand, p. 644.
19 28 Aug. 1931, Dalton MS. Diary, Dalton Papers.
20 *Hansard,* 8 Sept. 1931.
21 20 Sept. 1931, *Beatrice Webb's Diaries 1924-1932,* p. 287.
22 *The Times,* 26 Sept. 1931.
23 20 Sept. 1931, MacDonald MS. Diary, MacDonald Papers.
24 Marquand, p. 661.
25 Quoted in Nicolson, *King George V,* p. 491.
26 Henderson to Lord Sankey, 7 Dec. 1931, Sankey Papers.
27 Quoted in Hamilton, p. 408.
28 1 May 1932, MacDonald MS. Diary, MacDonald Papers.
29 Winkler, 'Arthur Henderson', p. 311.
30 MacDonald to Henderson, 8 March 1933, MacDonald Papers.
31 Reprinted in *Labour Magazine,* Feb. 1932.
32 George Lansbury to Stafford Cripps (undated), quoted in Postgate, *Lansbury,* pp. 279-80.
33 Reprinted as *Labour in Action* (1932).
34 8 Oct. 1932, Dalton MS. Diary, Dalton Papers.

35 *The Times,* 19 Oct. 1932.
36 Henderson to Lord Sankey, 27 Oct. 1932, Sankey Papers.
37 Winkler, 'Arthur Henderson', p. 341.
38 John W. Wheeler-Bennett, *The Disarmament Deadlock* (London, 1934), p. 164.
39 Cabinet Paper, 'Disarmament: Record of Conversation between Mr. Eden and Mr. Henderson, July 24, 1933'.
40 5 Aug. 1933, *Diary of Beatrice Webb, IV,* pp. 308-10.
41 League of Nations, 'Provisional Minutes of Meeting held on October 9, 1933'.
42 *Records of the Conference for the Reduction and Limitations of Armaments, Series C: Minutes of the Bureau* (5 June 1934), pp. 231-3.
43 *Preliminary Report on the Work of the Conference* (Geneva, 1936), p. 11.
44 League of Nations, *Official Journal* (1936), p. 59.
45 Henderson to Gilbert Murray, 6 Sept. 1933, Murray Papers.
46 Retrospective note on 1934, Dalton MS. Diary, Dalton Papers.
47 *Labour's Way to Peace* (London, 1935), p. 111. The book appeared as one of eight volumes elaborating party policies under the general title, *Labour Shows the Way.*
48 Reprinted as *Essential Elements of a Universal and Enduring Peace.*

Chapter 7

1 *Manchester Guardian,* 21 Oct. 1935.
2 11 Nov. 1937, *Diary of Beatrice Webb, IV,* p. 397.
3 Kenneth O. Morgan, *Labour People* (Oxford, 1987), p. 82.
4 Morgan, p. 87.
5 G. D. H. Cole, *A History of the Labour Party from 1914* (London, 1948), pp. 305-6.

Bibliography

Primary sources

There is no large Henderson manuscript collection, but a number of his letters can be found in other collections. Most are concerned with mundane Labour Party or government business, and scarcely any sheds much light on his personality or on his private life. For the early phase of his political career, there is material in the Bruce Glasier Papers (University of Liverpool Library) and in the Labour Representation Committee and the Independent Labour Party Papers (B.L.P.E.S., London School of Economics) and, more extensively, in the Labour Party Archive, Walworth Road, London. For the period from 1910 until his death there are a number of letters in the MacDonald Papers (P.R.O.), which also include MacDonald's manuscript diary. Its generally denigrating remarks, while often illuminating, reveal more about MacDonald than about Henderson. There is correspondence relating to his participation in the wartime coalitions in the Asquith Papers (Bodleian Library) and the Lloyd George Papers (House of Lords Records Office). Considerable information concerning Henderson's term as Foreign Secretary can be gleaned from Hugh Dalton's manuscript diary (L.S.E.) and from material in the Cecil of Chelwood Papers (British Library). Lord Sankey's manuscript diary (Bodleian Library) illuminates certain aspects of the 1931 crisis, as do the diaries of Dalton and MacDonald. Other collections which have proved useful include the Noel Buxton Papers (Redpath Library, McGill University), the C. P. Trevelyan and Walter Runciman Papers (University of Newcastle Library), the Gilbert Murray, Ponsonby and Horace Rumbold Papers (Bodleian Library), and the Algernon Simon Papers (State Historical Society of Wisconsin).

Beatrice Webb's diaries are full of incisive comments about Henderson at various stages of his career, but especially between 1918 and 1931. Most of these can be found in the two volumes edited by Margaret Cole: *Beatrice Webb's Diaries 1912-1924* (London, 1952) and *Beatrice Webb's Diaries 1924-1932* (London, 1956). Volumes III and IV of Norman and Jeanne MacKenzie, eds.,

The Diary of Beatrice Webb (London and Cambridge, MA, 1984-85) contain some references not included in the earlier volumes. Two other published diaries that add further information are Trevor Wilson, ed., *The Political Diaries of C. P. Scott 1911-1928* (London, 1970) and Thomas Jones, *Whitehall Diary Vol. I: 1916-1925* (London, 1969).

Secondary material

The only full-scale biography is Mary Agnes Hamilton's indulgent *Arthur Henderson* (London, 1938). Intelligent and informative, it stands up better than many political biographies of the period but lacks any scholarly apparatus. Based in part on personal recollection, it was written too close to his death to provide a detached perspective. Mrs Hamilton was also the author of the *Dictionary of National Biography, 1931-1940* entry. E. A. Jenkins, *From Foundry to Foreign Office: the romantic life-story of the Rt. Hon. Arthur Henderson* (London, 1933), written while its subject was still alive, was intended for popular consumption. An accurate summary appears in the *Dictionary of Labour Biography,* I (London, 1972) by John Saville. There is a useful, although generally uncritical chapter in Margaret Cole, *Makers of the Labour Movement* (London, 1948). Kenneth O. Morgan, *Labour People* (Oxford, 1987) contains a brief, but perceptive assessment.

Biographies of and autobiographies by Henderson's colleagues are an essential source of additional information on his career. Of these David Marquand, *Ramsay MacDonald* (London, 1977) and Ben Pimlott, *Hugh Dalton* (London, 1985) are central. Alan Bullock, *The Life and Times of Ernest Bevin, Vol. I: Trade Union Leader, 1881-1940* (London, 1960), Hugh Dalton, *Call Back Yesterday* (London, 1953) and *The Fateful Years* (London, 1957), Kenneth O. Morgan, *Keir Hardie: Radical and Socialist* (London, 1975), and Raymond Postgate, *The Life of George Lansbury* (London, 1951) are of considerable value.

The earliest phase of Henderson's political career is covered in A. W. Purdue, 'Arthur Henderson and Liberal, Liberal–Labour and Labour Politics in the North-East of England, 1892-1903', *Northern History,* XI (1976 for 1975), 195-217 and in Philip P. Poirier, *The Advent of the Labour Party* (London, 1958) and Frank Bealey and Henry Pelling, *Labour and Politics 1900-1906* (London, 1958).

Bibliography

For the First World War, involvement in the Coalition Governments, and Henderson's resignation over the Stockholm issue, see: Christopher Howard, 'MacDonald, Henderson, and the Outbreak of War, 1914', *Historical Journal*, 20, 4 (1977), 871-91; R. J. Q. Adams, 'Asquith's Choice: The May Coalition and the Coming of Conscription, 1915-1916', *Journal of British Studies*, 25, 3 (1986), 243-63; and J. M. Winter, 'Arthur Henderson, the Russian Revolution, and the Reconstruction of the Labour Party', *Historical Journal*, 15, 4 (1972), 753-73.

As an interpretation of Henderson's role in the development of the Labour Party Ross McKibbin, *The Evolution of the Labour Party 1910-1924* (Oxford, 1974) is definitive. Almost as useful is his article 'Arthur Henderson as Labour Leader', *International Review of Social History*, XXIII (1978), Part I, 79-101. A new revisionist analysis can be found in Christopher Howard, 'Expectations born to death: local Labour Party expansion in the 1920s', in J. Winter, ed., *The Working Class in Modern British History* (Cambridge, 1983), 65-81. Andrew Thorne, 'Arthur Henderson and the British Political Crisis of 1931', *Historical Journal*, 31, 1 (1988), 117-39 is an important recent contribution.

Henderson's evolving internationalism is discussed in Henry R. Winkler, 'The Emergence of a Labor Foreign Policy in Great Britain, 1918-1929', *Journal of Modern History*, XXVIII, 3 (1956), 247-58. Winkler provides a sympathetic assessment of Henderson's career as Foreign Secretary in an essay in Gordon A. Craig and Felix Gilbert, eds., *The Diplomats* (Princeton, 1953), 311-43. The fullest discussion of Labour's foreign policy between 1929 and 1931 is David Carlton, *MacDonald versus Henderson: The Foreign Policy of the Second Labour Government* (New York, 1970). A strongly partisan view by a participant is expressed in Hugh Dalton, 'British Foreign Policy, 1929-1931', *Political Quarterly*, II, 4 (1931), 485-505.

Of more general value are the following: R. Bassett, *Nineteen Thirty-One: Political Crisis* (London, 1958); H. A. Clegg, Alan Fox and A. F. Thompson, *A History of British Trade Unions Since 1889, Vol. I: 1889-1910* (Oxford, 1964); Hugh Armstrong Clegg, *A History of British Trade Unions Since 1889, Vol. II: 1911-1933* (Oxford, 1985); G. D. H. Cole, *A History of the Labour Party from 1914* (London, 1948); Richard W. Lyman, *The First Labour Government 1924* (London, 1957); Keith Middlemas, *Politics in Industrial Society* (London, 1979); Robert Skidelsky, *Politicians and the Slump* (London, 1967); F. P. Walters, *A*

Bibliography

History of the League of Nations (London, 1952); John W. Wheeler-Bennett, *The Disarmament Deadlock (London, 1934).*

Index

Adamson, William, 73, 79, 100-1, 112
Advisory Committee on International Questions, 103, 129
Anderson, Sir John, 126
Asquith, H. H., 45, 54-7, 59, 63, 123, 187
    AH's loyalty to, 60-1

Barnard Castle, 10, 14-18, 23, 28, 35, 38, 46, 88, 100, 123
Barnes, George N., 31, 35, 49
Bevin, Ernest, 95, 131-3, 144, 214, 218
Bolshevism, AH's attitude towards, 65-6, 76, 91, 96, 106, 108
Brailsford, H. N., 45-6, 131, 152
Branting, Hjalmar, 90, 92
Briand, Aristide, 153-5, 160, 162-3, 166-7, 173-4, 176, 178-9, 203
Brüning, Heinrich, 172, 176, 178, 204
Buchanan, Sir George, 64, 99
Burnley, AH as candidate in, 122-5, 130, 137, 169, 199-200
Burns, John, 30, 32
by-elections, 21-2, 34, 38, 43-4, 72, 101
    Barnard Castle (1903), 14-18, 21
    Widnes (1919), 98-100, 103
    Newcastle East (1923), 117
    Burnley (1924), 122-5
    Clay Cross (1933), 213-14

Cabinet, appointments to, 40, 55-6, 61-2, 119-22, 137-40
    resignations from, 59, 67-70, 141, 190
Cecil, Lord Robert (Viscount Cecil), 149-50, 170, 228 n. 20

Chamberlain, Sir Austen, 142, 144, 151-2, 215
Churchill, Winston, 32, 88, 123-4, 142, 198
Clay Cross, AH as candidate in, 213-14
Clynes, J. R., 88, 100, 112, 115-16, 119-20, 125, 131-2, 167-8, 194, 214
Cole, G. D. H., 73, 77, 93-4, 102, 206, 222
Communist Party, 91, 106-7, 110
conscription, 56-60, 96
Crooks, Will, 12, 16-17, 24, 30

Daily Herald, 81, 101, 106, 221
Dalton, Hugh, 93, 142, 148-53, 159, 170, 198
    quoted on AH, 141-3, 145, 153, 167, 171, 177, 193, 208, 214-15
Darlington, AH as mayor of, 11, 16
direct action, 82-4, 95, 97, 107-8
disarmament, 128, 146, 163-6, 203, 215
    AH as President of World Conference on, 148, 170-2, 201-6, 209-13, 220
'doormat incident', 67

Eden, Anthony, 211

Fabian Society, 29, 76, 102
Foreign Office, AH at, 126, 129, 139-41, 143-52, 169-70, 178-81, 219-20

general elections, (1892), 6, 9
    (1895), 9-10
    (1900), 12
    (1906), 27-8
    (1910), 34

(1918), 87-9, 198
(1922), 115-16
(1923), 118-19
(1924), 130
(1929), 137
(1931), 196-200
Geneva Protocol, 128, 130, 133, 138, 144, 147-8, 160
George V, 141-2, 158, 191, 230 n. 13
Gladstone, Herbert, 14-16, 22
Glasier, Bruce, 14, 21, 25, 32, 37
Graham, William, 183, 185, 190

Hardie, J. Keir, 1, 4, 15, 24, 29, 32, 35, 37, 42-3, 50, 80, 217
  critical of AH, 33
Hitler, Adolf, AH's meeting with, 210-11
Home Office, AH at, 126
Huysmans, Camille, 64, 89, 92, 110

Independent Labour Party, 8, 13, 16-17, 23, 26, 29, 33-6, 39, 42-3, 57, 59, 68, 71, 75, 77, 88-9, 104-5, 109-110, 119, 131-2, 134, 207
industrial conciliation, 8, 95, 115
International, *see* Socialist International
Ireland, AH's criticism of policy towards, 112-13
Ironfounders, Friendly Society of, 5, 7-8, 12-13, 19-20, 97-8
  AH as National Organizer for, 8
  AH as President of, 42, 54, 97

Johnston, Thomas, 188, 198
Jones, Thomas, 67, 73, 102

Kirkwood, David, 62, 116
Kitchener, H. H. (Lord), 57-8, 60

Labour and Socialist International, *see* Socialist International

Labour and the Nation, 134-5, 144-5, 147
Labour Party, 27-8, 34, 44, 47, 51-2, 72-9, 87, 101-4, 108-10, 118-19, 132-5, 192-3, 196-8, 208
  AH as Leader of, 50, 74, 87, 193-6, 200, 206-8
  AH as Secretary of, 29, 33, 35, 37-9, 53, 66, 79, 98, 101, 106, 111, 151, 214, 220-1
  AH's attitude towards, 29, 51-2, 81, 101-2, 111, 133, 220-1
  annual conference of, 45, 59, 62, 74, 77, 81, 84, 97, 101-2, 106-8, 110, 134, 143, 157-8, 198, 207, 214, 217
  constituency organization of, 47, 72-3, 75-6, 87, 109
  constitution of, 47, 73-7, 79, 86
  Head Office of, 36, 38, 98-100, 103, 111, 126, 151
  National Executive of, 33, 58-9, 61-2, 66, 74-5, 77, 88-9, 102-5, 107, 113, 126, 131, 133, 185, 187-8, 197, 207-8, 221
Labour Representation Committee, 12-15, 17-19, 21-8
  AH as Chairman of, 23, 28
Lansbury, George, 43, 46, 106, 116, 189, 191, 200, 207, 216-17
Laski, Harold, 198, 206
League of Nations, 90, 114, 127-9, 146, 159-65
  AH's belief in, 85-6, 129-30, 134, 144, 159, 178, 180, 219-20
  AH's performance at, 161-3
  Covenant of, 127-9, 147, 164-5, 178
Lindsay, Sir Robert, 149-50
Lloyd George, David, 40, 47, 55-6, 60-4, 66-70, 73, 80, 88, 92-6, 99, 113-15, 123-5, 198
  AH's conflict with, 67-70, 78, 84

Index

MacDonald, Ramsay, 15-17, 21-2, 28, 30, 32-40, 42-3, 47, 66, 70, 75, 79-80, 87, 89, 101, 105, 107-8, 114, 116, 119, 132-3, 214, 217
   as party leader, 35-7, 50-3, 113, 116, 131-5, 168, 197
   as Prime Minister, 119-22, 124-30, 137-41, 156, 165, 174-8, 182-99, 209-11
   compared to AH, 1, 3, 5, 19, 29, 49-52, 56, 78, 82, 101, 148
   conduct of, during First World War, 50-3, 61, 71-2
   relationship with AH, 22, 25-6, 33-7, 52-3, 71, 74, 113-14, 116-17, 121-2, 139-41, 143, 166-72, 175-7, 179-80, 188, 191-3, 202, 204-6
May Committee, Report of, 182-4, 186
Methodism, 2, 10-11
   AH's involvement with, 2-4, 11, 19-21, 123
Middleton, James, 69, 101, 111, 126, 168, 208
Morley, John (Viscount), 6, 9-10, 49
Mosley, Sir Oswald, 167-8, 221
Murray, Gilbert, 127-8, 145
Mussolini, Benito, 149, 166, 210

National Industrial Conference, 92-5, 115
National Joint Council of Labour, 104
National Union of Foundry Workers, *see* Friendly Society of Ironfounders
Newcastle, 1-2, 6, 9, 13, 117-18, 122-3
   AH elected to City Council of, 7
New Fabian Research Bureau, 206
Nobel Peace Prize, ix, 149, 215
Noel-Baker, Philip, 149, 228 n. 20, 215
Norman, Montagu, 176, 183

Optional Clause, 145, 147, 149-50, 152, 160-1, 164, 178

Parliamentary Labour Party, 29, 32-3, 35, 41, 43, 57-9, 96, 107, 112, 116, 168, 188, 194-6, 200, 208, 221
   AH as Chairman of, 32-3, 35, 55, 73
   AH as Chief Whip of, 29, 112, 116, 132
Parliamentary Recruiting Committee
   AH as Joint President of, 54
Pease, J. A., 10, 14-15
Pease, Sir Joseph, 10-12, 14-15
Pollitt, Harry, 214
Ponsonby, Arthur, 49, 70, 158, 192

reparations, 126, 153-5, 172, 179
Rumbold, Sir Horace, 164, 172, 176
Russia, AH's visit to, 64-6, 88-9, 99

Sankey, John (Lord), 92, 184, 186, 188-9, 191, 194, 199, 217
Second International, *see* Socialist International
Scott, C. P., 58, 73-4, 87, 114
Selby, Walford, 151, 181
Shackleton, David, 12, 16-17, 20-1, 23-5, 29-30, 32-3, 45
Simon, Sir John, 202, 205, 212
Snowden, Philip, 4, 17, 42-5, 48, 57, 114, 116, 119, 126, 129, 131-2, 167, 169, 194, 197, 199
   as Chancellor of the Exchequer, 138, 153-5, 176, 182-6, 190-1, 195
Socialist International, 41, 49, 68, 76, 85, 89, 106, 123, 144
   AH as Chairman of secretariat of, 117
   AH as President of, 111, 133
   Berne Conference of (1919), 89-92
   British section of, 29, 49, 55, 64, 89
   Hamburg Congress of (1923), 117
   Marseilles Congress of (1925), 133
Soviet Union, relations with, 106, 130, 155-9

Index

Stockholm conference proposal, 64-70, 88
Stresemann, Gustav, 127, 154, 160, 203

Taff Vale decision, 27-8, 30, 47
Tawney, R. H., 73, 93, 134
temperance, AH's identification with, 2, 32
Thomas, J. H., 95, 100, 115, 119, 138-9, 144, 183, 191, 202
Trades Union Congress, 8, 56, 74, 102, 104, 132, 188-9, 193, 207, 219
    General Council of, 104, 131, 134, 185, 187-8, 194
    Parliamentary Committee of, 97, 102
Trevelyan, Sir Charles, 70, 119, 207

Union of Democratic Control, 51, 70, 158

Vansittart, Sir Robert, 150, 169-71

War Emergency Workers' National Committee, 50, 54-5, 73, 102
Watson, Robert Spence, 6, 9-10, 15
Webb, Beatrice, 74, 93, 113, 131, 166, 211
    quoted on AH, 74, 80, 94, 100, 111, 119-22, 133, 195, 211
Webb, Sidney, 70, 73, 76, 82, 87, 93, 102, 119, 132
Widnes, AH as candidate in, 98-100, 115
women's suffrage, 43-6

Young, G. M., 65, 73

Zilliacus, Konni, 215